WHISPERIN' BILL ANDERSON

MUSIC OF THE AMERICAN SOUTH

WHISPERIN' BILL ANDERSON

AN UNPRECEDENTED LIFE IN
COUNTRY MUSIC

Bill Anderson

With Peter Cooper

The University of Georgia Press
ATHENS

*This publication was made possible in part
through a gift from Gus Arrendale and
Springer Mountain Farms®*

FRESH CHICKEN

Permission to print lyrics courtesy of Sony/ATV Music Publishing

Published by the University of Georgia Press
Athens, Georgia 30602
www.ugapress.org
© 2016 by Bill Anderson
All rights reserved
Designed by Erin Kirk New
Set in Minion Pro
Printed and bound by Thomson-Shore, Inc.

The paper in this book meets the guidelines for
permanence and durability of the Committee on
Production Guidelines for Book Longevity of the
Council on Library Resources.

Most University of Georgia Press titles are
available from popular e-book vendors.

Printed in the United States of America
16   17   18   19   20   C   5   4   3   2

Library of Congress Cataloging-in-Publication Data
Names: Anderson, Bill, 1937- author. | Cooper, Peter Michael.
Title: Whisperin' Bill Anderson : an unprecedented life in country music /
Bill Anderson ; with Peter Cooper.
Description: Athens : The University of Georgia Press, 2016 | Includes index.
Identifiers: LCCN 2015047528| ISBN 9780820349664 (hardcover : alk. paper) |
ISBN 9780820349657 (e-book)
Subjects: LCSH: Anderson, Bill, 1937- | Country musicians—United
States—Biography.
Classification: LCC ML420.a598 A3 2016 | DDC 782.421642092—dc23
LC record available at http://lccn.loc.gov/2015047528

To my children,

Terri, Jenni, and Jamey,

and my grandchildren,

Rachel, Caroline, Nick, Greta, Blake,

Gabe, Hallie, and Sophie

With all my love,

Dad/PawPaw

CONTENTS

ACKNOWLEDGMENTS

I've always felt that the acknowledgment section of a book should begin with an apology. There will be one sooner or later anyhow.

So I'll start by apologizing to all the people whom I should acknowledge here but unintentionally overlooked or forgot. Nothing was on purpose, and I love you and appreciate you just as much or more than I would have had I remembered to type your name.

Now, on to everyone else.

This book would have never happened without the encouragement and persistence of my former publicist and longtime friend Betty Hofer. It was her idea to involve Peter Cooper, and it was Peter's ability to see my life and my career from a different perspective than I might have seen it myself that has proven to be invaluable. He is a great writer with great vision and an uncanny knowledge of the country music business, both yesterday and today. Peter, thanks for choosing just the right pieces of my life to highlight and for all the time and energy you devoted to this project. It would have never been what it is without you.

Even though I graduated from the University of Georgia, it was through Lisa Bayer, a friend of Peter's, that led to the University of Georgia Press publishing this book. Who would have ever thought back in the days when people were laughing at me for wearing a red cowboy suit and white buck shoes in the freshman talent show that the esteemed university press would someday involve themselves with a book on the skinny kid from Avondale? I can't possibly recite the name of each press staff person whose hands touched this project, but I thank each and every one. Special thanks to acquisitions editor Patrick Allen, who never seemed to tire of answering my endless questions; Courtney Denney, whose copyediting skills amazed both me and Peter; Rebecca Norton, who helped shepherd the book into production; Amanda Sharp, who juggled promotion and marketing, and to

Chantel Dunham, the builder of more and better bridges between Athens and Nashville.

There are so many people who help keep my world turning on a daily basis. My thanks to Lee Willard, my tireless young manager; to Judy Price, my administrative assistant for all things Whisperworld; and to the members of my Po' Folks Band.

Unending appreciation to Troy Tomlinson, Terry Wakefield, and the staff at Sony/ATV Music Publishing, the best music publishers and song guardians in Nashville. To their New York counterparts, Caroline Bienstock, Bob Golden, and the staff at Carlin-America Publishing in the Big Apple. To my friends at BMI and CMA and ACM and ROPE and NSAI and RFD and WSM and all the other alphabet entities that I can't remember or spell; to Kirt Webster and Amanda Clark from Webster Public Relations for making sure this book was not a well-kept secret; and above all, to the fans.

I've never claimed to have had the largest number of fans in country music, but I have been blessed with some of the best and most loyal of them all. There are people reading these pages who have been following my career for almost as long as there has been one, people who don't need captions for any of the pictures.

To Larry Black, who gave me the opportunity back in 1997 to host for almost twenty years a television show called *Country's Family Reunion*. Modern-day country radio may have decided they don't need us old dinosaurs on their airwaves anymore, but Larry and CFR have helped prove that all our fans didn't disappear the day Garth Brooks moved to town.

To Colin Reed, Steve Buchanan, and Pete Fisher, along with Gina Keltner and Sandy Judge, who strive daily to maintain the legacy of the Grand Ole Opry while moving it forward toward its next ninety years. Thanks for continuing to allow me to take up space on that most hallowed of all stages.

To Stephanie Orr and Wes Buttrey, who created and maintain my website; to Gus Arrendale of Springer Mountain Farms chicken, one of the most generous people on the planet; to Mike Milom, the best music business attorney of all and the man charged with making sure all the i's got dotted and the t's got crossed; and to my booking agent and baseball-lovin' cohort, Nick Meinema, who works hard to make sure I don't ever get bored by spending too much time at home.

To the memory of Bob Tanner, who opened the first door for me, and to the legacies of industry icons Buddy Killen, Owen Bradley, Hubert Long,

Jim Fogelsong, and others who molded me. To absent friends like Roger Miller, Jimmy Dean, Conway Twitty, George Hamilton IV, Jim Ed Brown, and more whose music and stand-up character will remain with me forever. And to Bobby Brenner, Mark Goodson, and Jacquelyn Smith, who believed when many did not.

And to Vickie . . . for simply being you.

FOREWORD

By 1990, Bill Anderson was ten years past finished. Ten years past something to say.

He accepted this with a kind of agitated thankfulness. His life had been defined by what he'd had to say, and since the age of twenty, the things he'd had to say had been voiced in melody by some of the greatest singers ever to commandeer a microphone.

When Anderson was twenty years old, in 1958, future Country Music Hall of Famer Ray Price took his shuffling lament "City Lights" to the top of the country charts. After that, Aretha Franklin, Jerry Lee Lewis, James Brown, the Louvin Brothers, Connie Smith, Dean Martin, and many more sang his songs. Though he didn't have the vocal chops of those masters—his simple, low-key vocal style led to the nickname Whisperin' Bill—he did quite well for himself as a recording artist, singing eighty charting singles, thirty-seven country music Top 10s, and seven number one hits.

That's a good run, which is where the thankfulness comes in.

The dinosaurs had a pretty good run, too. By 1990, Anderson was one of them. He wasn't writing anymore. Bad investments left him teetering at bankruptcy's edge. His marriage was falling apart. And in Nashville, a music town where youth often carries the day, he was no longer relevant except as a nostalgia act, a museum piece waving from the stage of the Grand Ole Opry, and an affable host of country-themed television game shows.

The last time he'd told a music publisher that he had a good song for a female vocalist, the publisher wryly and callously replied, "Who do you want me to pitch it to, Kitty Wells?" Kitty Wells's last Top 10 record came in 1965.

Anderson was in his fifties and assumed he'd climbed all the mountains he'd been intended to climb. He was beginning his descent into whatever valley awaited. He felt old and apprehensive but in truth was younger and braver than he'd thought. The most thrilling, exhilarating, and unprecedented part of his journey lay ahead.

PETER COOPER

WHISPERIN' BILL ANDERSON

INTRODUCTION

In the early 1990s, my songs were just a bunch of old trophies on a shelf, up to be admired in passing while the real action took place as new music was written and developed and recorded. But one day, Terry Choate of Tree Publishing, which controlled rights to much of what industry folks would call my back catalog, called me and wanted to dust them off. He said, "I'd like to take a half dozen of your old songs and do new demos." (A "demo" is short for "demonstration recording." It's an inexpensive way to record a version of a song, meant to impress producers who might record a "master recording" for someone's album.) He took "You and Your Sweet Love," "I Never Once Stopped Loving You," and several others, including "Tips of My Fingers," which had been a hit for me in 1960, a hit for Roy Clark in 1963, a hit for Eddy Arnold in 1966, and a hit for Jean Shepard in 1975. A pretty good run, to be sure, but one that I was sure was over.

Patty Loveless, Ricky Van Shelton, and several other then-contemporary artists had hits in the 1980s with reworkings of old songs, but I had no confidence that anything like that could or would happen for me or for "Tips," a sad ballad of resignation that Terry wanted to pitch around Music Row at a time when up-tempo romps were in favor. Come to think of it, up-tempo romps are always in favor. "Sad songs and waltzes aren't selling this year," wrote my friend Willie Nelson. I'm not sure what year he wrote that. Doesn't matter, it's always true.

But when Terry came back to me with the demos, the old songs sounded up to date and viable. He'd wrapped a gleaming new ribbon around those old boxes. Suddenly, Terry's folly seemed less fanciful, and I said, "Man, get these out there where people can hear them."

He did, and they did, and a couple of big fish bit. One was Cleve Francis, a cardiologist-turned-country-singer who recorded for Liberty Records. Cleve recorded "Tips of My Fingers" (which, by the way, I'd first written and recorded as "The Tip of My Fingers"), and then I learned that an A-list

1

country star named Steve Wariner recorded it. Steve's producer, Scott Hendricks, played him the demo Terry Choate had put together, and they agreed Steve should record it. Scott asked if Steve wanted a copy of the demo, to learn the words and melody, and Steve said, "I don't need the demo, and I don't need a lyric sheet. I grew up hearing my daddy sing that song."

"Tips" became the biggest hit from Steve's 1991 album, *I Am Ready*. It was a number one country hit in 1992, thirty-two years after I first recorded it. My version hit the charts when Steve was five years old.

This was my first single as a songwriter in ten years, and at first I was more amused than excited, in part because I didn't realize the extent to which the economics of country music had changed. As Country Music Hall of Famer Tom T. Hall said, writing a hit single back in the 1960s might buy you a new car, but writing a hit single in the 1990s could buy you the whole dealership. Part of the way songwriters make money is from radio airplay, and the number of stations featuring country music had skyrocketed in the years that I was figuring myself too old and out-of-touch to write songs. There's a big difference in getting a song played on three thousand stations, versus three hundred. I didn't understand the significance of that at first. I realized it one day when I received a royalty check with enough zeroes that it was heavy to lift.

Aside from the money, it was wonderful to hear Steve Wariner sing my song. He was among the most talented artists of that era, and it was clear that he had respect and affection for what I'd written. For the first time in years, I felt like a contributor, not an interloper, on Nashville's Music Row. Yet it was tempered by the fact that I hadn't written anything new. What had I really proven? That I could write a hit song in 1960? That I used to be good? All this took a while to simmer and burn and sort out. The question was, could I do now what I'd done thirty-five years ago? I hadn't cracked the wall until I'd created something new. So why couldn't I create something new?

"Because, dummy," I told myself, "the game has changed. You don't know the guys who are writing and publishing the songs now. You don't know the record producers. Most of the people who were in control of the Nashville music industry back in your heyday aren't in control anymore. You don't know the ones in control now, and, worse, they don't know you. Your best days are behind you."

In some ways, I owe my second life in music to a hairstylist, and it has nothing to do with the way I look.

You see, Cheryl Riddle and her mom owned and operated a small salon upstairs in an old, nondescript glass building, smack dab in the middle of Music Row. Their clients were mostly women, but Cheryl's mom, Jackie, did Conway Twitty's hair for years, and Cheryl styled Randy Owen, the lead singer from the group Alabama, among others. I learned that Cheryl had been a big fan of mine for years. She had seen me in concert in her hometown of Charleston, West Virginia, back when she was in her early teens. She had a black-and-white picture of herself holding one of my albums. I liked her and felt comfortable around her and decided to give her hairstyling talents a try.

It wasn't long before she began telling me about a singer-songwriter in town whose hair she also was styling. "His name's Vince Gill," she said. "The two of you really ought to get together. I think you'd like each other a lot. He's like you, kind of quiet and soft-spoken. And he's a great songwriter. You two could write some great songs together."

I told her I was well aware of Vince Gill, was aware that he was the hottest thing in Nashville at the time, and was pretty sure he didn't know who I was. I told her I'd introduced myself to him at a celebrity softball game one time, and he wasn't particularly friendly.

"Oh, he's just shy. I'll give you his phone number. Call him."

I took the number, and didn't call. But Cheryl asked about it every time I saw her, and she said she'd told him I was going to call.

"But I've never done much co-writing," I said.

"Well, that's what everybody is doing these days. You need to give it a try."

She was speaking the truth. I thought of the royalties from the Steve Wariner record, and I knew the quickest way out of the financial troubles brought on by some ill-executed restaurant business ventures could be through songwriting. Plus, I wanted to do it. I had never stopped jotting down ideas for songs. I had desk drawers full of ideas. I had just stopped acting on them.

Songwriting is part art, part craft. The art comes in recognizing an idea when it's dangling in front of you in real life, in a conversation, or in something you read or something you see in the movies or on television. Taking that idea and turning it into a complete, marketable song is where the crafting comes in. Once you're a writer, you're always a writer. The desire to create never goes away, and mine certainly hadn't. But desire will only take you so far. I can desire to dunk a basketball all day long, and it's not going to help me until they lower the rim by half. Could I still craft a hit idea into a hit song? And could I do it with another writer, when I'd made my career by doing it myself?

Songwriting had always been something very personal to me. I had written many songs at three in the morning, in dimly lit rooms with the curtains closed and the shades pulled down. Could I bare my soul in front of another writer and create the same kind of emotion I had created many times in solitude? I had often told people that I didn't think you could punch a time clock and write songs. You have to strike when the juices start flowing naturally. They can't be forced.

But I looked around me, and the vast majority of hits on the current charts were co-written. In 1961, there were 1.12 writers per number one country song. By the 1990s, that figure had climbed to nearly 2 writers per song, and in the new century it has gone above that, to where many more hit songs are penned by a committee of 3 than by a lone songsmith. I ultimately reasoned that my strength as a songwriter was in lyric writing, not melody writing. Oh, I had put tunes to hundreds of songs over the years, but the newer music was a bit more sophisticated than my simple three- and four-chord compositions. Maybe I needed to work with someone who was more knowledgeable in that area. And Vince Gill was an extraordinary guitar player.

In most areas of my adult life, I've tended to do things slowly and deliberately. I've tried to think things out and not act impulsively. But once I make a decision, I make it and don't look back. One day, I woke up and decided it was time to make a change. I pulled the scrap of paper out of my wallet, took a breath, and dialed the number Cheryl had given me.

Straight to voice mail.

"Hi," went the outgoing message, spoken in a voice that was barely audible and strangely familiar. "This is Whisperin' Gill. I'm not here right now, but leave your name and number and I'll call you back. And God bless ye."

Best Bill Anderson impersonation I'd ever heard. I laughed out loud. And soon, the young buck and the dinosaur connected and made a writing appointment for early January 1994.

That appointment—the ease of it, the fun of it, and the love of it—was a pivotal point for me. It was the beginning of a new life for me in music.

Since then, stars from good ole Whisperin' Gill to Brad Paisley, Alison Krauss, Kenny Chesney, Elvis Costello, and George Strait have recorded my works. I've won two Country Music Association Song of the Year awards, been nominated for Grammys, won Song of the Year from the Academy of Country Music, and been named the first country music Songwriting Icon by Broadcast Music, Inc. In 2001, I was inducted into the Country Music Hall of Fame.

I write this roughly thirty-five years after I was finished, and two decades since I gave myself permission to try a new approach, to contribute and create rather than pine for what once was or what I thought ought to be. My late-life reality has been far richer than any ought-to-be I could have imagined. And I'd like to thank my hairstylist.

The beginnings of Bill Anderson's journey are certainly not without precedent, though they won't likely be replicated: The world
has turned too many times, and every time it comes back around
things are lost that won't be recovered. In the 1940s, radio was
a lifeline. Today, at best, it is an addendum. Boys don't grow up
idolizing men called Snuffy, Pappy, and Greasy. Grandfathers
with fifth-grade educations don't start insurance companies. And
baseball scouts in our times would never take notice of "the cautious left arm of Bill 'Hillbilly' Anderson": Starting pitchers with
"fastballs" that peak into the low seventies are now like defensive
tackles that stand five-foot-five and weigh 150 pounds.

   It's all different now, but reading Bill's account of his childhood
underscores his indefatigable adaptability. The boy who shared a
stage with Rufus Rainwater, the Red-Headed Rodeo Romper, and
who wanted to sing just like country music heroes Ernest Tubb
and Faron Young, went on to share stages with Tubb and Young.
And with Taylor Swift, Carrie Underwood, Brad Paisley, and so
many other modern-day superstars, some of whom have never
heard of a washtub bass and none of whom have ever given a
moment's thought to the late, great Byron Parker.

I have loved country music as long as I can remember. My parents tell me I could find the "hillbillies" (as they were called then) on the radio long before I could tie my shoelaces, so maybe it's a love I was born with. If so, it dates back to my birth, November 1, 1937, in Columbia, South Carolina. My mother said I was just another Bill that came on the first of the month. Actually, that's not true. My full name is James William Anderson III, and until I was eight years old I wasn't even a Bill at all. I was known as Billy. One day I decided that Billy didn't fit me and I refused to answer unless I was addressed as Bill. I'm sure I missed supper a few times when Mom or Dad would call out of habit, "Come to the table, Billy," but I wouldn't go until they said it right. Besides, I never thought Billy went with my last name. It always came out Billy Yanderson. Today a lot of people think Bill is my middle name. My first name, they think, is Whisperin'.

My mother and father, Elizabeth (Lib) and James William Anderson Jr. (Jim), had been married a little over four years when I came along. I was their first child. My sister, Mary Elizabeth, wasn't born until four and a half years later. Although I've written and sung many songs about coming from a large family, in reality there were only the four of us.

Daddy was not a farmer, as I sang in my song "Po' Folks," but rather an employee of the credit service company Dun and Bradstreet when I was born. He later became, like his father before him, an insurance agent. Mama's full-time job was taking care of Dad and us.

I don't know why I've always fantasized about coming from a large family and living on a farm. I wrote that not only into "Po' Folks" ("There was ten of us living in a two-room shack") but into "Mama Sang a Song" as well ("All daddy ever got was a bad-land farm and seven hungry mouths to feed"). I think that's why when I finally bought a home in the country in 1979, I looked on it as the fulfillment of a lifelong dream.

My parents were both originally from Georgia, having met as teenagers in the small mill town of Griffin, where my mother's father, the Reverend Horace Stratton Smith, had been sent to serve as pastor of the First Methodist Church. Mom was the third of four children born to her father and his wife, Mary Jessie Lewis Smith, and I heard her say many times over the years that she often felt like she was the third verse of a four-stanza hymn. "You know how a lot of times the preacher says, 'We'll sing the first, second, and last verses?'" she'd ask, smiling. "The third one is the one that always gets left out."

My mother's mother died when Mom was only sixteen, so I never knew her. Her father was an interesting man, though. He worked in the newspaper business for a while, was later employed as a school teacher, and might never have gone into the ministry except for a violent thunderstorm that swept across the Gulf of Mexico and onto the coast of Texas late one night. He was young and single at the time, going to school and living alone in a small room on the second floor of an old wood-framed rooming house in Galveston. For most of this particular evening he'd been lying across the bed in his room studying, listening to the wind howl around the corners of the ancient structure while the flashing bolts of lightning lit up the jagged coastline and the raindrops pounded viciously against the tiny window-panes. For some reason, around ten o'clock, he laid down the book he'd been reading, got up from his bed, and walked downstairs to the kitchen for a glass of milk. When he returned to his room moments later, one entire wall of the house had collapsed under the onslaught of the storm and debris was piled more than three feet high across his bed . . . right in the spot where he'd been lying. There was no doubt that if he'd stayed in his room he would have been killed.

He immediately began to ponder why he'd been spared. What made him rise from his bed and go for that drink of milk at precisely the moment he did? Was God trying to tell him something important? Did He have something special in mind for this young teacher to do with his life?

"I spent the rest of that night wrestling with the devil," he used to say, "and the devil lost." Grandaddy decided almost immediately to change directions in his life. He returned to Georgia and applied for a license to preach, joined the North Georgia Conference of the Methodist Church, and began his service as an ordained minister. From a fiery young circuit-riding preacher in his early days to a retired district superintendent many years later, he brought the word of God into thousands of lives. On his deathbed in 1965 at the age of eighty-eight, without his even knowing it, he touched thousands more.

"Billy," he said to me as I leaned over his bed and strained to hear his weakening voice, "I don't know much about this business you're in, but I do know one thing: You're in a position to touch more lives with one song, with one appearance somewhere, than I've been able to touch with every sermon I've ever preached in my life." His words stunned me.

I knew what he'd said was true, yet somehow it seemed so unfair. Here he was, a much more eloquent speaker, a much better person spiritually than I'd ever be, I knew, yet my opportunities would be so much greater than his. Several years later when I was given the chance to record an album of all religious music (*I Can Do Nothing Alone*) I used his last words to me as my inspiration and dedicated the album to his memory.

My dad's father, James William Anderson Sr., was born and raised on the red clay farm land of middle Georgia, and he worked as a farmer for most of his young life. Things weren't very easy, though, for people in that part of the country who tried to extract a living from unyielding soil. In 1920, my grandpapa, as I've always called him, sold the farm and the little wooden farmhouse in Pike County where my dad was born and moved his wife and their only child seven miles east into Griffin to take up the insurance business. Despite having no experience in the field and only a fifth-grade education, he helped to found Middle Georgia Mutual Insurance Company.

Grandpapa (his wife and friends all called him "Mr. Jim") was also an old-time fiddle player. He was part of a group that was widely known throughout the central part of the state as simply the Anderson Family Band. They played for every pie supper, cake walk, square dance, worm wrestlin', and goat ropin' that was held in those parts. Grandpapa had quit playing very much by the time I was born, but I felt the impact of his music many years later at my great-uncle's funeral when my dad introduced me to one of the neighbors, an old-timer who lived way back in the woods of that still extremely rural area.

"This is my son, Bill Anderson," my dad said proudly. "You might have heard of him. He plays up in Nashville, Tennessee, on the Grand Ole Opry." The old fellow, who had to be over ninety, looked me up and down, never showing any emotion in his craggy face at all. He spit a mouthful of tobacco juice on the ground in my direction and said, "Shoot, I don't care who he is. He can't make no music like Mr. Jim!"

My grandmother, Elizabeth Williams Anderson (everybody called her "Miss Lizzy"), was also a musician, a guitar player, although nobody seems to recall her ever performing in public. Like Grandpapa, she didn't play much in her later years, but I grew up feeling an extreme closeness to both of my Anderson grandparents. I've got to believe it was a bond created and strengthened somehow by the love we all felt for music and for singing, for the joy that only music can bring.

I was always particularly close to my grandpapa. He was a big, strapping man who stood well over six feet tall and weighed close to two hundred pounds. He thought his little curly-headed grandson hung the moon. He'd play ball with me in the front yard of his house in Griffin, he'd go to the movies with me and sit through a double-feature of Red Ryder and Little Beaver, and he'd let me help him mow the lawn, pick turnip greens from the garden, even sleep in the same bedroom with him when I'd go to his house for my summer vacation.

In those days there was a train called the *Nancy Hanks* that ran from Atlanta to Savannah on the old Central of Georgia railroad line, and I'd save my money every year just so I could ride on the *Nancy* some fifty-five minutes south to Griffin. I thought I was really hot stuff when Grandpapa would be there to meet me at the station in his 1941 green Ford coupe and carry me home to Grandmama's dinner table where I would invariably stuff my face so full of her good country cooking that I'd get sick. He'd pamper me all night, then take me to his office with him the next morning. He'd set me up in a back room with my own typewriter and a stack of paper, and I'd amuse myself for hours, typing all sorts of things and playing office. At night after we'd gone to bed, he'd lie on the other side of the room and tell me stories and give me advice.

"Billy, don't you be thinking about getting married now, you hear?" he said to me once when I was about ten or eleven years old and had told him about a pretty girl I liked in my sixth-grade class. And later on he said, "I know how much you like to play ball, Billy, but you be careful now and don't get athlete's foot." I had to laugh even then, but I knew no boy ever had a better friend than my grandpapa was to me.

People ask me all the time where I got my musical abilities and my desire to write songs and entertain. It goes back to my grandparents. When you combine an old-time fiddle player with a circuit-ridin' preacher who used to write for a newspaper, then throw in a guitar-pickin' grandma for good measure, you come up with whatever it is that I am.

My mother and dad got married in the parsonage of the First Methodist Church in Decatur, Georgia, where Grandaddy Smith had been transferred, the afternoon of September 27, 1933, then headed south to Savannah Beach for their honeymoon. They had barely gotten inside their hotel room, however, when a bellman knocked on the door and handed Dad a telegram telling him that the company he worked for was transferring him from Atlanta to Meridian, Mississippi, and that they needed him to report immediately.

Jobs weren't easy to come by in 1933, so, honeymoon or not, my parents-to-be decided they'd best leave Savannah right away. Driving Dad's little brown-and-tan Chevrolet coupe farther west than either of them had ever been in their lives, they wound their way to Meridian, a sleepy little east Mississippi town that had only recently achieved a certain amount of fame and notoriety as the hometown of country music's first superstar, Jimmie Rodgers. In later years, actresses Sela Ward and Diane Ladd, honky-tonk wailer Moe Bandy, and folk-rock songsmith Steve Forbert would be born in Meridian. Had my dad's company not changed its mind again and been so anxious to move him back east to South Carolina in 1936, ole Whisperin' Bill might have been born there as well.

My earliest childhood memories are set in Columbia, however, and I remember it as a happy place to have lived and begun growing up. It was hot as blazes in the summertime, and the streets were constantly filled during the wartime years with marching soldiers from nearby Fort Jackson. But I learned to play baseball at Shandon Park in Columbia, I saw my first college football game when the University of South Carolina Gamecocks defeated the Presbyterian College Blue Stockings (42–0), and I was valedictorian of my class in kindergarten. That meant I got to stand up in front of the rest of the kids and all the parents at our little graduation exercises and sing "Deep in the Heart of Texas" and recite a poem about how much fun it was to get mud between my toes.

I also got to go inside my very first radio station in Columbia. Our next-door neighbor's daughter was a receptionist at the biggest station in Columbia at the time, WIS, and she knew that from the time I was three or four years old I had sat faithfully by the radio every morning, noon, and night listening to a group called Byron Parker and the Hillbillies as they played and sang live country music on her station. They had three shows a day, sponsored by Seiberling Tires, Good Enough Flour, and Black Draught Laxative, and I never missed a one. I thought Byron Parker was the greatest man alive. He and General Douglas MacArthur were my first honest-to-goodness heroes.

I couldn't have been more than five or six the morning she asked me if I'd like to go to the radio station with her and see a live broadcast of my favorite show, but I remember it like it was yesterday. I was overwhelmed by all the microphones and the wires and cables and turntables in the control room, but what really got me excited was finding myself in the presence of the big man that loomed larger than life: Byron Parker, the man who talked to me and sang for me every day in my living room on Dad's little table-model Philco radio.

"Funny," I thought when I saw him for the first time, "he doesn't sound as big and fat on the radio as he looks in person." In your mind's eye, your radio heroes could look anyway you wanted them to.

Before he went on the air that morning at eight-thirty, Byron Parker came over to where I was seated in the corner of the studio and talked to me, asked me my name, then introduced me to some of the other musicians in the band. They were names I knew as well as I knew his: Snuffy Jenkins, Pappy Sherrill, and Greasy Medlin. When their show started, Byron Parker, the Old Hired Hand himself, even said my name on the radio so my mother and dad at home could hear that I was there. It was the happiest and most exciting day of my young life.

Byron Parker recorded a few songs for RCA Victor during his career, but he never became a star anywhere outside South Carolina, where his name was legend. I'd have given anything, though, if he could have lived long enough to know all the good things that have happened to me in my career and what a big influence he was on me. He died while performing on stage in the late 1940s, and I never had the chance to see him in person again. Yet there's another story involving him that gives me goose bumps every time I think about it.

In the early 1960s I was riding to a show date in Maryland with bluegrass greats Don Reno and Red Smiley on their bus. We had worked a show together the night before in North Carolina, and it was the first time Don and Red had ever seen me perform. Somewhere in the wee hours of the morning, Don got up from where he'd been sitting quietly in the front of the rolling bus and walked to the back where Red and I sat talking. He stood there without saying a word for the longest time and finally he looked down and said, "I've got it! It's been about to drive me crazy, but I've finally figured it out."

He was looking directly at me.

"What's that?" I asked, wondering what I'd done.

"I've been sitting up there all night trying to figure out who you remind me of. I saw you working onstage tonight and you reminded me of somebody and I couldn't think who it was. But now I know."

"Well, who is it?" I asked.

"Oh, you probably never heard of him," he answered. "He's not even alive now. He was just a local singer down in South Carolina that I used to listen to when I lived up around Spartanburg. But, boy, you sound like him and you move like him on the stage, and from what I saw tonight you handle an audience just like he did . . . and he was the best. It won't mean anything to you, but his name was Byron Parker."

I didn't sleep a wink that night.

I started school in Columbia and finished the first, second, and half the third grade at Schneider Elementary. In the 1970s, my mother was rummaging through her basement at home and ran across my last report card from there. In the section on the back where the teacher had space to write her personal comments to the parents, my teacher had prophetically written, "Billy whispers too much."

I was halfway through my third-grade year when Mom and Dad decided they needed to move back home to Georgia. Dad was becoming a bit restless in his job and wasn't sure he wanted to spend the rest of his life working for someone else. Too, his being an only child put extra pressure on him to return and live closer to his parents. His folks and Mom's dad and stepmother were all beginning to get along in years, so even though I didn't fully understand and begged and pleaded to stay in Columbia, I finally gave in and tried to smile when, in December 1945, we pulled up stakes and moved to Griffin, some forty miles south of Atlanta.

Actually, Griffin was only a pit stop. We lived there in the house with Grandmama and Grandpapa until the following February when the apartment Dad had rented for us in Decatur was ready. By the time my third-grade year was finally over, I had lived in three different towns, attended three different schools, each of which was teaching on a totally different level from the others, and had changed my name from Billy to Bill. I wasn't really sure at that point just who I was or where I belonged.

Dad had said Decatur would be a great place for us to live. It was only a ninety-minute drive from his parents, even closer to Mom's family, and "just a few miles outside of Atlanta," he told us. "It takes only a half hour to get right downtown, and you can ride the streetcar!" he'd say excitedly. "Plus, Decatur is a small town, not a big city like Atlanta. I want you kids to grow up in a small town." Of course, Decatur stayed a small town for about thirty minutes after we got there, and by the time I left home in 1955, Atlanta had dug up the streetcar tracks, replaced them with electric power lines for trackless trolleys, and swallowed up Decatur and a host of other little towns far beyond.

My childhood was, on the whole, what I'd call average. I wasn't really very different from most of the kids I grew up around. We didn't live in a house of our own until I was in the sixth grade, living instead in apartments or duplexes. We didn't have a lot of material possessions. Dad drove an old two-door black 1941 Chevrolet until I was well into high school, we never owned an air conditioner, we wore a lot of homemade clothes, and I got a lot of fifty-cent haircuts. But I never remember going to bed hungry. I made pretty good grades in school when I tried, but I didn't always try. I had a dog and a cat, and once I even decided I wanted to raise rabbits. I must have been pretty good at raising them, too, because I raised them faster than Dad could give them away.

I was in the 4-H Club, the Cub Scouts, and I played baseball and football in an honest-to-goodness cow pasture behind Ralph and Jerry Adams's house. I got interested in girls early on and spent many a Saturday afternoon on the back row of the old Decatur Theater watching cowboy movies, munching popcorn, and holding hands. I carried out groceries in a supermarket, delivered newspapers on my bicycle after school, mowed lawns, took pictures of the neighborhood kids at Christmas (for a small fee, of course), and once even started a neighborhood newspaper. I was always industrious and trying to come up with ways to make some spending money.

Money was something we didn't have very much of. Dad came home from work one evening not long after our move to Decatur and announced to the family over dinner that he'd quit his job. "What do you plan to do?" Mama asked nervously. "Oh, I don't know," Dad replied. "I've always kind of wanted to be in business for myself. I think I'll start my own company."

And with that, my father went into the insurance agency business in 1946. He called his firm "Jim Anderson and Company . . . All Forms of Insurance." "We can't say 'all kinds of insurance,'" he once told me, "because people will think we sell the good kind and the bad kind." The "and Company" was, in the beginning, the corner of our dining room table and a telephone I was warned never to answer. "It might be business," I was carefully told.

From those humble beginnings, Dad built a very successful agency, which he personally managed for over thirty years. He sold the company to a group of his employees the year he turned sixty-seven. To this day the company still bears his name, and to this day his is a good name.

I was his only son, and I guess it was natural for my dad to want me to follow his footsteps into the insurance business. I even worked for him one summer during high-school vacation, but I was a square peg in a round hole. I learned how to type labels for file folders and how to make bank deposits, but I never was too sure just what insurance was or how somebody went about selling it. It was apparent to me early on that I was simply not cut out to be, as many of the Georgia locals called it, "the policy man."

Over the years I've seen a lot of fathers try to force their sons into occupations the sons weren't really suited for. I've seen guys become doctors who wanted to fly airplanes, others become lawyers when they wanted to run off and join the circus. The greatest gift my dad ever gave me, the one he probably had to dig down the deepest to give but the one I'll always appreciate the most, was the freedom he gave me to be myself.

I did enjoy going to his office every day, however, for one reason. Upstairs over Dad's company was a radio station. The call letters were WGLS (they said it stood for World's Greatest Little Station!) and on my lunch hour every day I'd grab a sandwich and go running up the stairs to watch the disc jockeys and announcers at work. It was obvious that the show-business bug was beginning to nibble at me even then.

At night I'd sometimes hang around after the station signed off the air and watch people with colorful names like Cowboy Jack, George "Sleepy" Head, and Swain Sheriff and His Deputies tape record their early morning country music radio shows. They weren't very professional and some of them weren't even very good, but I didn't care. I loved the music they played and sang. They each had four or five local musicians who sold cars, laid pipe, or plowed all day, then picked 'n' grinned for a few extra bucks at night, and I'd sometimes sit there watching them for hours, tapping my toes, listening to the melodies they played and the lyrics they sang.

And, oh, how I wanted to learn to play the guitar like they did. I worked hard and finally saved enough money from my paper route to buy a cheap, flat-top model with the strings about an inch above the fretboard. Now, anyone who has ever tried to learn how to play the guitar will tell you that your fingers get mighty sore when you first start learning, even on a good instrument, but on this thing my fingers ached and bled so bad it nearly crippled me. I was determined I was going to learn a few chords, though, so I could accompany myself when I sang. By that time I could imitate any country singer you could name.

That was one of my problems. Being left-handed was another. My natural inclination was to turn the guitar around and strum it upside down, but something told me I'd never really learn to play that way. So I forced myself to flip my instrument back around and learn to play right-handed. To this day, playing a guitar is the only thing I don't do left-handed.

I soon learned to play well enough that I began picking and singing songs for my mama while she did her housework. I'd strum and sing up-tempo songs while perched on top of her old wringer washing machine, and she'd tap her toes, sing along, and get her work done in a hurry. If I started singing ballads, though, she'd slow down to the tempo of the music and the house would still be dirty when Daddy got home.

Dad would come in and hear me singing. If I was singing a Hank Williams song, I'd be trying my darnedest to sing it just like ole Hank. Or on an Ernest Tubb song, I'd try to sound like Ernest. Or Webb Pierce, or Carl Smith, or Faron Young, or any of the top stars of the day. I guess Dad enjoyed as much as he could stand, because one day he said, "Son, why don't you try sounding like Bill Anderson?"

I didn't understand what he meant at first and it hurt my feelings. "Listen," he said, "there's already a Hank Williams and an Ernest Tubb. Why do you want to sound like them? Try sounding like yourself."

Today, I'd say that was one of the two or three best pieces of advice I've ever received. Lots of people have said over the years that I sound "like the devil" when I sing, but nobody has ever accused me of being an imitator or a copier. You might not like Bill Anderson when you hear him sing, but you darn sure know who it is.

Actually, it wasn't until I began making up some songs of my own to sing that I was able to start sounding like myself. For the first time I was singing songs I'd never heard anybody else sing, because nobody else had ever sung them. I had to sound like me. I had nothing to imitate.

I was about ten or eleven years old when I wrote my first song. It was called "Carry Me to My Texas Home." I had never been west of Carrollton, Georgia, at the time, but Texas just sounded like something a true country artist ought to be writing and singing about. More than Decatur, anyway.

I was fifteen years old and in the tenth grade at Avondale High School when three buddies and I decided to form a band and enter the upcoming school talent show. I was selected to emcee our part of the show, play rhythm guitar, and sing. A genuinely talented boy a year or two younger named Charles Wynn would play mandolin and/or lead guitar and sing harmony. A short, chubby little guy my age whom we nicknamed "Meatball" Bell would be our fiddle player, while a big, lumbering, uninhibited goofball of a guy named Tom Schooley, who had no talent whatsoever but enough nerve and brass for all the rest of us combined, would do comedy and play wash-tub bass: a homemade instrument constructed by turning a galvanized tub upside down and drilling a small hole in the bottom, just big enough for a rope or a heavy string to slide through. One end of the rope is knotted underneath the upper side or bottom of the tub, while the other end is connected to a broom handle or stick, which then becomes the neck of the instrument. Musical tones can actually be formed by pulling or pushing the neck, which tightens or loosens the rope.

Schooley, unfortunately, never learned to match the tones of his bass with the tones the rest of the band was attempting to make, but a tenth-grader standing six foot two, weighing close to two hundred pounds, wearing bibbed overalls with freckles painted on his cheeks and his front teeth blacked out doesn't have to make beautiful music to get attention. We cleverly named him "Rufus Rainwater, the Red-Headed Rodeo Romper." We put a lot of thought into naming the band, too, and came up with the imaginative name the Avondale Playboys.

Meatball, whose real name was Jim, had been studying classical violin and never got around to telling his parents he had joined a hillbilly band. Somehow he feared that after all the money they'd spent on his music lessons they just might not understand. He'd never played any country music at all, so we bought him a copy of "Orange Blossom Special" and "Boil

Them Cabbage Down" and he listened to the records and actually became a pretty good country fiddler . . . as long as we didn't expand the repertoire too much.

I had written a song called "What Good Would It Do to Pretend?" and we decided to perform that and "Orange Blossom Special" for the talent show. The day before our big debut, we all went down to Decatur Street, in the heart of what was then the black section of segregated, downtown Atlanta, and found some matching brown cowboy shirts in the back of a dirty old pawn shop. The guy sold them to us for something like five bucks for the whole lot, and we thought we'd be the cat's meow wearing them in the show.

The act we put on for our teachers and classmates went over pretty well, especially my solo. After our part of the program was over, we went offstage and into the adjoining gymnasium locker room to change from our cowboy shirts and matching brown slacks back into our school clothes. We still had a full day of classes to attend. Suddenly I heard this tremendous roar going up out in the audience, screaming, clapping, cheering coming from every-where. In a minute somebody stuck his head in the dressing-room door and said, "Hey, you guys just won the show! They want you back out there!"

I got so excited that I forgot I wasn't fully dressed. I just grabbed my guitar and yelled "Let's go!" to the rest of the band, and we went parading back out in front of all our classmates, our teachers, and the principal of the school.

It wasn't until I reached the microphone at center stage that I began to feel a draft. I suddenly realized that while I did have my pants on, they were not zipped. For years, if you mentioned my name around any of the people who were there, they'd say, "Oh yeah, Bill Anderson . . . that's the guy who holds his guitar in a real funny position."

With all the excitement of winning the high school talent show still ring-ing in our hearts, minds, and ears, we decided to keep our little band together for a while, playing anywhere we could get anybody to listen. Tom Schooley's dad was one of the big shots at the local Chevrolet manufactur-ing plant and had just given his son a shiny new red convertible. We figured out a way to take full advantage of that. On weekend nights we'd gather the band together, roll back the top on Tom's car, and drive up into the parking lot of the Avondale Tavern, a beer joint / sandwich shop located along the main drag in the community of Avondale Estates. We'd turn a big cowboy hat upside down and set it out on top of the trunk, stand up in the back-seat with our instruments, and pick and sing for hours for tips. We didn't get rich, but the experience led to a regular Saturday night gig at a fancy restaurant east of town near Stone Mountain. We'd wander from table to table and play requests. We weren't guaranteed a salary, but the manager said we could take home as much money in tips as we could siphon off the customers. A big tip in those days was about a dollar.

One slow night around ten p.m. a large party of people from Wisconsin stopped in to eat, and we made a beeline for their table. "Would you folks like to hear a song while you wait for your food?" I asked. One of the men in the party, who had obviously had a bit too much to drink tore into his pocket and ripped out a crisp, new twenty-dollar bill. "You betcha," he shouted. "I'll give you twenty dollars to play 'On Wisconsin!'" All his friends started chiming in, "Yeah, play it . . . we wanta hear 'On Wisconsin!'" Trouble was, there wasn't a one of us Georgia boys who had any idea how to play "On Wisconsin!" But, oh, that twenty-dollar bill sure did look good!

"Sir, I'm afraid we don't . . ." I started to explain, heartsick to think that we were on the verge of missing out on the biggest payday we'd ever had. But before I could finish telling him we didn't know the song, I felt the sharp jab of a fiddle bow gouging me in the ribs.

"Oh yes, we do know it," Meatball interrupted. "I know it real well. You guys join in." And with that, he tore into playing the old country fiddle tune "Boil Them Cabbage Down" and began singing at the top of his voice, "On Wisconsin . . . on Wisconsin!"

It may not have been the worst attempt at making music I had ever heard, but it sure came close. There was no correlation between the lyrics and the melody whatsoever. It was just noise. The good news, though, was that the man with the twenty-dollar bill never knew the difference. In fact, he got so excited to be hearing a song about his home state sung 'way down south in Georgia that he started singing along. I can see him now, jumping up from his seat, dancing around the table, waving his money in the air, singing a college fight song to the tune of a hillbilly hoedown. And when we finished he applauded like he'd just heard Hank Williams yodel the "Lovesick Blues." Better than that, he gave us the twenty dollars.

Later that night, as the four of us sat around dividing up our loot, it dawned on me that I had just learned a valuable lesson: Music can be experienced in different ways by different people for different reasons. The notion of "good" is entirely subjective. We could have brought out a horn section and played a note-perfect version of "In the Mood," and it wouldn't have pleased our Cheesehead friend like our awful take on "On Wisconsin!"

The Avondale Playboys and I ended up with our own Saturday afternoon radio show not long afterward. It was on radio station WBGE, a small station located in the basement of the Georgian Terrace Hotel in downtown Atlanta. But had the program director of the station not had a good sense of humor, we might have lost our show before it ever got on the air.

We rehearsed for days and went down to the studios to audition early one evening. Everything came off perfect, so perfect, in fact, that we were hired on the spot and were told we'd be on the air for thirty minutes every week beginning at four-thirty the following Saturday afternoon. I was so excited I could hardly put my guitar back in the case. Meatball, however, was a bit skeptical.

"How powerful is this station?" he asked the program director moments after we'd been told we had the job.

"Two hundred and fifty watts," the P.D. answered. To which Meatball replied, "Good Lord, is that all? I've got lightbulbs at home that powerful."

Even with all the success we were having and all the fun I was finding in getting up on stage and performing, music was not my major concern at this point in my life. What I wanted more than anything else in the world was to be a professional baseball player.

I had played football for two years in high school but came to realize that I just wasn't aggressive enough to be really good at the game. Shortly after making first-string right offensive tackle in spring practice prior to my junior year, I quit the team.

But baseball, now that was something else. My freshman year in high school, I played first base, but not very much. Avondale won the State Class A Championship that year, and there were a lot of players on the team better than me. Three or four even signed professional contracts. But at practice one day during my sophomore season, I got to fooling around on the sidelines with pitching. I found I could throw a slow, tantalizing curveball and locate it just about anywhere I wanted it to go. I could break it out and away from a left-handed batter, in tight on a right-handed batter, or make it drop down like it was rolling off the edge of a table. I could make it do everything I wanted except go fast.

I worked hard at perfecting my newly discovered talent, and I became a pitcher. I guess I just pitched kinda like I sing . . . soft. My teammates used to tease that my fastball was so slow the school made extra money on the nights I pitched by selling advertising on the sides of the ball. But whatever I was doing it must have been right, because I started winning ball games doing it.

I moved into the starting rotation my junior year and ended up with a won-lost record of something like 10–2. I pitched both American Legion and Babe Ruth League ball the following summer, and by my senior year some of the pro scouts who combed our area seeking talent for the major league teams were beginning to take notice of me.

I was big for sixteen. I stood over six feet tall, weighed about 175 pounds, and it was obvious I wasn't through growing. The "bird dogs," as the part-time scouts were called, urged me to learn to throw more with my body and not put so much strain on my arm, but I was known for, as one newspaper writer put it, "the cautious left arm of Bill 'Hillbilly' Anderson."

The writers and most of the kids on the other high school teams knew of my interest and involvement in music through the various radio and TV programs I had begun doing around the Atlanta area (by my senior year in high school I'd had my own radio programs not only on WBGE but also on fifty-thousand-watt WEAS, as well as my own television show, on WQXI-TV), and when I'd pitch, some of the opposing players would really try to give me a hard time. They'd grab their bats over on the sidelines and act like they were strumming guitars. Then they'd start wailing some awful country song at the top of their lungs, trying to distract me. "Hey, Hillbilly," they'd yell, "sing us a song. Yodel-a-lady-who!" I'd just try to ignore them and keep on throwing roundhouse curves.

One of the scouts told me during my senior season that he could arrange for me to go to Mesa, Arizona, to the Chicago Cubs training camp the spring following graduation if I'd like to go and work with some of the pitching coaches there. Then, if things worked out—meaning if I ever learned to put my body weight behind my pitches and began throwing a protype fastball—he said the Cubs would sign me to a professional contract. Lord, I wanted to go, but the only thing my mom and dad had ever seriously asked me to do in my entire life was to go to college. They had let me play sports, they had let me run all over town at all hours of the night playing music while I was still in school (as long as I kept my grades respectable), but I knew I'd break their hearts if I tried skipping college to play baseball.

I wrestled with it long and hard and finally told the scout that I appreciated his offer but I intended to enroll that fall at the University of Georgia.
"Fine," he answered, "you play ball at Georgia and maybe when you get out
we can pick up some of your college expenses and you can still sign with
the Cubs." It sounded like a good idea to me.

On graduation night, the kids in my class all exchanged gag gifts with
one another. They called me up front and presented me with a little red-
and-yellow plastic guitar with a card attached that read: *To Bill Anderson
We Give This Guitar Because in the World of Music We Know You'll Go Far*.
I thought at the time, "Now that's silly. I'm not going to be in the music
business. I'm going to play professional baseball."

But a funny thing happened on my way to Wrigley Field . . .

In the summer before Bill Anderson's senior year in high school, four men—or rather, three men and a teenage boy—changed the world. They didn't know it at the time, but when producer Sam Phillips recorded Elvis Presley, Scotty Moore, and Bill Black playing a rollicking version of R&B song "That's All Right" at Sun Studio in Memphis, cultures shifted. Presley's sound would become known as rock 'n' roll, and rock 'n' roll would serve as a force for integration in the still-segregated American South. It would change the way people dressed, the way they dated and danced, and the way they spoke to authority. It would pose a significant threat to the health and commercial well-being of country music, resulting at first in straight-up hillbilly singers like Webb Pierce and Little Jimmy Dickens attempting to mimic Presley's hiccups, inflections, and gyrations, with sometimes laughable results. But soon enough, country singers and producers reacted to the rock 'n' roll onslaught by shifting to a smoother, pop-leaning style that became known as the Nashville Sound. One of the prime purveyors of that sound would be Whisperin' Bill Anderson, but that all came later. First, he had to enter the University of Georgia, endure a short-lived, ill-considered career as a Dahlonega, Georgia, sign thief, fail Music Appreciation class, and work as a disc jockey who was grudgingly allowed to play early rock 'n' roll but ordered never to air the hillbilly records that were his heart's delight.

2

I arrived at the University of Georgia in the fall of 1955, determined to get a degree in journalism as fast as I could and then run all the way, if I had to, to Mesa, Arizona, where the Cubs trained. A baseball player with a college degree. It had a nice ring to it.

I had decided on journalism as my major for two reasons. First, I'd always loved to write. I had been sports editor of the weekly DeKalb New Era newspaper in Decatur my last two years in high school and had even latched onto a stringer's job with the daily *Atlanta Constitution* on the side. "Stringer" meant I was given specific assignments to cover, in my case high school football and basketball games (notice I didn't say baseball . . . come baseball season I wanted not to write but to be written about), and I was paid by the job. Not much, mind you, something like five dollars per game, and out of that I paid my own expenses. But I enjoyed it. I even thought once or twice that in spite of the obvious lack of significant financial reward, sports writing might be an enjoyable way to try and make a living after my ball-playing career was over.

The second reason I chose journalism was because it was the only course I could find in searching through the university curriculum that didn't require any courses in math to graduate. In my sixteen years of schooling I flunked only two subjects: math and music. Actually the music course I failed was called Music Appreciation. One day the professor was telling the class something about Beethoven and I asked how that compared to something Hank Williams had once done, and he roared that I was never even so much as to mention the name Hank Williams in the same breath with Beethoven again. I decided not to return to Music Appreciation class after that. It was obvious I didn't appreciate their music and they darn sure didn't appreciate mine. Of course, math and music are the only two things from school that I've used since I got out.

I enjoyed my first year at Georgia. I lived in the freshman dormitory, sharing a small third-floor room and bunk beds with an older student and freshman counselor from Fitzgerald, Georgia, named Cliff Pickens. My sophomore year I became a counselor myself and shared the same room with a foreign exchange student from Tokyo named Hiroyuki Sugahara. You should have heard me trying to explain country music to him.

I studied hard most of the time, made fairly good grades, fell in love every couple of weeks or so, and tried to adjust to life away from home for the first time. I pledged the Kappa Sigma fraternity and, in an effort to prove what a good and loyal brother I'd be, I got myself thrown into jail on the Saturday night before my formal initiation into the brotherhood on Sunday afternoon.

Each of the pledges, most of whom were freshmen like me, was given what were supposed to be ridiculous but harmless little tasks to perform as part of our overall initiation rites. Each of us had a "big brother" in the fraternity, an older member to whom we were responsible, and it was the big brother's job to decide what each little brother's initiation chore was to be. My big brother was an upperclassman from Albany, Georgia, named George Thompson, and George had an old score he wanted settled.

Before he had transferred to Georgia, George had been a student at a military college in the little north Georgia town of Dahlonega, and he had gotten into trouble on more than one occasion while he was there. The commandant of the school, an army lieutenant colonel who lived in a nice house next to the campus, had meted out some pretty tough punishment on him a few times, and George had been carrying a grudge for years.

"The whole time I was in school up there," he said to me at the frat house on Friday night, "I tried to figure out a way to get back at that guy. Now you're gonna help me do it." There was a glow of sweet revenge in his eye.

"Right out in front of the house where he lives, on his lawn, is a little sign. It's nothing fancy, just a small white sign with his name and rank on it . . . and the word 'Commandant.' I used to pass his house and look at that sign every day, and I wanted to yank it up out of the ground and smash it to bits every time I looked at it. Now I'm finally going to get to do it, because you're going to go up there tomorrow and get that sign and bring it back to me. Aren't you?"

"Do I have a choice?" I timidly asked.

"No," Big Brother answered.

"Then, yeah, I guess I'm gonna go get it. But won't that be stealing?"

"Not if you don't get caught, it won't. But here's how you'll have to do it: Wait until after dark when everything in town is closed. That won't be very late 'cause they roll up the sidewalks in Dahlonega at ten o'clock. Then, when nobody's looking, you sneak up on the lawn, grab the sign, and run like the devil. It shouldn't take more than just a few seconds and you'll be gone. Bring the sign back here to me and I'll guarantee that you'll become a full-fledged Kappa Sig Sunday afternoon."

I wasn't sure what to say. I'd never stolen anything in my life, and I wasn't real anxious to start. On the other hand, I'd heard through the grapevine that some of my fellow pledges were going to have to eat raw eggs and swallow live goldfish as part of their initiation Saturday night, and stealing a little sign sounded kinda tame compared to that. I smiled at George, stuffed a couple of candy bars into the pockets of my coat, and headed for the dorm to get some sleep. At ten o'clock the next morning I was standing on the north side of Athens trying to thumb a ride to Dahlonega.

I had better luck than I had anticipated in flagging down a couple of cars, and I arrived in the former mining town (they discovered gold there back in the 1800s) in midafternoon. I decided it was too early for me even to begin thinking about carrying out my assignment, so I went to work on trying to pass the time. I wandered in and out of the drugstore a couple of times, checked out the dime store, then bought a newspaper and sat outside on a park bench and read for a while. I started once to go down to the barbershop and watch haircuts, but I never got quite that bored.

The local movie theater opened about seven, so I decided to take in the western that was playing. I bought a box of popcorn and a large soft drink and settled in for a couple of hours of watching the good guys run the bad guys out of town. I should have taken that as an omen.

True to George's prediction, thirty minutes after the movie let out around nine-thirty, downtown Dahlonega was deserted. I sauntered up the hill from the theater and tried to get the lay of the land. Sure enough, right at the top of the hill on the left side of the road was the commandant's house, and about thirty feet from his front door, square in the middle of his grassy, tree-laden yard, was my target, the little white sign. "Piece of cake," I smiled to myself. I looked to my left and then to my right. There wasn't a soul in sight. Then suddenly I realized I was about to act prematurely. My wait wasn't quite over. There were a couple of lights shining from inside the windows of the commandant's house. "Probably sitting up reading *War and Peace*," I surmised, and I walked aimlessly on up the hill.

It was a few minutes after midnight when I meandered back down by the house for the umpteenth time and saw that all was finally dark and still. "Perfect," I thought, and I tiptoed quietly up the little bank and into the yard. I slowly eased my way along, careful not so much as to step on a twig. I didn't want to arouse anyone's attention. I'd come too far and been too careful to blow it all now. I was starting to want the little sign as much as George did.

From one tree to the next, I inched my way, stopping to make sure no one was watching, creeping ever so carefully through the darkness. Ten feet away, then five, three, two, until suddenly I was standing poised directly above my prey. I looked all around one last time. No one was there. I reached for the sign and gave it a tug. It moved a couple of inches but that was all. "Hmmm, this might be a little harder than I thought," I conjectured, but I never got a chance to find out just how difficult removing the sign from the red Georgia clay might have been. I was suddenly distracted by the fierce glare of lights and the piercing scream of sirens!

The front yard of the commandant's house must have been wired like a mine field. All I know is that in far less time than it takes to tell it, I was standing dead solid center in the penetrating yellow beam of the army's or the sheriff's or somebody's hot, luminous spotlight and telling some big dude in a uniform that it was all a mistake. I wasn't trying to sabotage the United States Army, I was just a college kid from Athens trying to join a fraternity. You can imagine about how that went over.

In a minute here came the commandant roaring out his front door to see what was going on. He was dressed in bright red-and-white striped pajamas underneath a dark blue bathrobe. If I hadn't been so nervous, I'm sure I could have come up with a brilliant remark regarding his patriotic choice of nightwear.

"What's going on?" he thundered, and I launched into my story about George Thompson and Kappa Sigma and about how all I wanted was the sign for good ole George, but now that I'd had some time to think about it I really didn't want it all that bad, and why didn't he just keep his sign and go on back to bed and we'd forget the whole thing. About fifteen minutes later I was doing my whole routine again in front of an equally unappreciative audience down at the county jail.

But I've got to hand it to the chief or the sheriff or whoever was in charge, he was okay. He listened to all I had to say, kept me there for a few hours, probably to frighten me more than anything else, then just before daylight he let me go. Even sent me over to a legendary family-style Dahlonega eatery called the Smith House and instructed me to eat a good breakfast and be out of town by ten o'clock. I was out on the side of the road with my thumb in the air long before that.

Rides were hard to come by that morning, though, and I didn't make it back to Athens until just a few minutes before the formal oath-taking ceremonies at the fraternity house at two o'clock. And I walked into the house minus the sign I'd been sent to retrieve.

"It's a long story, big brother," I said to George as he rushed out to meet me, but he didn't even question me as to why I wasn't carrying his prize. He just reached up and hugged my neck. I found out later that he and all the other brothers had been so nervous as to my whereabouts that they didn't care whether I'd carried out my duties or not. They were just thankful I was alive. They had been looking at their watches since early morning and had about decided that I had been kidnapped, killed, or had run off to join the foreign legion. Not that they would have missed me all that much, but they would have been held responsible. If I'd never come back, the dean of men would have probably pulled the permit for their next beer party!

I grabbed a quick shower, put on a borrowed tuxedo, and became a full-fledged brother in Kappa Sigma that afternoon. I guess it was fun and I carry around some good memories from that period of my life, but it wasn't long afterward that I decided I wasn't really cut out to be Joe College. I was starting to get too many other things on my mind.

For one thing, there was a big freshman talent show coming up, and I wanted more than anything to enter. I did, wearing a bright red western shirt with matching fire-engine red pants, a white western belt, and a pair of white buck shoes with red soles. Can't you just imagine how that went over on a college campus? I played my guitar and sang the same song I had written and sung for the talent show in high school three years before, "What Good Would It Do to Pretend?" and actually my act went over pretty well. In fact, I won second place. A blind girl who played the piano and sang came in first. I learned another valuable show business lesson that night: Never compete against a kid, a dog, or a blind girl who plays the piano and sings. You'll come in second every time.

But the word quickly spread around campus that there was this oddball kid in the freshman class who went around wearing red cowboy clothes, picking a guitar, and singing through his nose. That prompted a phone call one day from a couple of upperclassmen who had been in the military and had come back to school to study under the GI bill.

"We're thinking about getting together a country band," they told me, "and wondered if you'd like to join us." I asked them, "Is a flat-top guitar flat?" Of course I'd like to join them. What they didn't tell me, though, was that each of them played nothing but guitar (neither of them exceptionally well), and with the addition of my talents, the band would consist of three guitars. That's all, just three guitars. And nobody really played lead. The strength of the group was obviously going to be in its rhythm section.

But we didn't let that stop us. We formed the Classic City Playboys, named after the town of Athens, which refers to itself as a "classic city": Norman Vaughn, later to be known as "Sleepy Norman" of all-night disc jockey fame on powerhouse WWVA, Wheeling, West Virginia; Chuck Goddard, who came to Georgia on a football scholarship and who would later introduce me to my first wife; and the young kid with the red clothes. Three rhythm guitars, a couple of weekend bookings at a local service club, and a half-hour show on radio station WRFC every Saturday afternoon. Yet, somehow, it lasted for almost a year.

Norman was also the early morning DJ on WRFC. Our band would go to the station once a week late at night to rehearse our show for the upcoming Saturday. One night in early January after we'd finished practicing, I asked Norman if he could show me how to run the station's control board. He sat me down, gave me a few pointers, and I went crazy. I can picture myself now sitting there between those turntables with a stack of records on one side and pages of news, weather, and commercials on the other and a set of those awesome-looking headphones ("We radio announcers call them 'cans'") stretched across the top of my head. I thought I was Superman. I knew that night that I had to get a job as a disc jockey.

I suddenly forgot all about baseball. The pitchers and catchers were beginning to throw and work out indoors, but I couldn't have cared less. I was too busy writing letters and making telephone calls to every radio station within a hundred-mile radius of Athens, trying to find somebody willing to hire an ambitious eighteen-year-old would-be disc jockey.

I got the same answer everywhere. "Have you had any experience?" they'd always ask.

"No," I'd always reply.

"Well, we're only hiring people with experience."

"How can I get any experience if I can't get a job?" I'd ask.

And they'd mumble incoherently and I'd start looking up the next number.

When school was out for the summer, I got in my shiny metallic-blue 1947 Ford, the one with just under two million miles on it, and drove to towns like Winder, Monroe, Madison, Griffin, Newnan, Carrollton, LaGrange, looking for a job as a disc jockey. Finally I found one right under my nose, at WGAU–AM and FM in Athens.

A genial, warm-hearted man named Burl Womack was station manager at the time, and he'd had a policy down through the years of hiring college students as part-time radio announcers. The first time I'd called on him he'd had no openings, but near the end of June another student announcer left town for the summer and I had a job. I still didn't have any experience, but I guess Burl figured I wouldn't be any better or too much worse than any of the others he'd hired. Or maybe he could just see in my eyes how badly I wanted to try.

My first duties at the station consisted of coming in at five-thirty every morning, gathering the news and weather for Burl to read on his *Breakfast with Burl* show, and reading a few commercials myself. Soon I was given a DJ show of my own on the weekends and finally the three to six p.m. slot every weekday afternoon. I was happier than a pig in a mud puddle.

Six weeks into my hard-to-come-by employment, however, my bubble burst. The station was sold to new owners and my friend Mr. Womack was fired. I was heartsick. I just knew I'd be back out pounding the pavement again any day. But, surprisingly, that didn't happen at all. A kind but firm man named H. Randolph Holder bought controlling interest in the station and for some reason didn't run the new kid on the staff out the back door when he came in the front. But he wouldn't let me play any country music.

"This is not going to be a country station," he said to me more than once in the deep, authoritative voice that had distinguished him for years as the town's leading newscaster at crosstown rival WRFC. "If you insist on playing country music, you can look for a job someplace else."

I had already seen that movie, so I followed orders and on my three-hour record show in the afternoons played only the songs listed in *Billboard*'s Top 100 pop records chart. Remember, though, this was 1956, and a new thing called rock 'n' roll was just beginning to burst upon the scene. I played

a lot of rock 'n' roll! On several occasions Mr. Holder would hear me playing records by Elvis or Carl Perkins and once even Fats Domino, and he'd
come charging into the control room to accuse me of playing country
music again. I'd calmly get out *Billboard* magazine, show him where the
song I was playing was ranked among the Top 100 pop records in the country, and he'd leave me alone. But he didn't like it.

At the time, WGAU was affiliated with the CBS Radio Network, and
we had a standard policy at the station that if anything ever went wrong
during one of our local broadcasts, we were to "hit the net," that is, punch
the button that would replace our local programming with the program
currently being aired on the network.

I was manning the control board late one Saturday night when an
Atlanta Crackers minor league baseball game we were carrying was halted
by rain. My specific instructions were right there in front of me written on
an alternate programming log: "In the event of a rainout or a rain delay,
continue with programming from CBS." What the person who typed the
log didn't know, however, was that on Saturday nights CBS broadcast live
from Shreveport, Louisiana, the *Louisiana Hayride*. And the *Hayride* was
second only to the Grand Ole Opry in those days as the top country music
show in America.

Well, the rains didn't let up in Atlanta and I did just as I was told. I
punched up the network and sat back in my chair grinning from ear to ear
listening to Johnny Horton, Slim Whitman, and all the *Hayride* regulars
singing their songs and doing their thing. And then the phone rang. Not
the request line nor the news line, but the hotline. The one that rang loud
and flashed bright red in the control room. The line the boss used when he
was mad. Or upset. Or both.

"What in the [blankety-blank] is that [blankety-blank] country music
doing on my radio station?" Mr. Holder bellowed into my ear. "If I've told
you once I've told you a thous—"

"But, Mr. Holder," I interrupted, "I only did as I was told. The log said to
go to CBS and this is what CBS is broadcasting."

On Monday morning Mr. Holder wanted to see me in his office. He had
calmed down but only slightly. "Look, I've been thinking about this, son,"
he said, "I know how much you love country music. But we're just not going
to play it here. That's all there is to it. We are not a country music station.
But I'll tell you what. A good friend of mine has just gotten his permit to

put a new station on the air up in Commerce, Georgia. I called him today and told him about you. He said he'd like for you to drive up next week and meet with him. I think you've got a good chance of being hired there. Of course, Commerce is just a little town compared to Athens, but you can play country music up there to your heart's content."

That was the nicest anybody has ever been fired. And although neither of us had any way of knowing it at the time, Mr. H. Randolph Holder had just proceeded to do Mr. James William Anderson III one of the biggest favors of his young life.

Led by Henry Aaron, who had escaped the Jim Crow South to become a major-league baseball star, the Milwaukee Braves were in first place in August 1957, the night Bill Anderson's life shifted on its axis. Aaron went hitless on August 27 against the New York Giants at the Polo Grounds, but Eddie Mathews drove in a couple of runs and "Spitter" Lew Burdette threw seven innings and got the win. Meanwhile, 691 miles away from Manhattan's Polo Grounds, nineteen-year-old Bill Anderson carried his guitar up to the roof of the Hotel Andrew Jackson in Commerce, Georgia. The words he scrawled on the back of a WJJC radio envelope imagined his three-story-high rooftop view of Commerce as something grander. There, in dirt-plain Commerce, he conjured something like gleaming Manhattan: "The bright array of city lights, as far as I can see," Anderson wrote. Those words would be his ticket to Nashville and his entry into the music business. Today, Aaron's MVP season of 1957 is deep history. There is no such thing as the Milwaukee Braves or the New York Giants baseball club. Mathews and Burdette are gone, and the Polo Grounds are dust. Ray Price, who would take "City Lights" to the top of the country charts, is gone, too. But those words that Anderson wrote . . . the ones about the lonely guy looking out at city lights . . . those words are still dancing off that WJJC envelope, singing to anyone who cares to listen, in a voice the nineteen-year-old Bill Anderson did not dare dream was possible.

Commerce, Georgia, was, in the late 1950s, a dingy, sometimes depressing little country town straddling U.S. Highway 441, eighteen miles north of Athens and just south of the foothills of the Blue Ridge Mountains. The most exciting thing a teenaged kid could find to do after work, if he wasn't into stealing hubcaps, was to go for a double-dip ice cream cone at the local Dairy Bar. There were three or four large textile mills in Commerce (at least one of them manufactured blue jeans), and much of the local citizenry was employed there. There was also a railroad track that ran parallel to the main street, dividing the heart of the business district, but in all the years I lived there I don't think I ever saw a train. Just the tracks. I used to try and figure out which was the right side and which was the wrong side of the tracks, but I never came to any conclusion. I lived on one side and worked on the other, so I really didn't care, but studying on it helped to pass the time.

Commerce was inhabited by approximately forty-two hundred of the kindest, friendliest, just plain nicest down-home folks I think I've ever known, and the radio station there, WJJC, "The Friendly Voice of Jackson County," turned out to be everything the station in Athens had not been.

I was there at WJJC from the very beginning. I had gone to work at the station in early June, a couple of weeks before we were scheduled to begin broadcasting. My primary job was to organize the record library. I was standing in the control room filing records the morning the telegram arrived from the Federal Communications Commission in Washington saying that as of that moment we were licensed to sign on the air. It was an exciting and tense time. There had never been a radio station in the little town before, and everybody was anxiously awaiting our first broadcast.

The owners of the station, Mr. and Mrs. Albert Hardy, had run the local newspaper in Commerce for years and didn't profess to know much about radio, so they hired a young station manager named Grady Cooper from

Cedartown, Georgia, and entrusted him with the job of getting us in business. Mr. Cooper, who turned out to be a very capable and dedicated manager (and in my case a very patient employer), decided we should sign on that first morning by playing a recording of "The Star-Spangled Banner," and then he thought maybe he'd like to open the microphone and say the first few words. That sounded great to me, and I stood nervously poised behind his chair as he flipped the switch to send our national anthem echoing out across the hills and valleys of northeast Georgia. It was a proud moment.

The record ended and Mr. Cooper opened his microphone. "Good morning, ladies and gentlemen," he said authoritatively, "this is Grady Cooper signing on WJJ—"

Then, click.

Then dead silence.

In all the excitement of trying to get our new radio station on the air, nobody had remembered to check the volume level of the microphone, and when Mr. Cooper threw the switch and started talking, the transmitter overmodulated something fierce. Our new little baby went right back off the air just as quickly as she had come on.

I could picture radios all over town having been jarred off their shelves by the roar and plummeting to the floor. All the planning, all the preparation, and our first broadcast had lasted less than three minutes. Fortunately, our engineer, Bill Evans, was standing by and quickly spotted the source of the problem. He turned down a couple of knobs, and we did it all over again. This time it worked to perfection.

In less than an hour, at eleven-thirty a.m. to be exact, I came on the air for the first time, hosting the station's first country music record show called, in the beginning, the *Dinnerbell Jamboree*. I loved my time on the air and the fact that finally, after more than a year of trying, I could at long last play country music on the radio, but every time I said the name *Dinnerbell Jamboree* I cringed. I didn't say anything about it at first, but after we'd been on the air for a couple of months and I had begun to build up both a bit of confidence and a bit of a following around the area, I began asking Mr. Cooper if we could change the name of my program. He wasn't too keen about the idea at first, but the more I badgered him the more I began to wear him down. Finally he gave in, more to shut me up than anything else, I think, and from that moment on the entire afternoon's programming became known as *The Bill Anderson Show*. I was off and running.

Mr. Cooper was a super boss, giving me a free hand not only to play the country music I loved but to develop myself into a full-blown radio personality as well. I took advantage (sometimes too much advantage) of my newfound freedom.

My new show came on the air every afternoon at one o'clock, and for the first two and a half hours of my shift I played country music. Nothing but country music, and all the country music I wanted. Then about three-thirty, when the area high schools began to let out and just as soon as I figured the kids had had time to get to their cars and head out of the parking lot, I rocked. I mean, up until the sun went down and our little thousand-watt daytime station signed off the air, I played Elvis and Jerry Lee and Chuck Berry and the Coasters and all the rest. And I liked it. Not as much as I liked country music, of course, but in those days rock 'n' roll was new and was a synonym for success. More than anything else in the world I wanted to be successful.

My radio program slowly but surely began to build an audience. The grown folks liked the country music I played and they seemed to respect my knowledge of the subject. The kids loved the loud rock and the fact that they never knew what I was liable to say or do next. I screamed and I yelled, I deliberately screwed up commercials, messed up artists' names and their song titles. I told jokes, I laughed when I should have been serious, and I played it straight when everyone else was cracking up. All over northeast Georgia it became the afternoon thing to do to turn the radio dial to 1270 and partake of the craziness.

There were even a few times when our signal wasn't confined to northeast Georgia. I snooped around and found out where the knob was on the transmitter that controlled the power output of the station, and I learned how to ease it up past our assigned thousand watts. It was illegal as robbing a bank, but when nobody was looking, I'd often do it. Some days when the ground was wet along the creek bank by our tower and nature was helping amplify our signal as well, listeners would phone me from parts of North Carolina, nearly one hundred miles away. I never got called on the carpet for tinkering, but it's a wonder. I could have cost the station a large fine and put our very license to broadcast in jeopardy.

I guess I was just too hyper and too young to realize that what I was involved in was something more than a big toy. To me it was all one big lark ... making a little money doing something I loved. I even went so far as to create an on-the-air sidekick, a talking duck named Josh.

Actually, Chuck Goddard, my old pickin' buddy from the Classic City Playboys, found the little rubber duck for sale in a store somewhere, bought him, named him, and taught him how to talk on the radio. Chuck and Josh manned the airwaves at WMGE radio in Madison, Georgia, about the same time I was at WGAU in Athens, and, quite truthfully, Chuck taught Josh most of his bad habits. In a couple of years Chuck got an opportunity to move up to WDOL in Athens, and they were so uptown they didn't allow ducks on their station. So I adopted the poor homeless creature and took him to Commerce.

Josh didn't actually speak. He just squeaked. I'd talk, squeeze Josh, he'd squeak his reply into the microphone, and I'd interpret for the listeners what Josh had said. Usually it was something outrageously stupid or else it was the duck trying to get the best of the disc jockey. It was really not much more than my sitting alone in a dark room and talking back and forth to myself, but I had a ball with it and so did the listeners. The younger kids especially loved Josh. Not long after the adoption papers had been filed and it was legally confirmed that Josh would be with me permanently, I had a contest on the air to give him a middle name ("Hey, gang, a duck this important needs a middle name. There's Harry S Truman, Dwight David Eisenhower . . . we've got to have Josh 'Something' McDuck!"), and I received thousands of entries, most of them from the kids. We ended up tagging him the distinguished Josh "Waddlesforth" McDuck, and pretty soon he was getting more fan mail than I was. When that started happening, I began to lie and tell the listeners that Josh was sick or out of town on business, and I'd do the shows by myself, leaving the duck on the shelf for days at a time.

I also became known in Commerce as "Peanut Butter Bill," a name that has, pardon the pun, stuck with me all these years in that area. I came upon it quite innocently. I had moved to Commerce by that time and drove to Athens every morning to attend classes at the university until noon. Then I'd drive back along the winding roads from Athens north to Commerce as fast as I safely could every afternoon and run into the radio station only a few minutes before air time, out of breath and always hungry. I'd keep a loaf of bread and a jar of peanut butter in a back room, and while my first record was playing I'd sneak out and make me a sandwich.

One day I mentioned on the air that I was eating a peanut butter sandwich. From that day on, whenever I'd make a mistake reading a commercial (they were all done live at small radio stations back then) or reading the news (another task I performed to justify my princely salary of fifty dollars a week), I'd just blame it on the peanut butter sticking to the roof of my mouth. Pretty soon I became "Peanut Butter Bill."

One day during the last Christmas season I spent in Commerce, I got a phone call from the local postmaster. "Come down here right now!" he ordered. "Everybody in this town must have sent you something made out of peanut butter for Christmas. Packages are piled everywhere. This whole post office smells like Peter Pan!"

Truly, it did. I found peanut butter cookies, peanut butter cakes, peanut butter candy, and I couldn't count the jars of just plain old peanut butter (both smooth and crunchy) that the listeners had sent me. In a way it was funny, but in another way I was genuinely touched. My listeners had cared enough about me and had identified closely enough with me for them to want to send something special for the holidays. It was my first introduction to the loyalty and the closeness that develops between the people in country music and their fans.

It was while I was in Commerce that I also began seriously trying to write songs. I lived in a tiny bedroom on the top floor of the tallest building in town, the Hotel Andrew Jackson. It was all of three stories high. Every night after I signed the radio station off the air, I'd go downtown and eat supper at the Piedmont Cafe or maybe across the street at Threatt's Restaurant. Then I'd go back to my little room, study as little as I could get by with, and then I'd pick up my guitar and start strumming. I loved to write, loved to create anything, and I began to put my thoughts down on paper and to make up little tunes to go along with them. One of those "little tunes" turned out to be my magic carpet to Nashville.

It was written on the back of a WJJC radio station envelope. In pencil. And because I dated all my compositions in those days, I know I wrote it August 27, 1957. Not in my room, however, but on the roof of the hotel.

It was a stifling hot night, and the little window air-conditioning unit in my room wasn't strong enough to cut through the abusive heat and the grueling Georgia humidity. On nights like that I'd often take my guitar and retreat to the top of the hotel, flop my long legs down across their one and only lounge chair, and sing my heart out into the darkness. This particular night there wasn't a cloud in the sky. I began looking up at what seemed like a million stars above and down on what few lights there were in Commerce,

Georgia, and I wrote: "The bright array of city lights, as far as I can see / The great white way shines through the night for lonely guys like me."

My dad said later that he knew I had the imagination it took to become a great songwriter if I could look at Commerce and write about a "great white way." It was more like two or three traffic lights, and even they didn't work all the time. But those few words opened the doors to the world of country music for his son.

And who would have dared dream, on that hot, muggy night in August 1957, that twenty years later the people of Commerce would erect a marble monument on a downtown sidewalk just a few blocks away from the old hotel:

> Bill Anderson, Country Music Hall of Fame Songwriter,
> Wrote His First Hit, "City Lights," in Commerce, Georgia.

What an unforgettable occasion it was for me the day the monument was unveiled. It seemed like everybody I knew in the whole world turned out for it. They proclaimed it Bill Anderson Day in north Georgia, and my then-wife, Becky, and I flew all night from California to be there.

By that time the little hotel where I'd lived and written my song was no longer in business; the building had been converted into a bank. The bank, along with WJJC radio, became the official sponsor of my homecoming and spared no effort in welcoming me back.

The bank lobby was filled to bursting with old friends, fans, and well-wishers when I walked in, almost two hours later than I'd been scheduled to arrive, thanks to some bad flying weather en route. But the people had stayed and waited patiently, and they cheered and applauded like mad when I finally got there. The bank officials unveiled a plaque that they said would be mounted in their lobby, marking the building as the spot where my first hit song had been written. Then, before I knew it, my old college buddy, newspaperman, disc jockey, and local entrepreneur Billy Dilworth, grabbed me by the arm and said, "Come go with me. We've got something else to do."

I didn't have any idea what was happening, but I followed him outside the bank, down the street a couple of blocks, and across the railroad tracks to the other side of the main drag, where another large crowd had already gathered. I looked out and saw my mom and dad standing there, both my daughters, all my band members, Buddy Killen from Nashville, Grady

Cooper (still the manager of WJJC), Bob Waters (the mayor of Commerce), and even the lieutenant governor of the State of Georgia, my dear friend of many years, Zell Miller. I still didn't know what was going on, but I figured something important must be about to take place.

Billy Dilworth moved to the center of the crowd, held up his hands for quiet, and began to talk, saying all kinds of nice things about me and about Commerce. Then the politicians talked, saying much of the same, and then somebody called my name and told me to step forward and untie a large rope that was holding a big piece of yellow canvas over the top of something standing five or six feet high in the middle of the sidewalk. I did as I was told, reached down and gave the cover a yank, and lo and behold beneath that canvas was the shiny marble monument paying tribute to me. I was flabbergasted.

I tried to talk, but the words wouldn't come. I was completely overcome by the excitement and the emotion of the moment. Later that night, we performed a benefit concert before a packed house at the Commerce High School football stadium, and I opened the show with "City Lights." I tried to tell the people then how much the monument and all the other events of the day meant to me. But I wonder if they ever understood how deeply I had been touched by it all.

You see, it was the people of Commerce, Georgia, who adopted me and believed in me long before anybody else did, and I've never forgotten that. I don't get to go back there very much anymore, but a big part of my heart lives there all the time. And it probably always will.

I finished writing "City Lights" the night I started it, and in a matter of just a few weeks I had made a recording of it in an unfinished TV studio in Athens and mailed the tape to Bob Tanner at TNT (Tanner 'N' Texas) Music, Inc., in San Antonio. I asked him if he'd like to publish the song and perhaps release my recording of it on his TNT label. He didn't exactly do cartwheels.

Bob had published and released the first song I'd ever had recorded back in 1956, "No Love Have I," by Arkansas Jimmy Burton, on TNT, and he'd released my first record, "Take Me," with "Empty Room" on the flip side, a year later. Nothing good at all had happened with either record, but he had encouraged me to keep writing and to send him anything new I came up with. "You never know where the next big hit is coming from," he had written in response to the first letter I ever wrote him. In those days I was seeking out the names and addresses of music publishers all over the country and writing them letters, begging somebody to please just listen to a few of my songs. Bob Tanner's name was just one of hundreds on my list, but of all the companies I contacted, he was the only one who even took the time to write me back.

Not very many people remember the first record of mine that Bob put out, thank goodness. It was pretty awful. I wrote both sides, "Take Me" (which Roger Miller used to love to call "Take That"), an upbeat, lyrically bland little ditty that *Billboard* magazine called "an Elvis Presley type country-rocker sung without Preslian power." On their one-hundred-is-perfect rating system for new records, mine got a sixty-five. Somebody once told me that the worst rating any record ever got was a forty. "Take Me" didn't beat that by much. "Empty Room," the ballad on the other side, was recorded about two keys lower than I was capable of singing. I can't believe I ever talked anybody into releasing it.

Looking back, I guess the most outstanding thing about my first record was the engineer. I cut the songs in the studios of radio station WEAS in Decatur and used one of their local DJs to set up the microphones and twist the knobs. He might not have wanted it publicized, but his name was Roy Drusky. He went on to have a pretty good career in country music as a singer/songwriter in spite of the fact that his being associated with my first record could have buried him early.

Bob Tanner most definitely didn't make any money on my first release, and he was understandably hesitant about the prospect of releasing the second one. Finally, I told him I'd buy a couple of hundred copies myself if he'd just press them, because I knew I could sell that many to my radio listeners. He owned a pressing plant, so he agreed and shipped me the first box a few days later.

Naturally, I played my new release on the air the first afternoon it came in, and by that night I had sold the first copy. Well, really, I didn't sell it; I traded it to a cute little waitress at the Piedmont Cafe for a plate of scrambled eggs and pork chops. I didn't put any green folding money into my pocket until several days later.

It seems strange recalling it now, but "City Lights" was actually released as the B-side of my record. Remember, the music of the late fifties was not hard-core country but rockabilly and rock 'n' roll. I had written a bouncy, driving little tune called "(I've Got) No Song to Sing" that was supposed to be my A-side. I had begun singing it on a few show dates around Georgia, and it was driving the kids in the audience wild. In fact, I worked a show in Swainsboro, Georgia, with Mel Tillis, who was then a struggling writer and performer himself, and when Mel heard the response to "No Song to Sing," he asked for a copy of my record. He took it back to Nashville and recorded the song himself on Columbia Records. It was not successful for him at all, and I teased Mel for many years, because had he taken the time to listen to the flip side, he might have recorded "City Lights" and had himself a number one smash.

Fortunately, a man in Nashville named Charlie Lamb did hear the B-side. At the time he was publishing a weekly trade publication called *The Music Reporter*, and I'd mailed him a copy of my record hoping to get a review in his magazine. There weren't nearly as many records released in those days as there are now, and when my record came across Charlie's desk, he took the time to listen closely. "City Lights" struck him as a powerful piece of material, and he knew my version on TNT Records wouldn't have more than limited distribution, so he took the song to Chet Atkins, the head of Artists and Repertoire for RCA Victor.

Chet listened to my record, agreed with Charlie on the commercial possibilities of the song, and in a matter of just a few days produced a great record of it on his label by a young stylist named Dave Rich. Dave was a singer like Willie Nelson, in that for many years he was simply ahead of his time. He was a tremendous singer, but the general public never quite caught on to the acrobatics he could perform with his voice. He had the vocal ability to move from one note to another in much the same sliding way as a pedal steel guitar, and he sang the living fire out of "City Lights." He took the word "array" in the first line and turned it into five syllables. He was incredible. Unfortunately, though, most people perceived him the same way as one lady who told me, "Gosh, he sure sings through his nose, doesn't he?" Dave eventually gave up on the country music business and went to preaching and singing only gospel songs, but I was thrilled to death by his recording of "City Lights," even by the sight of my name (B. Anderson) in little bitty letters on the RCA Victor label. If nothing else had happened, I'd have been satisfied.

But things were just beginning to happen. Dave Rich's record didn't set the world on its ear, but it accomplished one major thing: It got my song onto the airwaves of the leading full-time country music radio station in Nashville. And in Nashville you never know who's listening to the radio.

It turned out that Ray Price, who was just beginning to make his move into super-stardom about that time, was riding to the golf course one afternoon with the legendary Ernest Tubb when the disc jockey on WENO decided to play Dave's new record. The two of them turned up the volume and listened closely.

"That song sure sounds like one you could sing, son," Ernest said to Ray.

"Yeah, but I've already got my next record cut," Ray replied. "In fact, it ships next Monday."

"Well, if I were you I'd cancel that release and record this song," Ernest prodded. Throughout the entire round of golf that afternoon he never let up. Every time the two of them would meet on the green, Ernest would start in again. "You'd better cut that song, son," he'd say over and over until finally, and fortunately for me, Ray relented. He phoned Goddard Lieberson, the president of Columbia Records, and told him to hold up on releasing his next single. The following Thursday he called a special recording session and cut "City Lights."

I have since been told by several people who were at the session that it was a very emotional evening. After Ray and the musicians had rehearsed the song several times and had become confident that the arrangement was just the way they wanted it, Ray halted the proceedings and called all the musicians and background singers together in the center of the room.

"Now," he said, "I want you all to really think about what the ole boy in this song is going through. Listen and try to put yourself in his place. Imagine you're in Las Vegas, you're all alone, and it's cold and the wind is blowing and it's about to snow. You've just gambled and lost the last dime you have in this world. You don't know where you're gonna go, how you're gonna eat, what you're gonna do next. You pull the collar of your coat up around your neck and you walk out the door of the casino. All you see is 'the bright array of city lights' as far as you can see. Now . . . let's cut the song!"

And cut it they did. "City Lights" by Ray Price on Columbia Records was an immediate smash hit, rising to number one on the charts and staying in the charts for thirty-two weeks. Such diverse talents as soul singer Ivory Joe

Hunter and Debbie Reynolds covered the song in the pop field. In several of the year-end polls, it was voted both Song of the Year and Record of the Year for 1958.

The day I learned that Ray Price had recorded my song, I was on duty at WJJC. School was out for the summer, and I was working a split shift, signing on at five-thirty in the mornings, working until eight o'clock, then coming back at one for my regular afternoon show. For some reason, however, this particular morning I was still at the station around ten o'clock when the phone rang. The receptionist told me it was Roger Miller calling from Nashville.

Roger and I had met a few years earlier at the old Tower Theater on Peachtree Street in downtown Atlanta when he was stationed in the army at nearby Fort McPherson and I was a kid with a guitar wandering around town looking for someplace to play. We quickly became friends, meeting every time a big country show would come to town, standing off to the side of the stage in the darkened corners and singing each other songs we'd written, dreaming of the day each of us would become a big enough star to step out onto that stage and into the spotlight.

Roger said he was from Erick, Oklahoma, but what he wanted more than anything in the world was to say that he was from Nashville, Tennessee, and that he made his living writing and singing. Funny, I was beginning to want to tell people that's what I did, too, but for the longest time the closest either of us came to stardom was wandering through the corridors of the old building that had once been known as the Erlanger Theater, home of the famous WSB Barn Dance, and staring in awe at the performers who happened to be working there.

One Sunday afternoon Wanda Jackson was in town appearing as part of the *Hank Thompson Show*, and I nearly fainted when Roger got up nerve enough to knock on her dressing room door and ask if we might come in and talk with her awhile. She very graciously said sure, and while we were sitting there asking her all kinds of stupid questions about the music business, Roger spied her shiny new Martin guitar sitting in its case over in the corner. "Would you mind if I borrowed your guitar and sang my friend here a couple of new songs I've written?" he asked. Wanda, evidently taken back by such a request, said she didn't mind, but the look on her face told me she really did.

Roger grabbed the guitar and, not wanting to bother Wanda anymore, motioned for me to follow him out the door. He led me over to the edge of the stage where no one could see us, and he played and sang for me for about fifteen minutes. Then he handed me the guitar, and I played and sang to him for fifteen or twenty more. We were knocking each other out, telling one another how great we were, and marveling at how good Wanda's guitar sounded. Pretty soon, though, it started closing in on her time to go on stage, and she started looking around for the two clowns who had disappeared with her guitar. She couldn't find us anywhere. Finally she called her dad in on the case. He spotted me and Roger over in the corner pluckin' away. He walked over and, in a voice much calmer than mine would have been under the circumstances, asked us if we'd mind if his daughter got her instrument back. Please. Roger handed it to him like a parent giving up a baby for adoption. When her dad was out of earshot, he turned to me and said, "I'll have a guitar like that someday," and I said, "Sure, and so will I." We stood there looking at each other like a couple of lying fools and broke out laughing.

Roger moved to Nashville the day he received his discharge from the service and began to make his mark as a writer and as a performer not long afterward. He toured for a while as a fiddle player with Minnie Pearl, then became a member of Ray Price's renowned Cherokee Cowboys. Meanwhile, I went to Athens and then to Commerce. The miles came between us, but we always managed to stay in touch.

"Hey, Anderson, guess what," he roared excitedly over the long-distance wire. "Price cut 'City Lights' last night! It's gonna be his next release. I've got the other side, a new thing I just wrote called 'Invitation to the Blues.' How 'bout them apples?"

I was blown away! Roger and I hung on the phone like a couple of school kids, laughing and giggling and talking about how all our dreams were starting to come true. Then before I could come back down to earth the telephone rang again. This time it was Bob Tanner calling from Texas.

"Bill, I just found out Ray Price cut 'City Lights' last night. It's going to be his next release!" I dared not burst his bubble, so I acted surprised and congratulated him since he held the publishing rights to the song.

I was still bouncing off the ceiling when in less than an hour the phone rang for the third time. This time it was the head of Tree Publishing Company in Nashville, Buddy Killen. Roger had become a staff writer at

Tree and told Buddy he knew this young disc jockey down in Georgia who also wrote some pretty fair songs. Buddy had no financial interest in "City Lights" but called with the news anyway. "Congratulations," he said. I acted surprised again and answered, "What for?" as if I didn't know.

"Ray Price cut 'City Lights' last night, haven't you heard? It'll be his next release. Let me hear any new songs you might be writing, OK?"

I assured him that I would. Tree Publishing wanting to hear my new songs! What was going to happen next?

It didn't take me long to find out. About two o'clock that same afternoon Jim Denny, former manager of the Grand Ole Opry and president of the giant Cedarwood Publishing Company in Nashville, called. In his calm, understated yet very authoritative voice he said, "Bill, I think I've got something you'll be interested in."

"What's that, Mr. Denny?" I asked.

"Well, if you'll sign a contract to write all your future songs exclusively for Cedarwood Publishing, I think I might be able to talk Ray Price into recording 'City Lights.'"

Welcome to show business, Peanut Butter Bill.

Ray Price's version of "City Lights" came out in the summer of 1958, and it quickly rose to the number two position on the country charts. Then it stalled. And then it rose back up, to number one. And then it stayed there, for thirteen consecutive weeks. It was still number one as 1958 became 1959. By then, Decca Records was in the Bill Anderson business, releasing Bill's debut single, "That's What It's Like to Be Lonesome" to radio stations in time for Christmas. The singer was learning lessons both heady and humbling, working with his heroes onstage and in the studio, to varying degrees of public acceptance. His first tour was with George Morgan, Roger Miller, and the performer who would come to be known as Johnny Paycheck. Today, that sounds like an incredible melding of legends. At the time, it was cause for no great public concern.

As big a hit as "City Lights" was, it went against the grain of almost everything that was happening musically in the late fifties. It was a traditional, three-chord, cryin' country song, and it stood out like a sore thumb among the likes of "Wake Up Little Susie," "Whole Lotta Shakin' Goin' On," and "Great Balls of Fire" on the country radio airwaves. It was almost a throwback to another era. Maybe that's why it was such a smash. The public was obviously ready for a song of that type.

Buddy Killen, true to his word, did want to hear some more of my material, and I began making frequent trips to Nashville to show him the new songs I was working on. I was falling in and out of love on a daily basis surrounded by all the beautiful coeds at Georgia and the sweet, innocent little country girls from Commerce, and I never seemed to be lacking for new ideas for songs. Some were happy, some were sad, but nearly all my early writings had two things in common: They were based on my true experiences, and most of them were written to the exact same melody.

"Anderson, everything you write sounds like you stole the tune from the Baptist hymnal," Killen would say, and he'd sit patiently with me for hours, teaching me the art of crafting a song. He'd show me how one line had to build off the line in front of it and how a writer had to construct a song to reach a certain climax at a certain point. Mostly, though, he worked with me on my melodies. The lyrics always seemed to come easier to me, and I'd try to let the lyric "suggest" a melody. In other words, if I were writing a happy song, I'd try to come up with a happy sounding melody. The same would be true in reverse if I were writing a sad song. But I wasn't as creative melodically as I was lyrically. Truth told, I'm still not.

I signed an exclusive songwriter's contract with Tree Publishing Company, and Buddy and I became not only business associates but close personal friends as well. I confided in him one morning about the latest catastrophe in my love life, and before the day was over he and I had collaborated to write "I May Never Get to Heaven," a heartfelt ballad everybody from Don Gibson to B. J. Thomas to Aretha Franklin would record before Conway Twitty would finally take it to number one nearly twenty years later.

And it was Buddy Killen who in the late summer of 1958 asked Owen Bradley if he'd come by the Tree offices one afternoon and listen to some songs written by the skinny disc jockey from Commerce, Georgia, who wrote "City Lights," and, perhaps, to consider this DJ as a recording artist for Decca Records, where Mr. Bradley had recently been named chief of Nashville operations.

A great musician and record producer like Owen Bradley—one of the architects of the Nashville Sound—didn't need to make house calls, but out of respect for Buddy he came. And I sang, just me and my guitar, and he listened. After about a half hour or so Owen said, "Well, son, you're not the greatest singer I've ever heard, but you sure do write some terrific songs. And your voice is different. You certainly don't sound like anybody else I've ever heard. If you'll keep writing songs as good as these and if you'd like to try, I think we might be able to make some hit records together."

As simple as that I became Bill Anderson, Decca recording artist.

Owen and Buddy told me my job was to get busy writing some new songs for my first recording session; they'd take care of getting all the legal documents drawn up and the paperwork in place. I went back to Commerce and back to school. Once or twice I returned to the roof of the little hotel and tried to write, but lightning never struck there again. I did write some new songs but in other places. In a few weeks my recording contract arrived in the mail. I didn't even read it. I was so excited I just signed it and sent it back before anybody had a chance to change their mind.

I flew to Nashville and cut my first record for Decca in Owen Bradley's legendary Quonset-hut studio on Sixteenth Avenue South in August 1958, and before winter quarter began at school I had become the only student in the history of the University of Georgia to have a record in *Billboard* magazine's country music charts. Heck, I was probably the only student in University of Georgia history who had ever *heard* of the *Billboard* magazine country music charts.

Recording in Nashville with Owen Bradley for Decca Records was a far cry from recording in an empty TV studio in Georgia with a bunch of cronies and pals for TNT. I was scared half to death just looking around the room and seeing musical legends like Buddy Emmons poised behind his steel guitar, Tommy Jackson with his fiddle, Hank "Sugarfoot" Garland and Grady Martin on their guitars, Bob Moore on bass, and Buddy Harman on the drums. These were the cream of the crop, the pickers whose music I played every day on my radio show back home, and now they were in the studio waiting to play behind me.

And the equipment . . . I had never even seen a gold-plated German-made Telefunken microphone before, much less ever sung into one. And the first time I heard my voice played back on the huge studio speakers, in stereo, no less, it was almost more than I could comprehend.

Owen didn't hire a vocal group to sing in the background on my first session, and I was a bit disappointed about that. Groups like the Jordanaires and the Anita Kerr Singers had become the rage in Nashville, especially on records aimed at the new, lucrative crossover market, and I had had just enough local success with my rockabilly "No Song to Sing" to have my heart set on recording for Decca in a similar style.

"No, we're going to record you straight country," Owen said when the subject came up a few days before the session. He said it in such a decisive, forthright manner that I knew there was no room for argument. I'm glad now he never allowed me to voice my opinion. What if I had been able to change his mind? I might be a washed-up rock 'n' roller today.

We cut two sides on my first session, and both were songs that I had written. One was a straight-ahead country ballad very much in the vein of "City Lights" called "That's What It's Like to Be Lonesome." The flip side was a wordy, more up-tempo love song entitled "The Thrill of My Life." Instead of "ooohs" and "aaahs" and "doo-wops" in the background, though, Owen had Buddy Killen and a newcomer to Nashville named Donny Young blend with me on some high-lonesome three-part harmony on the choruses. In later years Donny Young was to achieve a certain degree of fame and notoriety under the name of Johnny Paycheck, but on this night, for my first recording session, he was my tenor singer.

As we all gathered around the giant stereo speakers in the control room and listened to the playbacks when the session was over, everybody felt "That's What It's Like to Be Lonesome" had turned out to be by far the stronger of the two sides we'd cut. Owen said it sounded like a hit to him and that he'd ask Decca to release and promote that side. He turned out to be right.

The record came out in late autumn and broke into the national charts on Christmas Day. By February it had climbed as high as number twelve. But, unbeknownst to me, Ray Price was once again somewhere listening to his radio, heard my new song, and recorded his own cover version to release as a follow-up to "City Lights." As soon as Ray's record reached the radio stations, most of the disc jockeys quit playing my cut and started playing his. Before it was over, Ray Price had his second consecutive hit with a Bill Anderson song.

A lot of people said to me, "Gee, that's too bad," when I told them Ray had covered my record, but I didn't feel that way about it at all. Actually, it put me in a no-lose situation. I wrote the song, and I knew I'd be getting much larger writer's royalties as a result of his record than I would have off my record alone. He was, after all, an established star who had just spent over half a year in the charts with a number one record. I'd be getting paid two or three cents for every copy of the record he sold whether it was on a single or in an album. In addition, I'd be receiving another few pennies from Broadcast Music, Inc., every time either my record or his was played on the radio or performed on television. It might not sound like much, but I knew a few cents here and a few cents there could eventually add up. Besides, my own record had already opened a lot of doors for me prior to Ray's cover. One of those doors came in the form of a phone call from a small booking agency in Nashville one day early in March.

"Bill, I just wondered if you'd like to go along on a little personal appearance tour I'm putting together for George Morgan in a few weeks." the voice on the other end of the line asked. "We're going out west for about twenty-one days, and your record's done real well out there, and we'd like to have you go with us. Whatta you say?"

I was speechless. Me, a student at the University of Georgia, a disc jockey in Commerce, Georgia, going on tour with Grand Ole Opry star George Morgan? I was just a greenhorn kid who had never been anywhere outside of five southeastern states. I nearly jumped through the roof. Would I like to go on a tour? Does a five-string banjo have five strings?

I told the agent heck, yes, I'd love to go. But as soon as I hung up the phone, I started wondering just how I was going to manage. I could take a leave of absence from the radio station, I knew that, but I had no idea how to get out of school. Finally I just said to heck with it, this is a once in a lifetime opportunity and I'm not about to pass it up. I've never regretted it either, even though by going on the tour I set my college graduation back a few months and ended up not earning the U.S. Army officer commission I was only a few weeks away from receiving through the ROTC program at Georgia. I was pickin' and grinnin' somewhere the day they gave the final Military Science exams, and I learned shortly thereafter that the army is a bit fussy about handing out officer commissions to young men who'd rather tote a guitar than a rifle.

My dad nearly had a coronary, though, because he just knew I'd end up as one of Uncle Sam's buck privates someday. I never did. In fact, I was never called into the service at all, but even if I had been, I honestly don't think I'd have cared. I figure I learned things out on the road on that trip that I couldn't have learned staying home and studying and taking exams for the rest of my life.

Besides, to this day, the memory of that first tour serves as a constant reminder of how bad things can get in this business, and it inspires me every day to try and never let my career deteriorate to the point that I might have to go through something like that again. The cast of the show consisted of longtime Opry great George "Candy Kisses" Morgan as the headline attraction and featured his all-star band of Little Roy Wiggins (legendary from his days with Eddy Arnold) on steel guitar, the incomparable Dale Potter on fiddle, Sammy Pruett (one of Hank Williams's original Drifting Cowboys) on lead guitar, veteran Bill Slayman on bass, Ken "Loosh" Marvin on rhythm guitar and as master of ceremonies, and a seventeen-year-old "rookie" named Willie Ackerman (later of *Hee Haw* fame) on drums. This group was hired not only to play behind Morgan but to play the music on my songs as well. They also were asked to back up two other young male singers and one female singer who had been invited to join the tour.

Each of the three young men on tour had had only one 45 rpm single record released at that time, none had ever recorded an album, and I dare say not one of the three attracted one paying customer to a single show. Later, though, they attracted plenty. Their names were Roger Miller, Donny Young (Johnny Paycheck), and Bill Anderson. The obligatory female was a tall, pretty lady named Wanda Jones, who never quite made it in the music business.

Morgan was one of the finest, purest singers country music has ever produced, but unfortunately had not had a big hit record in quite some time.

The tour opened at a club called Rosa's in Fort Worth, Texas, then swung out through west Texas into places like Sweetwater and San Angelo, on to Hobbs and Alamogordo, New Mexico, Phoenix, Tucson, Prescott, and Flagstaff, Arizona, before mercifully ending some twenty-two days later back at Cain's Academy ballroom in Tulsa, Oklahoma. In three grueling weeks, we hadn't drawn, as Loosh put it, "enough people to flag a hand car." And there's nothing worse, I found out, for your ego or your pocketbook than to be thousands of miles away from home singing your heart out in an empty club, auditorium, or arena night after night after night.

But crowds or no, I was having a ball. Every day was full of new excitement, new adventure, and I came to respect George Morgan to the point of almost idolizing him. I'd stand in the wings during the shows and watch his every move, watch the way he could touch whatever audience we might have with just the right combination of seriousness and humor, and I'd yearn for the ability to be able to do the same. I was so in awe that I never spoke to him much, but he was watching me. One night after a show in a nearly empty roller rink in Alamogordo, New Mexico, he came up to me and in his most sincere manner put his arm around my shoulder.

"Anderson," he began earnestly, "I've been watching you. I've been watching all you guys, in fact, and I've decided you are going to be the biggest star of all three."

I beamed. I glowed. I swelled with pride. "Thank you, sir," I managed to whisper.

"Do you know why you are going to be a big star?" he asked.

"No sir, why?"

"Because you are different. You may be, in fact, the only guy in the history of country music who can hit an E chord on his guitar and come in singing in the key of C."

I was crushed for days.

A lecture in intonation, a big dose of U.S. geography, and the knowledge of how to survive on two cheap, thin hamburgers a day weren't the only lessons that I learned from my first tour. I also got exposed to a few things my somewhat sheltered life had thus far protected me from. In particular, those staples of the road: pills, booze, and women.

We weren't fifty miles west of Nashville riding in Miller's blue 1954 Cadillac with the clear plastic seat covers and the four recap tires when one of the band members turned to me, opened his hand to reveal a half-dozen or so little yellow pills, and said, "Wanta bennie?"

So this was what they looked like! Benzedrine, I think, was their proper name, and I knew musicians often took them to offset the rigors of travel and the pressures of the road. I also knew they could keep you awake for days at a time. I'd never taken one, and just the thought frightened me. What if I liked them? What if I never wanted to go to sleep again? What would my conservative Methodist mother say? So I politely declined. To this day I've never taken an upper, although Miller swore that one night when he and I were en route to a show in Florida, I took a No-Doz pill with a cup of coffee, got back in the car, rolled down the window, beat out wild rhythms on the dashboard, and sang at the top of my lungs all the way to Panama City. If that's true, then I'm glad I never tried anything stronger.

Actually, I didn't need a thing on that first trip to keep me awake. The thrill of being on the road, sitting in the backseat of that big blue car, knowing I was heading for Texas was all the upper I needed. When the tour opened at Rosa's in Fort Worth, I found myself smack-dab in the middle of a world that was as foreign to me as downtown Moscow. I wouldn't have admitted it at the time, but I had never actually been inside a nightclub until that very moment. Not only had I never performed in one, I had never been in one, period. Oh, I had played in a few American Legion halls and AMVETS clubs back in Georgia, but not in a real, honest-to-goodness Texas-style honky-tonk.

I'm sure my naïveté showed in my performance, too. I wasn't used to people drinking beer and dancing and hollering and carrying on while I was trying to sing. And the people who came to Rosa's hadn't come for prayer meeting. They said they liked our music, but I wasn't sure they even heard any of it. When it got to be my turn onstage, I sang a couple of songs and then tried telling a few jokes, but nobody paid any attention. Finally I decided to just shut up and sing. It took years for me to adjust to the audiences in Texas and some of the other southwestern states because the biggest compliment they can pay an artist there is not to applaud him but, rather, to like his music enough to stop talking and get up and dance to it.

And then there was the drinking. Liquor was something I'd never been around much either. I'd seen and smelled lots of it when I'd been in college, but drinking had never been a part of my family, and it seemed to go against all my upbringing. But they drank lots of beer and booze in Rosa's and in most all the other places we worked on that first tour. As our crowds shrank and our expenses mounted, the liquor got to flowing rather heavily among some of our cast members as well. I never was tempted to join in, though. Fact is, I was almost twenty-seven years old before I ever let my hair down far enough even to taste beer, wine, or hard liquor.

I'll never forget the first time I ordered a drink. I was in New York City, working as part of a gigantic two-day country music spectacular at Madison Square Garden. At the time, I don't think a larger country show had ever played the Big Apple. It was an exciting time, and after the Saturday night show my wife and I decided to go out to a nice restaurant to celebrate.

We found a quiet, intimate spot with a small band playing softly in the corner. The waiters were all dressed in tuxedoes, and the food coming out of the kitchen smelled delicious. I was feeling great. I decided it was time for the bashful kid from Georgia to broaden his horizons a bit. I signaled for the waiter, but when he got to our table I realized I hadn't the foggiest idea of what to order or how to go about ordering it.

"Uh, sir, you see, I've never ordered a drink before," I stammered, "and I don't really know what I want. We're here to celebrate, though, and . . . well, we'd just like something to relax. What do you suggest?"

He looked at me with that sardonic New York look on his face and said, "Why don't you try dancing?"

I ended up ordering a whiskey sour and nursing it for three or four hours. I wasn't much of a drinker then, and I've not become much of one since. Today I drink very little and never when I'm working.

Texas dance halls, clubs, honky-tonks, skull-orchards, or whatever you want to call them were not only loud and boisterous. They could also be the smokiest places in the world. It could be awfully rough on a singer when he's up on the bandstand inhaling all the fumes floating around him. Especially one like me who has never smoked himself.

Cigarettes, like liquor, have just never been much of a temptation for me. I tried them, like every kid did, when I was a teenager, but I never liked them very much. I recall vividly the last time I ever lit one up. I was fifteen or sixteen years old, about the age when a kid thinks he knows everything, and I'd gone down to radio station WEAS in Decatur to watch a disc jockey/recording artist named Texas Bill Strength do his afternoon DJ show. Bill was quite well known in those days, particularly in the South and Southwest. He'd made a few records for some of the major labels, guested on the Grand Ole Opry a few times, and as such he had become one of my heroes. For no real reason he had always been extremely nice to me, inviting me to his home on several occasions, and always letting me come out on stage and sing a couple of songs as a warm-up act when he'd promote concerts by the major stars around the Atlanta area. If Texas Bill Strength had told me to jump off a cliff, I'd probably have asked him "Which one?" and done it. I looked up to him that much.

But ole Texas Bill, as I suspected then and confirmed in later years, was quite a rounder. He smoked, he drank, he partied a lot, and he didn't care who knew it. So when I walked into the radio station with a cigarette in my hand this particular afternoon, I didn't think anything about it. I was just doing something I'd seen Texas Bill do on many occasions.

"What are you doing with that cigarette, boy?" he growled when I came into the control room, where he was seated between the turntables spinning the top country hits of the day. "Don't you want to be a singer when you grow up?"

"Yes sir," I answered timidly.

"Well, put that damn thing out and don't you ever let me catch you smoking another one, you hear me?"

"But you smoke," I protested.

"Yeah, and you know what? I can't hit the high notes like I used to either. And I cough a lot, sometimes right in the middle of a song. And it's 'cause I've messed up my throat with them [blankety-blank] cigarettes. Nobody ever told me like I'm telling you not to smoke. I wish they had. Now put it out!"

I did, and I was never tempted to smoke again.

I once heard a major country music star tell a disc jockey, when questioned on the air about his personal habits, "I don't take pills, I don't drink, I don't smoke, and three out of four ain't bad!" I've always assumed the fourth vice to which he could not claim abstinence was women.

I'll admit I've always enjoyed the members of the opposite sex myself. As the old stage gag goes, "I've liked girls ever since I found out they weren't boys!" By the time of my first tour, I had dated quite a bit, gone steady a few times, been "engaged to be engaged" once, whatever that is, and had my heart broken on more than one occasion.

But at the same time, I was still quite naive where the ladies were concerned. Remember, this was the late fifties and where I came from girls didn't even call boys on the telephone. So the first time a sweet young thing in skin-tight blue jeans and high-heeled cowgirl boots waltzed her curvaceous little body up to me in one of the nightclubs where we were working and said, "Dance with me!" I didn't know whether to wind my watch or take a bubble bath.

To say that my first tour was a financial disaster would be to say the burning of Atlanta was a nice little bonfire. I had been promised fifty dollars per working day by the promoter, and out of that I was to pay my share of a hotel room and buy all my own food. My transportation was to be furnished. It wasn't much money, but for a kid who'd been used to making fifty dollars a week as a disc jockey (in cash so that nobody in the local bank could see my check and know how little I made), I thought I'd struck gold. What the promoter didn't tell me or George Morgan or any of the others on the tour, however, was that he was depending totally on the gate receipts from the shows to pay the talent. He had no cash reserves, and, as it turned out, most nights he didn't have any money to pay us.

Today, a booking agent would never allow his acts to leave town without the promoter having put down a sizable cash deposit for the tour, but country music booking agents weren't nearly as sophisticated in those days as they've become in recent years. Too, in the years immediately following the rock 'n' roll explosion, long country music tours just weren't that easy to come by. It was almost a case of the artists taking whatever they were offered, and once the promoter got the acts out on the road, they were pretty much at his mercy. Every day our promoter would lie and tell us, "Boys, we've got a great advance sale building up in the next town. Hang in there with me one more day and everything will be all right." And we'd eat another hamburger and keep heading west.

About two weeks into the tour, tired, broke, and hungry, we found ourselves in Tucson, Arizona, without enough money even to buy breakfast, much less a tank of gasoline to get us to our next gig a couple of hundred miles north in Prescott. It really looked like the end of the line. To make matters worse for me, the night before I had walked into the cold, cavernous dressing room backstage at a place called Tucson Gardens, where we were performing, and been greeted by a letter from the dean of the journalism school at the University of Georgia. He had written to tell me that he'd been trying to find me since the end of the winter term. Somehow my credits had been added wrong, and while I had been told I was going to graduate when I got home in June, in reality I was still some six hours short of having earned the required credits. Not only were we broke, not only was I tired and hungry, but now they were telling me that the college diploma I thought I had coming, and which I always figured I could fall back on in the face of disaster, was really not mine at all. I was still on cloud nine from having been on the tour, but I was confused by some parts of "big-time" show business. It made for a bittersweet time.

Fortunately, things got better. Before leaving Nashville, Roger Miller had crammed a small record player into the trunk of his car saying, "We might want to listen to our records while we're gone." I had laughed.

The record player had never been out of the trunk until Tucson. But early that morning while we were all sitting in the hotel coffee shop pondering our fate and slowly wilting from hunger, Roger hit upon the solution. "Be right back," he announced and left the rest of us sitting in a booth sipping ice water and stalling the waitress. In a few minutes he returned, proudly waving fourteen crisp new one-dollar bills in the air. "Eat up, guys, we're rich!" he exclaimed. "I hocked the record player!"

We didn't know it at the time, but there actually would be a decent crowd waiting to greet us that night in Prescott. We'd still be cutting it close, but by watching the nickels and dimes we'd be able to make it back to Nashville in just a few more days. A belly full of Rice Krispies and two cups of strong, hot coffee later, I put my college diploma way back in the corner of my mind. I walked outside with my buddies, kicked off my shoes in the front seat of the old Cadillac, propped my feet up on the dashboard, and rode off into the sunrise one more time, doing something I've been doing all of my life . . . humming an old country song and chasing a dream.

Candlestick Park in San Francisco. Major League Baseball All-Star Game. Tuesday, July 11, 1961. The 1950s version of Bill "Hillbilly" Anderson figured his cautious left arm would have landed him on the mound that day, battling Whitey Ford, Mickey Mantle, and knuckleball master Hoyt Wilhelm. But by 1961, Hillbilly Bill was no more, and Bill Anderson had become a country music star who wrote hit songs for others and who sang one of them—"Po' Folks"—himself. At Candlestick, the National League got out to an early lead, as Roberto Clemente scored on a sacrifice fly. Two thousand miles away, Bill Anderson's telephone rang in a Nashville suburb. Grudgingly, weary of distraction from the big game he was watching, he picked up the phone and heard a man named Ott Devine ask him to become the sixty-first member of the Grand Ole Opry. Two seconds later, he said, "Yes." Then he hung up and hollered in triumph. Later that day, Clemente's tenth-inning single to right brought home Willie Mays with the winning run, but Bill Anderson had long since turned the game off.

In a way I've always been thankful that my first tour turned out the way it did, because as soon as we limped back into Nashville riding on skin-slick recap tires and one patched up inner tube, totally exhausted and stone broke, I got myself back down to Georgia and back into school.

I looked for the shortest summer school session I could find and located one that lasted only five weeks at tiny Oglethorpe University in north Atlanta. The credits I earned there could be transferred toward my degree at Georgia. I paid my tuition with my second royalty check from TNT Music for "City Lights," something like four hundred dollars. My first royalty check wouldn't have covered it. It was for exactly $2.52. I never even cashed it. I put it in a frame.

I had no intention of becoming a full-time student again, but in order to get the few remaining credits I needed for graduation, I knew I had to hit the books hard and heavy one last time. I had seen firsthand that all that glitters in show business is not gold, and I figured I was going to need all the formal education I could get. The tour had given me a large dose of the informal kind. I didn't tell anybody in Nashville about it for a long time, but I managed to graduate from college in August 1959.

While I was back in Athens for the graduation exercises, my life took another strange turn. The night I got to town I phoned to talk to my buddy Chuck Goddard, only to have his wife, LeeAnn, tell me that while I'd been gone on tour she and Chuck had separated and he had moved away. She thought he was in Swainsboro working at the radio station.

"But please come by while you're here," she said encouragingly. "I'd love to see you and, besides, Bette's here. I know she'd like to see you too."

Bette Louise Rhodes was LeeAnn's youngest sister from Atlanta. Chuck had introduced us several years earlier on one of her weekend visits to Athens, hoping to spark a romance, I think, but I'd always considered her just a friend. I thought there was too big an age gap between us. That is, until I went to see LeeAnn the night before graduation.

Bette had grown up. She was in nurse's training at Georgia Baptist Hospital in Atlanta, and suddenly we had a lot more to talk about than we'd ever had before. We spent almost the entire rest of the night doing just that, talking. After LeeAnn had gone to bed and we'd emptied the pantry of all the cookies we could find and drunk up all the Cokes in the house, we walked outside into the front yard, leaned up against my car, and talked some more. I told her all about the tour I had been on with George Morgan, how much fun I'd had, and how little money I'd made, but how, in spite of that, just as soon as I got my diploma that next morning I was going to move to Nashville and try to get into the music business full time. I was sincere when I told her I hoped she'd write me and stay in touch. She assured me that she would. Several dozen letters, a couple of hundred phone calls, and four months later, Bette Rhodes and I got married.

It's easy to see now that we simply weren't old enough (she was nineteen and I was all of twenty-two) and didn't know each other nearly well enough to have taken such a big step. She was an attractive girl, tall, brunette, a bit shy, and in spite of our brief courtship we made things work pretty well for a while. We even became the parents of two beautiful daughters, but Bette and I came from backgrounds that were very different. Our expectations of life turned out to be quite different, too, and we eventually grew to be two entirely different people from the kids we were in 1959. There's a line in an old country song that says, "We didn't grow together so we grew apart." That pretty accurately describes what happened to us.

Bette's father had been a city policeman in Atlanta all of his adult life. She grew up with a man-figure who left home at six-thirty in the morning, worked eight hours at his job, came home at three-thirty in the afternoon, didn't bring any of the problems of his job home with him, and built barbeque pits and poured concrete patios for his family in his spare time. A hillbilly singer-songwriter doesn't exactly keep those kinds of hours nor have the hands-on abilities of a cop. At least, this one didn't. When we bought our first house, I had a hard time digging the hole in the ground for our mailbox to sit in, and I nearly got an ulcer trying to string a clothesline between two poles.

For a long time Bette tried to understand me and my way of life, but I think show business and its high-profile lifestyle confused her. It was so different from anything she'd ever been around. I probably didn't help a whole lot myself. I was so intense and so intent on making it big that I know I often neglected to put my arms around her and guide her slowly into this strange and foreign world as I should have. There were other problems, of course, there always are, but had I not been cut out of such ambitious cloth and had I realized that life moved at any speed other than full open throttle, our marriage might have lasted a bit longer than it did. Bette and I began to drift apart around 1964. We separated in 1968, and a year later, in June 1969, our divorce became final.

Fortunately, my career was headed in a more positive direction than my personal life. I was living in Nashville full time, and the hit songs were pouring off my pen: "The Tips of My Fingers" for me and Roy Clark and Eddy Arnold, "Riverboat" and "Face to the Wall" for Faron Young, "I Missed Me" and "Losing Your Love" for Jim Reeves, "Happy Birthday to Me" for Hank Locklin, "When Two Worlds Collide" for Roger Miller, and, in 1961, a hit of my very own called "Po' Folks."

I say "of my very own" because up to that point it seemed like every time I wrote a song and recorded it myself, a more well-known artist would cut a "cover" version of the same song and theirs would become the better-selling record. Owen Bradley was frustrated, saying, "We're cutting the best and the most expensive demos in town!" But nobody tried covering "Po' Folks," thank goodness. For the first time a song finally gave me some identity as a recording artist and not just as a songwriter. And so many of the good things that have ultimately happened to me in my life and my career started with "Po' Folks." For one thing, it was the song that led to my being invited to join the cast of the Grand Ole Opry.

I was guesting as an opening act on a big star-studded Opry package in Panama City, Florida, one Saturday night when "Po' Folks" was right at the peak of its popularity. I didn't know it at the time, but the manager of the Opry, Ott Devine, was in town for a fishing trip in the Gulf of Mexico, and he had heard about our show and decided to come in off the water long enough to see us that night at the city auditorium. It was a great night for me in that the audience wouldn't let me leave the stage. I was called back time after time for "just one more verse of 'Po' Folks'" before the crowd finally stopped applauding. Mr. Devine saw it all and evidently was impressed. He came backstage after the show to congratulate me and to tell

me I'd be hearing from him soon. I simply assumed he meant he'd be calling and inviting me to do another guest appearance on the Opry, since he
had already been quite generous in that regard for the past several months.
I thanked him but soon learned that I did not attach nearly enough significance to his remark.

I was sitting at home a few weeks later watching the All-Star baseball
game on TV (they played them in the daytime back then) when the phone
rang. I almost didn't get up to answer it. Who would have the nerve to call
in the middle of such an important event, anyhow? I finally pulled myself
away from the game and caught the phone on the fourth or fifth ring. "Bill,
this is Ott Devine," I can still hear him say. And without wasting any time
on pleasantries, he added, "How would you like to become a member of the
Grand Ole Opry?"

Me? A member of the Opry? That was like asking me if I wanted to go
to heaven when I die! I mean, this was the same Grand Ole Opry, wasn't
it, that my mother and daddy had brought me to Nashville to see the
summer before my junior year in high school? The one where we had the
seats downstairs under the old Confederate Gallery balcony at the Ryman
Auditorium and somebody upstairs spilled a soft drink on the floor and it
leaked down between the cracks and dripped all over Mama's pretty new
dress? The same Grand Ole Opry that I used to listen to down in Georgia
by pinching the aerial on my little Arvin radio and twisting and turning the
receiver until I could get the signal from WSM in Nashville strong enough
to hear Red Foley and Hank Williams and Minnie Pearl above the static.
Did I want to become a part of that show? Is a G chord made with three
fingers? (Note to non–guitar playing readers: It is.) I hung up the phone
and screamed loud enough to be heard in downtown Atlanta.

They made me the sixty-first member of the Opry onstage at the his-
toric old Ryman Auditorium a couple of Saturday nights later. There was
no elaborate ceremony, no coronation of sorts, just a simple introduction
by host Billy Grammer and a million butterflies in the pit of my stom-
ach. I wore my shiny purple western suit with the gold trim and the white
snowflakes all over the front and my white boots. I sang "Po' Folks" and the
audience called me back for an encore. I don't think I've ever experienced
a bigger thrill, though my twenty-fifth and fiftieth anniversary Opry shows
were mighty special as well.

Not just anybody can become a member of the Grand Ole Opry. It's nothing that can be achieved, nothing that can be earned. An artist has to have had a certain amount of success in the country music field, of course, even to be considered for membership, but that membership is issued by invitation only. It does not automatically come with x number of hit records or x amount of sold-out concerts. You must be invited to join. That's part of what makes being an Opry member something so very special.

Nobody ever forgets the first time they walk out onto the Opry stage. For me it happened almost five years before I became a member of the cast, and on my first trip across those hallowed boards I didn't even carry a guitar.

I carried a camera.

My Georgia buddy Chuck Goddard had been invited to come to Nashville as the guest of the folks at WSM Radio to spend a weekend serving as their "Mr. DJ, USA," an honor the station bestowed each week upon a disc jockey somewhere out across the land who played country music records on his station back home. At the time, Chuck played a lot of country music on WMGE in Madison, and he was thrilled to death over the prospect of plying his craft for a couple of hours on the fifty-thousand-watt, clear-channel powerhouse in Music City. But I told him the minute he called and said he'd received the invitation that there was no way he'd be going to Nashville without me. I packed my bag on Thursday after school, drove to Athens to meet him as soon as he got off the air, and the two of us roared out of town at sundown heading for Tennessee.

We were in the hallways of WSM before the early morning announcers even logged in on Friday. We had no idea what lay in store, but we quickly learned that the station sure knew how to roll out the red carpet. Chuck was the one who was their special guest, of course, but they treated both of us to a super weekend.

On Friday night, he got to spin records and interview several country music stars live over WSM. I stood over in the corner of the studio completely awestruck, listening, hanging on every word. Saturday evening Chuck was the special dinner guest of veteran Opry announcer Grant Turner at one of Nashville's finest downtown restaurants. After dinner Grant presented him with a sterling silver medallion, engraved with the date, the WSM insignia, the words "Mr. DJ, USA," and Chuck's name on the back. But the biggest moment of all was yet to come. At ten-thirty Saturday night at the Grand Ole Opry itself, Grant Turner would introduce Chuck to the audience and invite him to walk out onto the Opry stage and say a few words. From the minute Chuck found out that was going to happen, he was a nervous wreck, but when the time actually rolled around it was hard to tell who was more nervous, him or me.

"Here, Willy, take my camera," he said to me hurriedly just seconds before Grant was to head for center stage to call his name. "Go out in the audience and take my picture. I've got to have a picture of me onstage at the Grand Ole Opry. They'll never believe it back in Madison."

I took the camera and started to walk toward the backstage exit and out into the auditorium when Grant grabbed me by the arm. "You don't have to go out there to take his picture," he said. "Here, follow me." And he started walking out in front of the open curtain and onto the left-hand side of the stage.

"Whoa . . . I can't go out there," I protested.

"Why can't you?" Grant asked. "Sure you can. I said it was all right."

"But . . . but that's the stage of the Grand Ole Opry!" I cried. "I can't go out there."

Grant didn't have time to stop and argue with me. The song preceding Chuck's introduction was almost over, and Grant was about to take charge. So instead of his trying to convince me any further, he simply walked around behind my back and gave me a shove that literally pushed me from the wings out onto the most special stage in all the world. Then he calmly walked to the microphone and introduced Chuck.

I nearly broke my fingers trying to get the camera set and in focus to take Chuck's picture. I snapped it twice and took off running back behind the curtain as fast as I could go, shaking like a leaf. Never in my wildest dreams had I ever imagined that I would someday walk out on the stage of the Grand Ole Opry. And I surely never thought after that night that I'd ever go back out there again.

But I did. Less than two years later, in fact, I was back, this time as Mr. DJ, USA myself. The following year I made my first guest appearance on the Opry as a performer. Four months later I was invited back for my second visit, this time as the featured guest on the NBC network portion of the Opry that was broadcast on radio stations all around the world. And now here I was just two short years after that becoming a regular member of the Opry cast. A little less than five years from cameraman to star. Don't tell me dreams don't come true.

The Opry has provided me with some of the most memorable of all the moments in my singing career. One night at the Ryman I was in the middle of a song, went to take a deep breath, and a bug flew right into my mouth and down my throat. I began coughing, then choking, struggling to get my breath, and I know the audience must have thought I'd flipped my wig, especially the radio audience who couldn't see any of what was going on. One of the musicians from someone else's band was standing not far behind me on stage and realized immediately what had happened. "Hey, Anderson," he called out, "let the bug sing!"

Standing ovations at the Opry are rare, but I've had a few and I'll never forget them. My first one came one Saturday night at the Ryman when my mother was in the audience and I did "Mama Sang a Song." I received several more when my record of "Where Have All Our Heroes Gone?" first came out. But the most memorable of all the standing ovations I ever witnessed at the Opry came not when I was on the stage performing but when I was out front watching the show from the audience.

It was in the spring of 1974, and it was one of the most emotional and historically significant weekends in the history of country music. This was the time when the Opry was about to leave its home of more than thirty years at the Ryman Auditorium and move across the Cumberland River into the sparkling new facilities of Opryland USA.

It was a move that had to be made. The Ryman, an old gospel tabernacle built in the late 1800s by a former riverboat captain named Sam Ryman, had grown too tired, too worn to keep up with the music industry's burgeoning growth and its impending charge into the last quarter of the twentieth century. For one thing, the old building could be adapted for television only very painfully. The wiring was antiquated, the production space backstage was severely limited, and there was no air conditioning whatsoever to offset the heat from both the sweltering Tennessee summers and the searing TV lights. There was virtually no convenient parking for the performers or the fans, the area immediately surrounding the Ryman was rapidly becoming overrun with seedy bars, strip joints, and adult book stores, and with country music gaining acceptance and respectability on an ever-widening front, its vanguard show had to keep pace. So on Friday night, March 15, 1974, we stood on stage, all holding hands, and sang "Will the Circle Be Unbroken?" as the tattered old curtain came together in the building that had come to be known as the Mother Church of Country Music. The following night we stood proudly but misty-eyed as Roy Acuff sang "The Wabash Cannonball" and the rich velvet curtain rose high into the rafters above the stage for the first time in the glistening new Grand Ole Opry House just a few miles north at Opryland. As a symbol of the circle remaining truly unbroken and as an assurance that the Opry would never lose touch with its past, a large circle of wood had been cut out of the old Ryman stage and implanted into the center of the new stage at the very spot where the stars would stand to perform.

There has never been a night at the Opry filled with quite as much electricity as opening night at the new Opry House. All the regular members of the cast were there; dignitaries and VIPs came from everywhere. Even the embattled President and Mrs. Nixon flew down from Washington for the festivities. I was so excited I forgot for a moment that I was one of the stars of the evening. All I wanted to be was a fan.

I was scheduled to be the second person to sing on the new stage, but I didn't want to wait my turn standing in the wings. I wanted to see and hear the opening song and the inaugural ceremonies just like the folks out in the audience. So I left my comfortable perch backstage and made my way out into the crowd. I still get goose bumps when I think about what I saw.

The auditorium was packed. There was a pulsating feeling in the air, an excitement I had never felt before, and when the house lights dimmed and the first strains of music began to filter down from the magnificent cluster of speakers hanging high above the stage, forty-four hundred people rose as one and began applauding . . . softly at first, then louder, and then louder. And I stood right out there among them and applauded just as loud as anyone.

But the first few notes of the music we heard were not being played live on the stage. A large, thin white scrim had been hung like a movie screen down across the front of the stage, and a movie projector out in the house was flashing old black-and-white motion pictures of a young Roy Acuff and his Smoky Mountain Boys off it. They were playing and singing "The Wabash Cannonball" in a scene from a movie they had made in Hollywood back in the early forties. The Opry stage itself was totally quiet and completely dark.

And then slowly but surely a few beams of light began to appear behind the scrim. Faint at first but growing brighter, then brighter. And the strains of the recorded music began gently to fade as the first notes of live music started to flow, rising softly at first, then louder, then louder. The same song, the same key, the same singer. Even many of the same musicians.

And the scrim began slowly to rise. The Roy Acuff of the forties, dressed in a plaid shirt and overalls, began to disappear and the Roy Acuff of the seventies—white-haired, distinguished, dressed in a bright yellow sport coat and tie—strode to center stage and took over right where his image on the screen had left off. I'll never forget that moment as long as I live. I laughed and I cried. Mostly I just stood there and cheered.

But then I had a song to sing. I stopped applauding and took off running as fast as I could from my spot out in the audience up through the backstage door and into the wings. I had only a minute to catch my breath before they introduced me. When my name was called, I bounded out into the spotlight and headed straight for the old Ryman circle. Somehow I felt that if I could just make it to there, I could relax. I'd be home.

I welcomed the crowd and told them I wanted to sing "Po' Folks" because that was the song that had been responsible for my being on the Opry in the first place. I sang it and received a warm round of applause. A short while later I came back onstage again and stood with the rest of the cast as we watched Mr. Nixon yo-yo with Roy Acuff and joke with him and talk and get caught up in the spirit of this momentous occasion. Then I joined in with everybody else and sang along as the president played the piano and led everyone in singing "God Bless America."

The great Ernest Tubb, who had been an Opry member since the early forties, was standing next to me onstage, and it suddenly struck me to turn to him and ask him a question.

"Ernest, did you ever dream back in those early days that the president of the United States would someday come to the Grand Ole Opry?"

He thought for a minute. "No, I didn't," he replied softly, "and I'm glad he's here. But to tell the truth, I wish it had been another president."

A few months after having had the hit record "Po' Folks" and having joined the Grand Ole Opry, the biggest things of all began happening in my career. In early 1962 I wrote and recorded a semiautobiographical recitation (the first of many talking songs I'd be doing over the years) called "Mama Sang a Song," and it surpassed anything I had ever done, climbing all the way up to the top of the national country charts. It was my very first number one record. It was such a smash hit that it even entered the pop charts, not only my version but a cover version by jazz legend Stan Kenton (he might have been a great bandleader, but he did a lousy country recitation) and a later version by Walter Brennan, who put all the emotion and feeling into the song you'd expect from an actor of his stature. There were several weeks when all three of our records were high in the pop music charts despite the song's heavy religious overtones. I didn't know it at the time, but the stage was set for the big explosion in my career.

Owen Bradley, however, clearly saw what was going on and put it into words.

"Well, Bill," he said after "Mama Sang a Song" had reached number one and had begun to slide back down the charts, "we've finally had a number one country record, and I'm happy for you. But, because you're primarily known as a country artist and because 'Mama Sang a Song' was so religious in nature, your record couldn't go any higher in the pop charts or sell any more records than it did. But now we've got some momentum going for us. If you can write a love song that fits the same formula as 'Mama Sang a Song'—you know, a little singing and a little talking—I honestly believe you're ripe to bust the country charts and the pop charts wide open."

I listened intently.

"Now, don't make this song you're going to write religious," he emphasized. "Make it about a man and a woman. We want the appeal to be as broad as we can get it."

"Gosh, Owen," I said, "That's a big order. I don't know whether I can do it or not."

"Sure, you can," he encouraged me. "You can do it and it'll be the biggest thing you've ever done." He was prophetic and 100 percent right.

Fortunately, the song I needed to write almost wrote itself. The best ones often do. And like most of my best songs, it was inspired by something that actually happened.

I had gone back to Atlanta to visit my folks in the fall of '62, and while I was in town the producer of the leading local morning television show phoned the house and wanted to know if I'd come by the station sometime during my visit and do a live interview. Sort of a "local boy makes good" type of story. I said sure, I'd be glad to, but it wasn't until after I'd accepted the invitation and hung up the receiver that I remembered one of my former girlfriends from college worked at that very station. I hadn't seen her for several years, and I wasn't too sure I wanted to.

You see, there had been a time when I had been crazy about her, but she had jilted me—a small-town country disc jockey in Commerce—to run off to Atlanta, take a job at the city's largest TV station, and marry the station's top-rated local weatherman.

Yet, just a few years earlier, she and I had almost run away together ourselves. In those days when you "ran off together" you usually got married, so I guess we'd have probably done that too.

Because of the regional success of my record of "City Lights" on TNT, I'd had a feeler from the *Louisiana Hayride* in Shreveport concerning the possibility of my joining the *Hayride* as a performer and joining the staff of the *Hayride*'s originating radio station, KWKH, as an announcer and disc jockey. Being terribly in love and not wanting to go all the way to Shreveport alone, I considered making the move only if this lovely woman-child would agree to go with me. She worked in radio as well, and I figured she could get a job somewhere in the market herself and bring in a few extra bucks to help put groceries on the table. It sounded too good to be true. Turned out it was. Enter the weatherman and a long spell of cold, rainy weather for me. I never did get to check out the climate in Shreveport.

And now, four years later, I was agreeing to go to the television station where she and ole Partly Cloudy himself both worked and do an interview? My first thought was to call the producer back and cancel my appearance. Then common sense and pride took over. "Hey, dummy," I said to myself, "she's probably not even working there anymore. And what if she is? All that stuff was over years ago. Act like a man. Go!" So I went, but all the way to the studio I wondered how I'd feel and how I'd act if I did happen to run into her.

I didn't have to wait very long to find out. I pulled my car into the parking lot and, not being familiar with the layout of the building, began searching for anything that looked like an entrance. Suddenly my eyes came to rest on a double-wide plate glass door behind some high shrubbery, and I eased my car closer in order to get a better look.

And there she was, standing right behind that very door, peering out.

I stopped and stared at her through the window of the car, through the glass door, and I could tell every inch of her was still the beautiful, vibrant young woman I remembered. Then I thought of how quickly the worm had turned and how I was now a much bigger star than her weatherman. And I smiled as I pulled my Cadillac into the parking space next to her Chevrolet.

Up to that point, everything was fine. But I had my car radio on, and, as fate would have it, just as I went to get out of the car and stride confidently into the television station, the disc jockey on the station I was listening to decided to play George Jones's record of a Cowboy Jack Clement song called "Just a Girl I Used to Know":

> Just a girl I used to spend some time with
> Just a friend from long ago
> I don't talk about the nights I cry without her.
> I say she's just a girl I used to know.

I came bounding back down to earth in a hurry. That song had always moved me, but this time it was like an earthquake. I started thinking, started remembering, and I wondered if I was as over my old girlfriend as I had thought I was.

But I took a deep breath and walked right on in through the wide double doors. I smiled, we said hello, made a little small talk, and she led me to the studio where my interview was to take place. The show came off without a hitch. I made it through the interview just fine, made it through seeing her again with no problems—I made it through everything—everything, that is, except the night.

I drove back to Nashville late that afternoon, went home and tried to pretend the whole day had never happened, but when it came time to try and fall asleep, I couldn't do it. Finally, around three o'clock in the morning with my brain racing ninety miles an hour down a dead-end street, I climbed out of bed, walked into my little pine-paneled den, and in almost less time than it takes to tell it I sat down at my old manual Underwood typewriter and wrote the words and music to a song called "Still":

> Still . . . though you broke my heart
> Still . . . though we're far apart
> I love you still.
> Still . . . after all this time
> Still . . . you're still on my mind
> I love you still.

I've been asked a thousand times over the years who I wrote "Still" for and for years I carefully dodged the question. Actually, I didn't write "Still" for

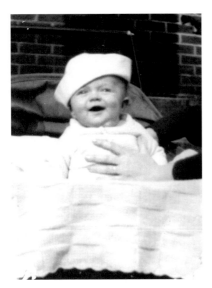

Columbia, South Carolina, 1938

Columbia, South Carolina.
Sister Mary and me, 1944.

Columbia, South Carolina, 1942.

The Avondale Playboys, 1953.
Front row: Jerry Jones, me, Charles Wynn.
Back row: Billy Moore, Jim "Meatball" Bell.

"The cautious left arm of Bill 'Hillbilly' Anderson."
Avondale High School, Avondale Estates,
Georgia, 1955.

After winning the annual Lions Club talent show, Athens, Georgia, 1956.
Millard Seagraves of the Lions Club is presenting the award.

First disc jockey job. WGAU, Athens, Georgia, 1956.

The original copy of "City Lights," on TNT Records, 1958.

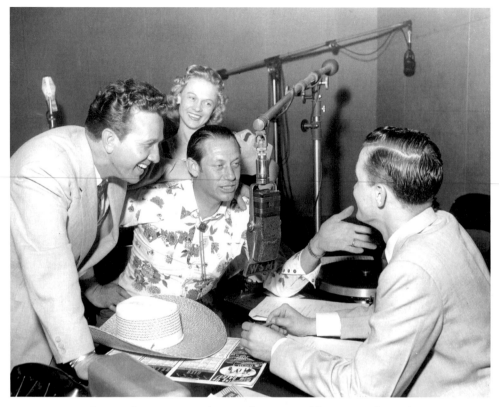

On WSM's *Mr. DJ USA* show, with Marty Robbins, Jean Shepard, and Hawkshaw Hawkins, 1958.

First professional publicity photo, 1958. TNT Records.

First time on *Louisiana Hayride,* 1960.
Tommy Tomlinson playing guitar in background.

With Patsy Cline at wsix television studio, February 26, 1963,
one week before she died in a plane crash.

Bill Anderson with the original Po' Boys band, 1964.
Lake Winnepesaukah amusement park, Rossville, Georgia.
With Weldon Myrick, Jimmy Gateley, Len "Snuffy" Miller,
and Jimmy Lance.

With Ray Price at East Point City Auditorium, East Point, Georgia, 1964.

Faron Young, me, and Ernest Tubb.
Getting a *Music City News* Songwriter of the Year Award,
at the Ernest Tubb Record Shop, Nashville, 1964.

With the Reverend Billy Graham at WBT television studios,
Charlotte, North Carolina, 1965.

Onstage at the Grand Ole Opry, Ryman Auditorium, 1968.
Jimmy Gateley is on the left.

With Roy Rogers on *The Bill Anderson Show*, Nashville, 1968.

Cast of *The Bill Anderson Show*, late 1960s.
Front row: Jan Howard, Jimmy Lance.
Back row: Me, Jimmy Gateley, Sonny Garrish,
Len "Snuffy" Miller.

With Jan Howard and Johnny Cash on the set of ABC's *The Johnny Cash Show*,
Ryman Auditorium, January 1971.

Largest crowd I ever played for. Sanford Stadium, November 4, 1972.
Left to right: Jimmy Gateley, me, Larry Fullam. Waving to my parents,
who were seated on the back row of the stadium.

First country music show broadcast live via satellite from the United Kingdom to the United States. London, 1975. Jimmy Gateley at left.

Harlan Howard presenting me with a Nashville Songwriters Hall of Fame trophy, called "the Manny," short for "manuscript," in my Nashville office, October 1975.

Signing autographs in the mid-1970s.

With Sarah Purcell on the set of
The Better Sex, late 1970s.

On the set of *Fandango*, 1983.

With songwriting awards, late 1970s. Photo by Dana Pembrook Thomas.

With Little Richard and Governor Zell Miller at the Georgia Music Awards, 1984.

With President Jimmy Carter and First Lady Rosalynn Carter,
White House, 1978.

With umpire Ronnie Milsap, who calls 'em like he sees 'em. Late 1970s.

With Glenn Hubbard, Chris Chambliss, and Rafael Ramírez,
Atlanta Fulton County Stadium, 1982.

On the set of *Family Feud*, March 1984.
Porter Wagoner, Boxcar Willie,
Dottie West, me, Minnie Pearl, and
host Richard Dawson.

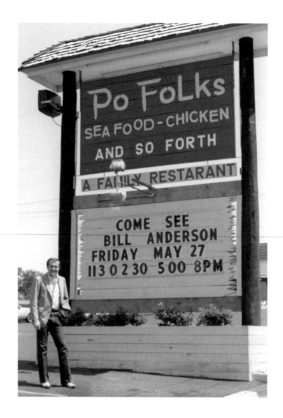

Outside a PoFolks
restaurant, 1984.

Bill's rebirth as a songwriter was influenced heavily by Steve Wariner and
his recording of Bill's classic "The Tips Of My Fingers" in 1992.

My favorite picture of my
mother and father.

With guitar, 2000.

With Garth Brooks onstage at the Grand Ole Opry, 2001.

Brad Paisley, me, Buck Owens, and George Jones.
Getting the 2001 Country Music Association Vocal Event of the
Year Award for "Too Country" at the Grand Ole Opry House.

With Country Music Hall of Fame plaque, 2001.

Bill Anderson Boulevard, Commerce, Georgia, 2002. Photo by John Kelley.

Frances Preston presenting me with Nashville's first BMI Icon Award, November 5, 2002.

Winning the
Country Music Association
Song of the Year for
"Whiskey Lullaby"
on November 15, 2005.

On Jimmy Dean's boat with President George H. W. Bush.
Kennebunkport, Maine, 2006.

Vince Gill introduced Bill to the world of cowriting songs,
and later Bill inducted Vince into the Country Music Hall of Fame.

anybody. I wrote it because of somebody and because of a situation I found myself in. I was not still in love with my former girlfriend, but I had experienced the feeling of being in love with her again, and that's what I wrote the song about. It's a thing called empathy, and it's the greatest friend a songwriter can have. I'll discuss it in more detail later.

To be honest, in the beginning I didn't think "Still" was all that great of a song. Even today I think I've written several songs that are a lot better. But somehow I was able to write into this very vanilla lyric ("Remember, vanilla still outsells all those thirty-one other flavors of ice cream," Owen Bradley loved to say) the feelings, the thoughts, and the emotions of hundreds of thousands of people. I can't begin to tell you how many people have come up to me over the years and said, "My husband and I fell in love to your song 'Still'" or, "We were about to get a divorce and he/she sent me a copy of that record and we got back together," or, "That was our song while I was in Vietnam . . . it kept us going." Somehow my song struck a nerve with virtually every segment of the population, every age group. If I knew how to do it again, I'd do it every time I write a song. So would every writer. It's that magical little something that you search and search for, and if you're lucky you find it once in a lifetime.

"Still" has been recorded by many other artists. My favorite cover of that song may be from my fellow Georgia Music Hall of Famer James Brown.

"You know, a good friend of mine, a country and western star, a beautiful man, brother Bill Anderson, he said this," James said, midsong. "And Bill told me, through a dream I had, he said, 'Brother Brown,' he said, 'Go on and tell the world . . .'"

If "Still" was a good song, then Owen Bradley turned it into a great record. First, he encouraged me to slow down the tempo. I had originally written it a bit brighter, but he knew it needed to be a more mellow ballad. Second, he added a few passing chords to the melody that I didn't even know how to find on my guitar. And they were beautiful. Third, he worked and worked the day of the session with both the engineer and the Anita Kerr Singers to get that bright little ringing sound every time the group sang the word "still." He called it "like a little bell," and nobody before or since has been able to duplicate it. Many have tried but none has succeeded. The secret lay in the fact that Owen didn't really have the group sing the word as much as he had them say it on pitch and then let the echo chamber take over and make the word ring.

"Still" did exactly what Owen had predicted it would do. It streaked up the country charts all the way to number one in almost no time, and it stayed there. Then, because of that just-right combination of elements he'd gone searching for and found, the record slowly began to be accepted by the pop audience as well. At first it was just a city at a time. Today Toledo, tomorrow Cleveland, the next day Pittsburgh, the next day Philadelphia. Then one day somebody at the powerful WMCA Radio in New York City got turned on to the record somehow and decided to air it on that station. From then on it was Katy-bar-the-door. By the time the dust settled some eight or nine months after the record had first been released, "Still" had reached number one on the country charts, number five on the pop charts, sold a million copies, been translated into several foreign languages, inspired both parody and answer records, and changed my life forever. After all this time, the one song people around the world most closely associate with ole Whisperin' Brother Bill Anderson is still "Still."

When the song was at its peak, I was running back and forth across the country, promoting it everywhere I could. I was booked onto every major country music tour I could possibly be a part of. I toured the South with a big rock 'n' roll review featuring many of the top pop stars of the day. I went with movie star James MacArthur to Rochester, New York, to perform at another rock extravaganza, and he and I stood backstage and wondered how two fish like us managed to get so far out of our native waters. While some teenaged bebop group was blasting away on stage, we gave up, snuck out a side door, and went back to our hotel.

The crowning jewel for a singer with a pop hit in the late fifties and early sixties, however, was to be booked for an appearance on Dick Clark's *American Bandstand* television show. There was no bigger show anywhere for a recording artist to be on (with the possible exception of *The Ed Sullivan Show*), and I was thrilled the day the *Bandstand* producer called and said they wanted me. But the week they'd be using me, he said, Dick would not be doing the show from his customary studio in Philadelphia. Instead, he would be on location outdoors on Miami Beach. That sounded even better to me. Lie on the beach, soak up a little sun, and appear on national TV. What else was there?

ABC flew me to Miami, put me up in a swanky hotel, and I went out and bought a new sport coat to wear. I mean, this was major league, and I didn't figure the purple suit with the snowflakes was exactly what I needed for a teenage dance party by the sea.

I was scheduled to be the last artist to appear on Dick's final show of the week on Friday afternoon, and I was some kind of pumped up. The cameras were set up outside around the swimming pool at the hotel, the Atlantic Ocean rolled gently in the background, and as we rehearsed that morning the bright blue Florida sky glistened overhead. There couldn't have been a more beautiful setting.

The show went on the air live, coast to coast, around four o'clock that afternoon. I stood off to the side and watched the other performers who went on ahead of me, my heart pounding loud enough to wake up people sleeping in Fort Lauderdale. Finally there was nobody left to go on but me, and I stepped from the shadows out onto my mark. Dick spent what seemed like five minutes introducing me, saying all kinds of nice things. Finally he called my name, the recorded music started rolling, and I was on.

"Still . . . though you broke my heart / Still . . . though we're far apart." Everything was going perfect. But suddenly from out of nowhere came a sound that I'd never heard on the record before. Then I heard it again. In less than a heartbeat I knew exactly what it was. It was thunder.

I wasn't two lines into the recitation on the first verse of my song when the heavens opened up and the bottom fell out. It rained like I had never seen it rain. Rain on my face, rain on my hair, rain all over my new sport coat, rain on the cameras, rain everywhere. And we were on the air, live. What was I supposed to do?

Dick Clark provided the solution. Pro that he was, he quickly motioned to one of the cameramen to swing his camera off of me and turn it instead on him. He was just as soaked as I was, but as the camera picked him up he took off running madly away from the swimming pool and directly toward the open waters of the ocean, slinging water everywhere. The rain was coming down in sheets by now, and here was this nationally known TV celebrity streaking wildly over the sands toward the Atlantic, still dressed in his dark, conservative suit and tie.

He never broke stride. He dove like a porpoise headfirst into the breakers, came up for air, waved good-bye to the camera, and the credits rolled and the show went off the air. I stood dripping wet back by the swimming pool, bewildered, wondering if my career had also just gone out with the tide.

But Dick was marvelous. He came back up onto the patio area wringing wet and apologized to me like the rain had been his fault. And he promised me that when my next record came out, my follow-up to "Still," whatever it might be, he'd have me back on his show from drier quarters in Philadelphia. And it wouldn't matter, he said, whether the song was in the pop charts or not. He'd still have me back.

He kept his word. The following winter I had a song out called "8 × 10," and I flew to Philadelphia and performed it in a nice warm, dry *American Bandstand* studio.

Back in 1963, there was no such thing as a country music awards show on network television. There was not much country music on television, period, particularly at the network level, which was another thing that made my two appearances with Dick Clark so very meaningful. When it came time to pass out the plaudits for achievement in the country music field each year, everybody just gathered in Nashville in late October or early November for the annual Disc Jockey Convention and Grand Ole Opry birthday celebration. That's when the performing rights society, Broadcast Music, Incorporated—the organization that collects the monies and pays the songwriters and music publishers for the radio and television performances of their songs—held their small, annual banquet open only to a few composers, publishers, and invited guests, and handed out their Citations of Achievement to the people responsible for creating the biggest hits of the year. The various music trade publications, like *Billboard*, *Cashbox*, *Music Vendor*, and *Music Reporter*, banded together during that time as well to present their trophies and plaques. These were the only country music awards back then. The Country Music Association wouldn't enter the awards business for another four years. I've often wondered what the impact would have been on my life and my career had "Still" come along after the nationally televised CMA Awards became the career-making event it is today.

The best you could hope for back in 1963 was to have your name called out at a breakfast for convention participants held in the cavernous Nashville Municipal Auditorium. If you won an award, you walked on stage in front of a few hundred folks who put down their sausage and biscuits long enough to applaud politely. Then you posed for a few snapshots, talked into a few tape recorders, and that was about it.

The breakfast and awards presentation that year happened to fall on November 1, my twenty-sixth birthday. And because of "Still," I won just about everything they gave away. *Billboard* named it Song of the Year and

Record of the Year. *Cashbox* said it was the Most Programmed Country Record of the Year on radio stations. *Music Vendor* saluted me as Male Vocalist of the Year, and *Music Reporter* honored me with their most prestigious award, the Number One Award, for being as they called it, "The Number One Artist of the Year." "Still" also won for me as a composer both a country citation and a pop citation from BMI. I had never had a birthday party quite like it, and even though I've had three or four extremely memorable birthdays, nothing will ever quite match that one as far as gifts are concerned. I left the auditorium carrying so many prizes I looked like I'd just robbed a jewelry store.

The ever jolly and always acerbic Faron Young spotted me as I was leaving the breakfast, struggling to make it out the door and to my car with all the loot. In the midst of all the well-wishers and right into a battery of open radio microphones, his voice loud enough to be heard in Memphis, he bellowed, "What's the matter, Anderson? Is that all you could win? Hell, I thought for sure you'd figure out a way to win Female Vocalist of the Year, too."

Every now and again, people ask Bill Anderson how he learned to write songs. He tells them he had to teach himself. The truth is, he's had a thousand teachers. He learned songwriting from ex-wives and from dry cleaners, from Chuck Berry and Roger Miller, from his dear mother's abiding faith and lousy singing voice. In considering Bill's formidable catalog of original songs, some have credited his intellect. Others point to his empathy and his ability to remain present in most any moment. But with a thousand teachers, how could the guy possibly miss?

There was no doubt in my mind, nor, perhaps unfortunately, in anybody else's, that the key to my budding success in the music business was my songwriting. All my early hit records—"Po' Folks," "Mama Sang a Song," "Still,"—were songs I had composed. As a recording artist, I'd begun to develop a bit of a style, but I knew I wasn't a great singer. Chet Atkins once told me the world is full of great singers but the only ones who are successful are those who have a supply of great songs to sing. He was right.

For some reason, there seems always to have been a universal fascination with the business of writing a song. It appears to be an easy enough thing to do, and if you're not too picky about the end result I guess writing a song is relatively easy. But writing a good, solid, commercial song with the potential to become a best-seller is not easy at all.

The two questions I've been asked more than any others over the years are "How do you write a song?" and "Of all the songs you've written, which one is your personal favorite?"

There are as many different ways to write a song as there are different songs to be written. There's no formula, no roadmap. I can speak only for myself and from my own experience, but I find that writing from a lyrical idea or from a catchy phrase or hook line is the best place for me to begin. If I have real-life inspiration like "Still" or an experience similar to the one on the hotel roof that produced "City Lights," then I'm that much farther ahead of the game. But I've never been the kind of songwriter who had to get drunk to write about getting drunk.

To me, the greatest asset a songwriter can have is empathy, the ability to put himself in another person's place, to think like another person thinks, to feel what that other person feels. Empathy, that's the thing. The biggest compliment I can be paid as a songwriter is for somebody to come up to me and say, "You must have written that song just for me. Your song says exactly what I feel but I didn't know how to say." That's when I know I've hit home. When John D. Loudermilk was writing some of the best songs and biggest hits coming out of Nashville in the sixties ("Waterloo," "Then You Can Tell Me Goodbye," "Tobacco Road") he'd often go downtown and hang around the blue-collar bars or spend the night just sitting in the local bus station talking to drunks in search of that very thing, empathy. I guess it worked for him, but I always preferred to close my eyes at home and imagine myself in those places. I got more rest that way, it was cheaper, and, with a little creativity I always felt I could transport myself mentally to the places I needed to visit.

When you write songs from an idea, you find that the whole world becomes one big constant song idea flowing through your mind. A talented painter looks at a gorgeous sunset and sees brilliant yellows, bright oranges, soft pinks, and vivid blues dancing in front of his eyes. And by simply picking up his paint brush he is able to transfer those images beautifully to canvas. That's his world, colors and images, captured by the touch of a master's hand. As a songwriter, however, I could look at that same sunset and not be able to draw even a good broomstick cowboy but I might write:

> I watched the sun go down this afternoon
> And paint the city's face all red,
> Then I wished upon a silver star
> That crept into the pink sky overhead.

The painter and the songwriter saw the very same sunset. We were both moved to want to preserve the beauty of the moment forever, and each of us attempted to do so in our own way. He painted with colors and I painted with words. Maybe it's called having "songwriter's eyes." To me, it simply means looking at everything that you see, hear, and feel in the world around you and thinking at least subconsciously how those things might fit together in a song.

I was having dinner in a restaurant one night at a big round table packed with friends when suddenly one of the guys pushed back his chair, tossed his napkin onto his plate, and announced, "Well, gang, I've enjoyed as much of this as I can stand." And he got up and walked away. Everybody else at the table roared with laughter, but I simply reached into my coat pocket, took out a pen, and scribbled the words he had just spoken onto the back of a scrap of paper. Before the night was over I had composed a song that would soon become a number one record for Porter Wagoner called "I've Enjoyed as Much of This as I Can Stand." Any one of the other people at that table could have written down that same phrase, but nobody else heard it in the same light that I did. I was just accustomed to listening with songwriter's ears and observing through songwriter's eyes.

I went into a small dry cleaning establishment out on my end of town one day to pick up some clothes. When I walked in the door, I noticed the owner of the shop standing there with a bewildered look on his face. "What's the matter?" I asked.

"You won't believe what just happened," he said, his eyes glazed over in bewilderment. "This guy walks in here about five minutes ago and asks to pick up his cleaning. I bring it to him . . . it was a pretty large bundle . . . and he turns and walks outside to put it in his car. I assume he'll put it down and come back in here to pay me. Instead, he gets in his car and roars out of the parking lot. Stiffs me on the ticket. I can't believe it."

"You know the guy?" I asked.

"Never seen him before in my life," he answered. Then he shook his head, shrugged his shoulders, and said, "Well, I guess if he can live with it, I can live without it."

Bingo. What a great title for a song, except not about a guy stealing his laundry but about a romantic relationship where one breaks off the marriage or the commitment and splits. And the one who's left behind says, "Well, if you can live with it, I can live without it. / If you can face your conscience, I can face my pride." I have a plaque on my wall that says it was a pretty good idea. I wrote the song, recorded it myself, and it went to number one in the charts.

When you look at and listen to the world constantly thinking song, song, song, you find that ideas for songs are all around. They're in advertisements for products, in the scripts of television shows and movies. They're in newspaper articles, magazine stories, and all over the Internet.

Sometimes ideas for new songs are even buried deep inside the lyrics of old songs. I got the idea to write "I Love You Drops"—one of my best-known songs and biggest hit records from the midsixties—by picking out an obscure phrase in Chuck Berry's classic rocker "Memphis." There's a line hidden deep in the words of that song where he talks about "hurry home drops on her cheek," and when I listened closely and realized what he was saying, I thought to myself, "What an unusual way to describe tears." He called them "hurry home drops" and it stuck with me. There was nothing illegal or immoral about my using that one phrase and writing a totally new song called "I Love You Drops." I didn't have to split the copyright with Chuck Berry, nor would he have expected me to.

I've had people write songs from phrases and thoughts I've put into my own songs many times. You can copyright a song, but you can't copyright a song idea. And a song title is not exclusive to only one musical work either. Years ago, a pop group called the Commodores had a big hit with a song called "Still." It was the same title as my most famous song, but all I could do was hope maybe I'd accidentally get some of their royalties. I couldn't stop them from putting it out. One of Billy Joel's biggest hits was titled "My Life." I had the number one country record of the year by that same title in 1969. (I really did get some of his performance royalties by accident, but somebody caught on and I had to give them back.) And a rock group once cut a song with the title "Wild Weekend." In country circles that title is synonymous with Bill Anderson, but again there was nothing I could do but wish them well.

I once wrote another hit for Porter Wagoner called "I'll Go Down Swinging." Baseball nut that I am, I had heard that phrase all my life, but it wasn't until I heard a tag line at the end of a Hank Snow record called "Breakfast with the Blues" that I realized "swinging" didn't necessarily have to involve a ball and bat. My song had nothing to do with our national pastime.

The Charlie Louvin number one hit "I Don't Love You Anymore" was inspired by a joke I heard Ray Price pull on one of his band members during a show one Sunday afternoon at the Queen Elizabeth Theatre in Vancouver, British Columbia, Canada. I was standing in the wings watching his show when I heard Ray tell the audience that one of his band members didn't drink anymore. "Of course," Ray added, "he doesn't drink any less!" My songwriter's antenna went up instantly, and I transposed the drinking to loving and went back to my room at the Georgian Hotel and wrote a song about a guy who says he doesn't love his lady anymore. "Trouble is," the lyric goes, "I don't love you any less."

One of my very first fans and dearest friends over the years, Mrs. Margaret Patterson, was taking me to the bus station in her hometown Roanoke, Virginia, late one night following a show I'd done there early in my career, and she got to telling me a bit about her family. She'd gone through a long list of sons, daughters, aunts, uncles, and cousins when she came to a person she said was the black sheep of the family. "Oh, he'd probably be all right," she said, "if he wasn't afraid to go out and get a little dirt on his hands."

Again, whammo, home run. I asked her if I could borrow a piece of paper and a pencil, and in the back of a dark, rockin', rollin' Greyhound between Roanoke and Bristol, midnight and dawn, I wrote "Get a Little Dirt on Your Hands," a song I recorded once as a solo and once as a duet with David Allan Coe. It was a reasonably successful song in the United States, but it was recorded in Australia by a pop group called the Delltones, and in that country the song is legendary.

My ex-wife and I were having dinner one evening in the Peddler, a little restaurant across the street from the church we attended, and we were enjoying a glass of wine with our meal. Suddenly I looked up, and several of the church members were coming in the door. My first inclination was to slide my glass of wine behind the menu propped up on the table. I wasn't sure I wanted the elders and the deacons to know I was imbibing.

But my then-wife refused to be a partner in my little act of subterfuge. "Hey, the Lord knows I'm drinking," she said. I got mashed potatoes and gravy all over my elbow falling across the table reaching for a paper napkin, while Becky calmly finished her meal. I totally lost my appetite. I was too busy writing on the napkin the words to a song about an ole boy who was having a few drinks in a little neighborhood bar one night when a "self-righteous woman" from the church came in and started preaching to him about his sinful ways. He told the lady, just as Becky had told me, "Hey, the Lord knows I'm drinking." That was the hook line, the title of the song, and I've got all kinds of awards hanging on my wall today attesting to the fact that a lot of people identified with the message. The song was a number one country hit for Cal Smith and even earned me a pop award from BMI due to the tremendous amount of airplay it received from all formats of radio. There's even a plaque up there on the wall of that restaurant—now called the Hermitage Steakhouse—commemorating the writing of "The Lord Knows I'm Drinking."

Not everybody writes songs the same way. Some writers compose a melody first and then add lyrics to it. I'm sure that works fine for them, but it's never been comfortable for me. Then again, melodies have never been my long suit.

I've heard people who knew Hank Williams say that he believed if a song couldn't be written in twenty minutes it wasn't worth writing. I agree up to a point. Sometimes when an idea strikes, it hits so hard the song almost seems to write itself. One minute you're staring at a blank piece of paper, the next minute the words to a song are staring back at you. Nearly every successful writer I've ever talked to has at one time or another experienced the overwhelming phenomenon of suddenly having a song appear and not being able to recall writing it. Yet nobody has ever been able to explain how it happens. In my religious song "I Can Do Nothing Alone," I wrote, "I held the pencil, but He wrote this song." How else can a writer explain a song suddenly arriving on an empty sheet of paper? I believe there are definitely times when a composer's thoughts and inspirations come from a higher power.

Mel Tillis, who has written some of the greatest country songs ever composed, evidently agreed. When I asked him if he'd been writing any new songs, he shook his head and said, "No, I haven't."

"Why not?" I asked.

"I'm not real sure," he replied. "It could be that the Lord only gives you so many. Maybe He's already given me all of mine."

Of course, not all good songs or successful songs are written in twenty minutes. Many are just as much perspiration as they are inspiration. I have written songs in less than twenty minutes, and I once agonized over a song for three years before I was finally able to finish it. And it was one of the simplest songs I've ever put together in terms of the silly idea and the plaintive sing-along chorus.

The song was called "Peel Me a 'Nanner," and it was an award-winning song for me thanks to the fine recording of it by Roy Drusky. For three years I carried these lines around in my head, unable to add anything to them:

> Peel me a 'nanner . . . Toss me a peanut
> And I'll come swinging from a coconut tree.
> Peel me a 'nanner . . . Toss me a peanut
> 'Cause you sure made a monkey out of me.

As you might expect, I've been teased and kidded about that song for years, but if you knew all the trouble I had writing three verses to go with that crazy little chorus you wouldn't laugh at all. It nearly drove me nuts. First, the chorus and the idea are both so ludicrous that the temptation was to try and write nonsensical verses. But I'm no comedian, and how much "silly" can one song stand anyhow? So I tried writing the verses in a serious vein. But how serious can you be when you're writing about monkeys swinging from trees? After struggling with this thing off and on for over three years and not being able to get it off my mind or come up with a solution, one day I was driving along in my car when *zap!* out of the blue I hit on the way to connect the chorus and the verses. The result was part serious, part foolishness, but it worked:

> There I was in all my innocence
> Loving you with all of my might.
> Come to find I didn't have any sense
> You had a different darling every night.

Although nobody will ever confuse "Peel Me a 'Nanner" with Beethoven's Fifth Symphony, I was happy with it when I quickly added two more verses and realized all the pieces finally fit. I tell people it's a song that took me three years and twenty minutes to write.

Until the 1990s, I never worked very much with co-writers. There were a few exceptions along the way, however, the most notable being a song written years ago in the backseat of Roger Miller's bright green Rambler station wagon in the middle of the night somewhere between Nashville and San Antonio, Texas.

Roger had seen the science fiction movie *When Worlds Collide* not long before and had become convinced that the title of the movie could and should be transferred to a country song. "You know," he'd say, "it'll be about the separate worlds of a man and a woman being on a collision course." And I would argue, "But we can't steal the title of a movie and make it into a song."

"Okay, so we'll change it a bit," he agreed, and we did. When the song came out, it was called "When Two Worlds Collide," and it became a big hit for Roger himself and later for several other artists, including Jim Reeves.

The night we finally got it written, we were traveling to a string of personal appearance dates in Texas and had a young singer named Johnny Seay in the car with us. Roger was under the wheel, Johnny was riding shotgun, and I was in the backseat directly behind the driver when the juices began to flow. Roger immediately stopped the car and told Johnny to slide under the wheel and drive. He reached into the back of the wagon and pulled out his guitar, climbed into the backseat with me, and I grabbed a piece of paper and a pen. The only light we had was from the headlights of an occasional passing car and a big silver moon high in the sky overhead. Roger would come up with a line and I'd write it down. Then I would think of a line and feed it to him, and he'd keep singing it over and over for fear he'd forget the melody. There was no such thing as portable battery-operated tape recorders in those days, and since neither one of us actually composed music, we just wrote down the words and hoped we wouldn't forget the tune before we reached a place where we could record it. We were so knocked out with what we were writing that even though we finished the song somewhere around midnight, we didn't dare go to sleep for fear we wouldn't remember it when we woke up the next morning. When we pulled into San Antonio around eight a.m., neither one of us had closed our eyes all night. But we knew our new song awfully well.

We checked into the old Gunter Hotel, Roger singing the song over and over—in the lobby, on the elevator, all the way up to our floor. As soon as we reached our room, he got on the telephone and called a disc jockey buddy of ours in town named Neal Merritt (who was later to write a hit song himself called "May the Bird of Paradise Fly Up Your Nose") and instructed him to "Come over quick and bring a tape recorder!" Neal did, and there in that little hotel room Roger and his guitar cut the original demo of "When Two Worlds Collide." Only when we were finally assured that the machine had worked and the song was safely on tape did we allow ourselves to fall limply across the beds and go to sleep.

Co-writing songs is the mandate in Nashville songwriting circles these days, but back then it was rather rare. There were only a few people I felt comfortable enough around to want to share my very heart and soul and guts with. And that's exactly what you do when you compose a song. You pour it all out, and it's not easy working on a song, creating your own little "baby," only to have somebody listen to what you've written and say, "Hey, your kid is ugly!" You've got to have a special relationship with someone to open yourself up that far. And they've got to trust you as well.

Jerry Crutchfield, who became one of Nashville's top record producers, wrote some songs with me in the early sixties, the most memorable of which was a Brenda Lee hit called "My Whole World Is Falling Down." We intended to write that song to the tune of "London Bridge Is Falling Down," but we got our nursery rhymes mixed up and it came out to the tune of "Mary Had a Little Lamb" instead. Jerry and I wrote mostly what I'd call "light" songs and nothing very heavy lyrically, but we had a few hits.

Buddy Killen and I wrote several songs together, usually combining my lyrics with his melodies. "I May Never Get to Heaven" was probably our most successful. Most of the other songs on which I'm listed as a co-writer were one person's idea (usually the other person's) and my actual composition.

Steel guitarist and record producer Walter Haynes brought me a song in 1964 called "Just an Old 8 × 10," a story about a child finding a faded photograph of his parents. I didn't care for the song very much, but the phrase "8 × 10" really caught my eye, especially the way it was written with the letter *x* being used for the word *by*. I took that germ of an idea and wrote my hit "8 × 10," which by the time I finished it had become not a song about mom and dad but a lament of lost love. I figured it was more commercial that way. A lady named Jerry Todd, a fan of mine from Cleveland, Ohio, later brought me a song called "Three A.M.," but there was nothing whatsoever in her lyric that I could use. But, again, as with "8 × 10," there was something about "Three A.M." that jumped off the page and hit me square in the face. I wrote my own song from her idea, and it, too, was a big record for me. Jerry and Walter are each listed as co-writers on the songs for which they supplied the ideas, and they have, over the years, shared in the royalties the songs have earned.

There is a difference, however, between the case of somebody who deliberately sets out to give a writer an idea for a song and that of someone who casually makes a comment in passing and the songwriter later takes that comment and turns it into a song. The former should definitely be listed as a co-writer and expect to participate in whatever monies the song might bring in. But a person who casually says, "Boy, it's a beautiful day," to someone who then goes home and writes a song called "Boy, It's a Beautiful Day," should not necessarily expect to be rewarded with a co-writer's percentage of that song. The writer might be generous and offer a share to the person, but that's up to the writer's discretion.

I was once in the right place at the right time and got partial writer's credits on a song that I had nothing to do with conceiving but which turned out to be an award-winning smash. Don Wayne had written the first two-thirds of a clever story song called "Saginaw, Michigan," but as he began to reach the end of the song, he didn't know how to bring his story to a conclusion. The idea was that a young couple lived in Saginaw and fell in love, but the girl's father was very much against her being with a poor boy. So in an effort to impress the father with both his resources and his ingenuity, the young man left Saginaw and went to Alaska in search of gold. It was Don's idea that the young man return from Alaska to face the father and claim the girl, but at that point he hit a stone wall. He just wasn't sure how to make it all come together.

I suggested the idea of having the boy come back and tell the father that he'd found this tremendous amount of gold up in Alaska but for a price he'd be willing to sell the rights to his claim to the father. The old man fell for the lie hook, line, and sinker, and took off to Alaska himself "looking for the gold I never found." While he was gone, of course, the boy and girl got married and began to live happily ever after.

In the beginning I didn't even consider my being listed as a co-writer on the song because I had intended to record it myself. I figured the work I had done on it would be more than justified if my recording turned out to be a hit. But I made a big mistake. I took the song to my next record-ing session but never got around to cutting it. Instead, I recorded a song I had written about another town, "Cincinnati, Ohio." Before I could set up another session, my publisher, Buddy Killen, pitched "Saginaw, Michigan" to Lefty Frizzell and it became the last number one record of Lefty's illus-trious career.

After Lefty cut the song, Don Wayne did a very kind and honorable thing. He offered me a percentage of the song and had my name added to the copyright as co-writer. Unfortunately, the first copies of Lefty's record had already begun to ship to the radio stations and record stores by this time . . . without my name on them. I received credit on later pressings of the single, and my name was always listed on the album copies, but for a long time I had trouble convincing some people that I wrote part of "Saginaw, Michigan." If you have a copy of Lefty's original single, you might want to check and see if there are two writers listed or only one. If there's no "B. Anderson" on the label, it could be that you have one of those rare early pressings.

It's not always easy to write an ending to a song. Many's the time I've written myself right into a corner with a song, much like a painter might back himself into a corner while he's painting a room. And there have been times when there has appeared to be no exit.

That's exactly what happened when I was writing one of my favorite songs, "The Cold Hard Facts of Life," a third composition of mine that Porter Wagoner took to the top of the charts in the late sixties. I began the song by telling the story of a man who had been out of town, presumably on business, but had come back home a day before he'd planned to. He thought about calling his wife to tell her he was home but decided to surprise her instead. The surprise turned out to be on him, however, when he found her at their house having a wild party with lots of friends and "a stranger."

In my lyric, the hero of the song stops in "a little wine store on the corner" to buy a bottle of champagne to take home for his wife. While he's there he overhears another man asking the clerk for "two bottles of your best." The man tells the clerk, "Her husband's out of town and there's a party. He winked as if to say 'you know the rest.'" Our hero leaves the store "two steps behind the stranger" and realizes that the stranger is headed to his house to see his wife. The story was gripping and spine-tingling as I was writing it, until I suddenly realized I didn't have the foggiest idea how my little soap opera was going to end. I had exactly sixteen bars of music, about four lines of lyrics, and possibly a tag line with which to wrap the whole thing up, and I wasn't sure quite frankly if it could even be done.

I tried every angle I could think of, then finally decided to have my hero burst into his own home and confront both his wife and her lover face to face. Throughout the story the singer had been referring to the entire scenario as his "witnessing the cold hard facts of life." So, I felt it only fitting in the climax of the song to write:

> Lord, you should have seen their frantic faces.
> They screamed and cried "please put away that knife."
> I guess I'll go to hell ... Or I'll rot here in this cell.
> But who taught who the cold hard facts of life?
> Yes, who taught who the cold hard facts of life?

Where in the world I came up with the "who taught who" line I'll never know, but it was perfect. It was my payoff. And it got me out of my corner. But it's also a lot easier telling it here than it was coming up with it then. It was just one of those fortunate things that happened when I needed it to happen most.

When a young, aspiring songwriter comes to me for advice on how to perfect his craft, I stress three things. First, I talk about empathy, but I've about decided over the years that empathy is something you either have in your psychological makeup or you don't. I'm not sure it can be taught or acquired.

Second, I tell would-be writers, "So what if you can't be great? You can be original. And, who knows, that originality might just be your key to greatness." They didn't understand Willie Nelson flailed and failed around Nashville for years, but it wasn't because he wasn't just as great then as he is now. He was just so very original that the rest of the world needed more time to catch up to what he was doing and join in his parade.

I saw firsthand Roger Miller's struggle for acceptance, writing those crazy little "Do Wacka Do" type songs. When the world finally caught on to what he was up to, they said, "Gee, how original!" But it took time. And Roger and Willie and all the others who've been successful with their originality also never gave up. That's the third thing I stress—total dedication and commitment. Without that, you may as well hang it all up.

I've often wondered if a song lyricist's craft isn't more difficult to perfect than, say, a newspaper columnist's or a novelist's, because a songwriter has such a limited number of subjects he can write about. Whereas a writer of prose can go on forever writing about nuclear waste dumps and old men chasing whales at sea, a songwriter must operate inside much more restrictive and confining barriers, both in terms of subject matter and style. Nobody tells a novelist, for example, that he can only write X number of pages that can be read in X amount of time. But a songwriter has three or four minutes at best in which to get his entire point across. Plus, his words have to rhyme and conform to some kind of meter and cadence.

Still, the greatest challenge a writer of songs has is to say what he wants to say in a way that it's never been said before. His primary objective must always be to think original, write original, and be original. It's tough, but if it's any comfort, it's exactly what every successful songwriter before him has had to face as well.

I once had a young soldier in uniform bring me a song he had written that he said would be perfect for me to record. I played his tape and read along with his handwritten lyrics. It took only the first eight lines or so for me to tell it wasn't anything I'd be interested in. But I kept on listening, nonetheless, because there was something about his melody that struck me. That's really a nice tune, I began thinking, and then suddenly I realized I'd heard the melody before.

"Hey, that's the tune to the old Hank Williams song 'You Win Again,'" I said.

"It sure is," the soldier beamed proudly.

"But you can't use that," I informed him.

"Why can't I?" he asked defensively.

"Because . . ." I replied, not sure this conversation was actually taking place, "it was Hank Williams's melody. It belongs to him."

"Hell," the soldier answered. "If it was good enough for ole Hank it's good enough for me!"

It did better for Hank.

I didn't get into the songwriting business for the money or the glory, though those things turned out to be a lot of fun. But I never sat down to write a single song with the idea of making money from it, or winning an award. Why then, I've asked myself, do I write? Not everything I have written comes under the category of "art," yet I do think I've lived the life of an artist. I once read a newspaper article from Sydney J. Harris that asserted that an artist will write, paint, or compose even if his family suffers, if his wife leaves him, or if the world finds him loony.

"I'm not saying that these are optimum conditions," Harris wrote. "I'm not saying . . . that such scorn and sacrifice are 'good' for the artist. I'm simply pointing out that these are the dynamics of his nature."

I'm the only person in the history of Des Moines, Iowa, to be inducted into the Nashville Songwriters Hall of Fame.

I was on stage at the Veterans' Auditorium in Des Moines, in the middle of singing a song, when one of the emcees from the local radio station walked up beside me and pulled the microphone right out of my hand. "Ladies and gentlemen," he announced to the stunned audience, "I hate to interrupt Bill's show like this, but we have just received a very important phone call backstage from Nashville, Tennessee." I could hear a big gasp rise up from within the crowd. It was like they expected to be told of some great tragedy.

"It seems that while this man has been here on this stage singing his songs for you tonight," the emcee continued, "back in Nashville he has been named the newest member of the Nashville Songwriters Hall of Fame!"

I stood there totally speechless. Twelve thousand people rose to their feet and began to cheer and applaud wildly. I looked around behind me and every member of my band was standing and applauding too. I tried to talk, but I wasn't able to do a very good job of it. A big tear welled up in my eye and trickled slowly down my cheek.

And I stood there thinking that this wasn't what I'd had in mind at all that night up on the roof of the hotel in Commerce when I'd written "City Lights." Nor was it what I'd thought about the afternoon I'd wheeled my car into a filling station in some little town in Michigan, grabbed a paper towel that was supposed to be used for cleaning windshields, and leaned over onto the roof of my car and written a song called "Then and Only Then," a hit for Connie Smith. I hadn't thought of awards or the Songwriters Hall of Fame then or on a single one of the hundreds of other days or nights that I'd stopped in the middle of whatever I was doing, wherever I happened to be, and begun to write a song. I had written for all the other reasons . . . the musts, the self-propulsion, the dynamics of nature. But I had to admit that it sure was a nice, warm feeling to be standing there on that stage in Des Moines and be told in such a meaningful and lasting way that what I had done had been recognized. And appreciated.

There are two of my compositions that I feel deserve a little more attention, even though I've referred to them earlier. One is "Po' Folks" and the other is "Mama Sang a Song." Both of these songs have been extremely important in my career.

People have asked me for years, "Were you really as poor as you sing about in your song 'Po' Folks'? And if you weren't, how could you write about it like you did?"

The answer is no, I did not grow up as poor as the lyrics of "Po' Folks" might suggest. But I know people who did, and I called on that feeling again—empathy—and I tried to write those lyrics with the same feelings and sensitivity I would have felt myself had I grown up that way.

When I first started writing the song, it wasn't even called "Po' Folks." My working title was "The South Side." I had written:

> There's a whole lot of people lookin' down their noses at me
> 'Cause I didn't come from a wealthy family.
> There was ten of us living in a two-room shack
> On the banks of the river by the railroad track
> And we kept chickens in a pen in the back
> 'Cause that's how it is on the south side.

I liked the first few lines but somehow the title didn't seem to click. There was no snap to it. I decided to keep working on it, though, and carried the idea with me on tour to California. One day I was visiting Johnny Cash at his home in Encino, and I picked up his guitar and sang him the first few lines. "What do you think?" I asked him. "Is there anything here?"

He smiled and said he liked it. He took the guitar and fooled around with it a while and said we ought to call it "One Mule Farmer" 'cause it reminded him of back home in Arkansas where a lot of people had to work big farms with no machinery at all and only one ole mule to plow. We kicked that idea around for most of the afternoon, but somehow it didn't really seem to work either.

One day after I got back to Nashville, I was singing the first few lines around the house, still trying to make them connect, when my mother-in-law overheard me. "Sounds like you're singing about po' folks to me," she said innocently. My search for a title was over.

I wrote much of "Po' Folks" with my tongue planted far over into my cheek. The part about "If the wolf had ever come to our front door he'd have had to brought a picnic lunch" was only my exaggerated way of trying to inject a little humor into the song while attempting to illustrate a point. The real objective of what I wanted the song to communicate was, "Hey, it doesn't matter one iota about the material things we may or may not have in this life. What matters is how we feel about ourselves and about each other." So when I ended the writing, "We patched the cracks and set the table with love," I summed up everything I intended for the song to say.

(A fan once sent a handwritten note to me on stage at a concert wanting me to sing "Po' Folks," but she couldn't think of the title. "Do that song," she wrote, "where you sing about if the fox had ever come to the back door he'd have brought a bucket of chicken!")

"Mama Sang a Song" is probably my favorite of all songs I've ever written, and for years I've introduced it on stage by saying it's a page out of my life.

And it is. Actually, it's more than that. It's many pages out of many different parts of my life.

SUNG:
God put a song in the heart of an angel
And softly she sang it to me.

SPOKEN:
I get to thinking lots of times about back when I was a lad
Of the old home place where I grew up . . . Of the days both good
     and bad.
My overalls were hand-me-downs, my shoes were full of holes.
I used to walk four miles to school nearly every day
Through the rain, the sleet, and the cold . . .
I've seen the nights when my daddy would cry
For the things his family would need
But all he ever got was a badland farm
And seven hungry mouths to feed.
And yet . . . and yet our home fire never flickered once.
'Cause when all these things went wrong
Mama took the hymn book down . . . And Mama sang a song.

SUNG:
"What a friend we have in Jesus"

SPOKEN:
Oh, I've been rocked to sleep many a night to the tune of
"What a Friend"
And then come morning and "Rock of Ages" would wake me gently
     once again.
And then I remember how Daddy would reach up and he'd take the
Bible down . . . And he'd read it loud and long
And I always felt our home was blessed when Daddy would say,
"Mama, sing a song."

Sister left home first I guess . . . And then Bob, and then Tommy, and
     then Dan.
By then Dad's hair was turning white and I had to be Mama's little man.
But, you know, it seemed that as Daddy's back grew weak, my mother's
     faith grew strong
And those were the greatest days of all . . . when Mama sang a song.

SUNG: Rock of Ages . . . cleft for me
Let me hide myself in Thee.

SPOKEN:
I guess the old house is still standing . . . I don't get to go home much
    anymore.
No voice is left now to fill those halls . . . And no steps to grace the floor.
For you see, my mama sings in heaven now . . . Up around God's golden
    throne.
But I'll always believe this old world is a better place
Because one time . . . My mama sang a song

SUNG:
"Precious memories flood my soul"

Again people are always asking, "Is that song really about your mother?"
And the answer is yes. But it's also about my grandmother, both my grandfathers, my father, and perhaps even one or two other people who have
touched and influenced my life. And it's only about one side of my mother.

Mama was the first to admit that she never was what you'd call a very
good singer. To be honest, she couldn't carry a tune in a bucket. But anytime she sang, you always knew it came from deep down inside her heart.
When she'd sing, "Just as I am . . . without one plea," you knew she was honestly and sincerely bringing herself and her problems to the Lord without
any pomp or frills. She came just as she was.

Having grown up as the daughter of a minister, Mama always had a deep
and abiding faith in God. At the same time, it would be very unfair for me
to give the impression that all my mother ever did was walk around with
an open Bible singing hymns. She was one of the most fun-loving, full-of-
life people I've known. Life to her was a treasured gift and she lived every
day of it to the fullest. I heard her say many times that she didn't believe the
Lord wanted his children to walk around with long faces. He wants us to
be happy. And even though life dealt her some tough blows, like losing her
mother when she was in her teens, leaving Mom to raise her baby sister as
if she were her own daughter, Mama managed to be a positive, upbeat lady.

One year when I was about ten years old, I decided the greatest gift I
could give her on Mother's Day was to take her to a baseball game. Heck,
that's what I'd have wanted someone to give me. It never dawned on me

that the reason Mama had never seen a baseball game in her life might be because she had never wanted to. I saved my money and bought us two box-seat tickets right behind first base to see the Atlanta Crackers play the Nashville Vols at old Ponce de Leon Park in Atlanta. I bought her a score-card and told her who all the players were, and during infield practice the Nashville shortstop threw a ball over the first baseman's head and it landed squarely in Mama's lap. It wasn't thrown hard enough to hurt her, thank goodness. She quietly picked the ball up and looked at it, much like one might inspect an egg if a bird suddenly flew overhead and laid one on an unsuspecting soul below.

Not having a lot of use for a baseball, not even an official Southern Association model, and knowing her son and his friends often played with a ball held together by large globs of black tape—plus just being the sweet-heart she was—Mama gave the ball to me.

Later, she became the biggest baseball fan you ever saw. And come football season, she and Dad traveled all over the country following the University of Georgia Bulldogs. They had season tickets to the games in Athens and always seemed to have some kind of business that needed tending to in the very same towns where the Dogs just happened to be scheduled for their road games. Every two years, I knew they'd be coming to see us in October, because Georgia would be in Nashville to play Vanderbilt. When I think of all the gifts my parents received on their fiftieth wedding anniversary, I believe the one they enjoyed the most was the trip my sister, Mary, and I gave them to California to see the Rose Bowl.

When Mary and I were growing up, Mama never went anywhere, seldom even downtown to the movies, but later she and Dad traveled to just about every state in the union and visited all kinds of exciting places overseas. She'd talk to me in one breath about riding to town in a horse and buggy when she was a girl and living in a house with no electric lights, and then in the next breath she'd tell me about flying across the Pacific Ocean in a 747 and visiting the Royal Palace in Tokyo. I constantly marvel and am continually thankful for the scope, the depth, and the fullness of the life my mother lived.

When Mom and Dad got married in the early 1930s, the years following the Great Depression, things weren't easy. They both had to work long and hard for what they achieved, and they sacrificed constantly so that my sister and I might have a few of the advantages in life that they had never enjoyed. I know now that it was Mama's faith that got her through many of her most trying hours.

Mary told of coming home one night not long after we'd moved from South Carolina to Georgia and seeing Mom standing on one leg in the tiny kitchen of the small apartment where we lived, shelling beans, for supper. Her other leg was draped over an open cabinet door, the varicose veins bulging so badly that she couldn't bear to put weight on the leg at all. Dad had quit his job, lost the medical insurance coverage he'd had through his company, and his new business wasn't yet bringing in a dime. The last thing our little family could afford was an operation for Mama. She knew that. So she endured.

Many nights as a boy I watched Mama stand over a sink full of dirty dishes, washing and drying by hand, masking her anxieties by singing "What a Friend We Have in Jesus" or "Rock of Ages" or "Amazing Grace," songs she had literally rocked me to sleep with when I was a child. Those songs seemed to calm her fears, sustain her hopes, and restore her strength. And they made a deep, lasting impression on me.

My dad was a fine Christian man himself. His integrity, his loyalty, and his honesty were shining examples to everyone who came in contact with him. He started his own business on a shoestring when he was thirty-five years old, with not much more going for him than a dream and a heart full of persistence. He had to work hard—he had a wife and two children to support—but he always seemed to find time to serve in the latest county-wide Red Cross campaign or the Lions' current drive to raise money to aid the blind, or any of a number of other local campaigns and causes. And he always found time to take me to the Sunday afternoon double-header baseball games at Ponce de Leon Park. When people ask me who my heroes are, he is always at the top of my list.

At the same time, he was not in reality the one who "took the Bible down and read it loud and long," as I wrote in my song. That would have been my grandfather, the minister. And many's the time when I, as a little boy, was sure I was going to starve to death at mealtime waiting for him to quit praising the Lord and blessing the food. Once when I was very young, I even interrupted his Bible reading one morning. "Grandaddy," I said with all the innocence and guile of a four-year-old. "You read the Bible at the table. My daddy reads the newspaper."

I was actually inspired to write "Mama Sang a Song" while sitting around my house one afternoon not long after I'd moved to Nashville, thinking back on an old-time camp meeting revival we'd once had at our church when I was in my early teens. The Reverend Homer Rodeheaver, a well-known evangelist, songwriter, and singer, had been in town all week conducting the services, and a big part of what he did every night before preaching his sermon was to break out his big, loud trombone and lead the congregation in singing the old gospel-type hymns.

The sanctuary of the church my family attended at the time was shaped like a capital letter T. When you walked in the rear door, you were standing at the bottom of the T, and the pulpit was directly in front of you. That meant that as the minister faced the congregation there was a section of the church off to each side of him that could not be totally seen by others seated in the back of the building. There was also a small balcony above the main floor in the rear.

The Reverend Rodeheaver always made a big issue out of dividing the congregation according to where the people were seated and having each section of the church try to "out sing" the others. And he was in rare form this particular night. I had gone to the services with some of my teenaged friends, and we were seated off to the right-hand side of the pulpit on the back row. From where we were, I could not see around the corner and into the rear of the church very well, and I could not see the balcony at all. Therefore, I had no way of knowing that my mother and my sister had come into the services late and were the only persons seated in the balcony.

The hymn Reverend Rodeheaver had picked out for us to work on was the old favorite "Brighten the Corner Where You Are."

"Let's just see which corner of this church we can brighten the most!" he cajoled us. "Let's see which group can sing the loudest!" And with that he began blowing his trombone, the organist joined in, and the rafters really started to ring.

"OK, we'll start with the left side," he said, and everybody over there opened up with "Brighten the corner where you are" at the top of their voices. "Now, the right side," he said, and my buddies and I let fly. "Now, the main floor," and finally, "Now, the balcony!"

Well, you can imagine what it sounded like after all the big booming voices filled the church with their rich baritones, basses, altos, and sopranos, when my mother, the only adult seated upstairs, came out singing by herself about four keys flat: "Bry-tun thuh caw-nuh (I forgot to mention her deep Southern drawl!) whah-uh you ahhh!" My buddies fell to the floor laughing. I wanted to crawl under the pews and never come out. Mary said everybody in the main sanctuary suffered whiplash from turning around to see where that awful voice was coming from.

But thinking back on it years later as an adult, I realize that my mother had simply done what she'd always done. She had brought her faith and her love to the Lord the only way she knew how. There were dozens of people there that night who sang that song right on pitch but didn't have any idea what they were singing or why. My mother did, and the corner where she sang was truly brightened.

I've got to believe that God probably laughed a little bit at the time, but I'll bet later on He gave her an E for effort. That's why I ended my song by saying, "This old world is a better place . . . because one time . . . my mama sang a song."

Bill Anderson will tell you it was awful. The unending miles, the cramped quarters, the dangerous back roads, and the meager financial returns made touring in the early 1960s a wrenching and regrettable thing. Bill will tell you all of that, and describe a world that is, thankfully, long gone, replaced with safety and comfort, good money, and some measure of privacy. But then as he talks about that horrible life on the road of more than fifty years ago, he'll get to smiling. He'll tell you about his friends, about the drummer who feared a road wreck that would snuff out the whole band, and about the fiddle player who calmed him in every tense moment. He'll tell you about the old Green Goose, and the tobacco-spitting old man who wasn't impressed by any transportation shy of a Cadillac. And after a while, he'll admit to a joy in the whole endeavor that outweighed any of the hassle.

7

I've always felt that I got into the country music business at the best of all possible times. The late fifties marked the end of the hillbilly era, the end of the "Let's tie the big upright bass fiddle to the top of the car and go out and hit the road" mentality that had ruled country music since day one. (Actually, on our famed western tour, we did tie the big upright bass to a luggage rack mounted on top of Roger Miller's faded blue Cadillac. That worked fine until it started to rain and we had to bring Big Bessie inside the car to ride with five cramped and extremely irritable musicians. I'm convinced the two greatest inventions in the history of show business have been the electric bass and the blow dryer.) The early sixties turned out to be the formative years of both the art form and the country music industry as we know it today. I got to Nashville just in time to see it from both sides.

I never thought about it at the time, but my compadres and I had come to launch a whole new generation of country music. The torch was about to be passed from the legends of the thirties, forties, and fifties to a totally new group of players. Within a matter of just a few years Nashville became home to Bill Anderson, Roger Miller, Harlan Howard, Hank Cochran, Dolly Parton, Willie Nelson, Mel Tillis, Tom T. Hall, Loretta Lynn, all energetic, creative young people who came to town and changed the face of the music they composed and performed. It was the new day of the singer-songwriter, the creator who wrote the song then went into the recording studio and out onto the stage and performed it. It was a fun time, inno cent in a way because none of us were very sophisticated musically, yet the words we wrote and the melodies we sang in those days have withstood the test of time.

I'm sure the young entertainers who come into our business today would find a lot of the things we did back then strange, awkward, and hard to believe, particularly those of us who tried to build careers as singers as well as songwriters. Today, a record company offers a new artist a recording contract; then either the company or some wealthy group of investors puts up money for tours, buses, bands, and all the rest. In 1964, I was coming off my third consecutive number one record, "8 × 10," and I was struggling to make ends meet with a two-piece band.

Can you imagine a major country star attempting to tour with a two-piece band today? But back then that was all I could afford. In the new century, if an artist has had three consecutive number one hits, one of which was a gigantic crossover smash in the pop field, he'll have six or seven musicians touring with him, and he'll be commanding upwards of $500,000 per performance. He'll have numerous buses, a sound and lighting truck complete with crew, a separate truck and crew to merchandise his souvenirs, at least one manager on the road with him, a half-dozen or so gophers and flunkies to cater to his every whim, and he'd be working more or less when and where he chooses. I was so excited that I threw a party in 1964 the night I worked my first gig where I got paid the princely sum of $500.

Actually, $500 a day in 1964 was really pretty good money. The top acts in the business were only making $750 to $850 per working day. That would have been the headline attractions like Faron Young, Ferlin Husky, Carl Smith, Kitty Wells, Marty Robbins, and others. I think I heard someone say once that Jim Reeves had cracked the $1,000-per-day barrier at some point before his death in August of that year, but Don Helms, the great steel guitar player with Hank Williams's Drifting Cowboys, told me that so far as he knew Hank never made as much as $1,000 for any one show he performed his entire life.

I realize that $500 a day sounds like decent money even now, but let me break that down a bit. First, an artist had to pay around 10 to 15 percent of his fee to a booking agent for arranging the performance. Let's say it's 10 percent to the agent and another 10 percent to the artist's manager, who stayed home and handled all the various details of the artist's life and career. On a $500 appearance, that leaves only $400 of "real" money. Now, let's say the musicians were making $40 a day, which is about what the American Federation of Musicians union scale was in the early sixties. With a four-piece band, that brings the artist down to $240 or less, depending on whether or not one member of the group gets paid a little extra to serve as band leader and/or road manager. Then, the artist had to furnish both the transportation and the lodging for his musicians. That meant a car, car insurance, gasoline, oil, tires, maintenance, and all that goes with providing transportation, including the possibility—no, the probability— of two or three breakdowns during the year and the artist having to rent cars or furnish airline tickets. Hotels could run anywhere from the top of the line to the bottom, but stars weren't going to put their musicians nor stay themselves in fleabag hotels. Putting four musicians into two double rooms and himself into a single cost another $75 to $100.

Musicians were responsible for their own food on the road but not their own stage costumes. Unless you let your group work onstage in the same clothes they'd been traveling in all day (and I've never allowed that), there goes some more of the profit. You can readily see that while the artist working for $500 a day might clear a few bucks, at the end of the day he'd be a long way from being rich.

But I don't know of a single artist in the entertainment business who got into this line of work to make money. I certainly didn't. Most people play music for one reason and one reason only: because they love it. And the money, as somebody else once said, is just one way of keeping score. At the same time, if we lost money every time we went out to sing, none of us could afford to stay in the business very long.

One key to the tremendous difference between what country stars made in the sixties compared to what country stars make today lies in the fact that what it cost a fan to see a country concert back then was a drop in the bucket compared to what it costs today. I have a poster advertising a tour I worked through Iowa and Minnesota in the late sixties. I was the headline attraction, Hank Williams Jr. was my opening act, and the ticket prices topped out at $4 for the best reserved seat in the house. General admission tickets were $2.50 and children's tickets cost $1. I thumb through magazines today and routinely see country concert tickets selling for well over $100. Plus, the arenas are much larger now and can accommodate many more people.

But, of course, it's not just country music that's more expensive, it's life. What did a loaf of bread cost in 1967? A tank full of gasoline? A sideman (a musician working in an artist's band) only made $18.75 per working day when I first came to Nashville in 1959. Some salaried players working the road now pull down well over $100,000 a year. Ted Williams was the highest paid baseball player of his time, and people cringed with disbelief when he signed a contract in 1957 guaranteeing him $100,000 for the season. A major league ballplayer making $100,000 today is . . . well, none exist. In 2015, the big league minimum salary was $500,000.

I hired my first two musicians in the summer of 1963. One was Weldon Myrick, recognized today as one of the premier steel guitar players in country music history, but at that time a newcomer to Nashville, fresh off the police force in Jayton, Texas. The other was a young lead guitar player from near Steubenville, Ohio, named Jimmy Lance. I put them on a weekly salary. I honestly don't remember how much I paid them, but I'm pretty sure there's not much there to remember. I do remember hoping every week that I'd be able to meet the payroll.

I wasn't yet able to afford the luxury of hiring a bass player or a drummer and, as you might suspect, that made for a lot of fun-filled and exciting evenings on the bandstand. Weldon, Jimmy, and I would roll into a strange town, and if we weren't working as part of a package show with other Opry stars where we could borrow a couple of pickers from their bands, we'd have to get on the phone and try to pull a couple of musicians out of a local group someplace. More often than not these guys would be God-awful bad. Maybe it was my material. My songs were not the type many local bands included in their repertoire like they did the Buck Owens and Ray Price songs of the day, and when we'd start into songs like "Still" with all its passing chords and "Mama Sang a Song" with its intricate arrangement, the local players would usually throw their hands up in horror. Finally, after almost a year of trying to make it with only two musicians, I had no choice. Extra expense or not, I knew if I was going to survive in this business I had to have my own band. In self-defense if nothing else.

I started out by adding to Weldon and Jimmy a chubby, reticent former record salesman from Atlanta named Len Miller to play drums and a guy I had grown up watching on Red Foley's *Ozark Jubilee* TV shows, Jimmy Gateley, to play bass, fiddle, and front the band. ("Fronting the band" was country for "emceeing the show.") Because of my 1961 hit and another real lack of creativity on my part, I cleverly named my newly formed group the Po' Boys. They said based on the way I paid them in the beginning, the name was fitting.

At the start, the five of us traveled in my car pulling a luggage trailer behind us loaded down with our costumes and instruments. I was proud of that little trailer (I bought it used from former Opry great Carl Smith) because having it meant we no longer had to tie anything to the roof of the car. I had my name and the name of the band painted on the sides of the trailer and across the back in big black letters that glowed when hit by the headlights of a following car: BILL ANDERSON & THE PO' BOYS / GRAND OLE OPRY / NASHVILLE, TENNESSEE. I thought I was the king of the road until we pulled into our very first motel to check in.

"We're Bill Anderson and the Po' Boys from the Grand Ole Opry," Jimmy Gateley said proudly to the lady at the front desk. "That's our trailer out there!"

"Whatcha got in it?" was her caustic, uninterested reply. "Ponies?"

You've never lived until you've taken off on a thousand-mile journey across North America in a car packed with five itinerant musicians. It sounds glamorous in the beginning—seeing the country, riding the wind, singing your songs—but it's amazing how quickly it turns into mile after boring mile of sitting upright in one uncomfortable but fixed position, the radio blaring loud enough to clear your sinuses and cure your grandpappy's gout ("We don't want the driver to fall asleep, now do we?"), and you so exhausted that you finally nod off to sleep on the shoulder of the guy sitting next to you, only to be awakened by the slamming of the brakes, the screeching of the tires, and the screaming of the driver: "Damn, I almost hit that pig!" And it slowly dawns on you that you're a slave to the habits, idiosyncrasies, and manners of the others cooped up inside that tiny, ever-shrinking vehicle with you. If they smoked, you inhaled. If they passed gas, you hoped you were sitting by the window.

There was rarely any time built into your travel schedule to stop and eat a meal at a decent restaurant, so it was a lap full of fast food on the run and catsup running down your pants leg. There was no such thing as pausing en route between towns to shave, change a shirt, or take a shower. It was hurry up and get to the next place you were playing so you wouldn't miss the show . . . and miss getting paid. The most exciting part of your day came when you saw a sign reading "Rest Area Next Exit" and you knew the driver needed to "rest."

When you added to that mix one band member, the drummer, who was so jittery he talked nonstop, mile after mile, day after day, who screamed in fear every time you met a passing car, and who kept his drumsticks lying loose in the area up behind the backseat so that every time the car goes around a curve they r-r-r-rolled to one side and then on the next curve they r-r-r-rolled back to the other, your father's insurance agency back in good ole Decatur, Georgia, or your Uncle Cyrus's feed 'n' seed store down in Gum Log, Arkansas, started looking better and better all the time. From the very beginning, Len Miller was a nervous wreck. He couldn't relax no matter where he sat in the car or what time of the day or night it happened to be. He was constantly afraid we were about to have a wreck.

And he'd try to cover up his anxiety by talking. He would jabber non-stop at the top of his voice mile after mile after mile. For the rest of us, there was no place to hide. A car doesn't exactly come equipped with private soundproof compartments. One night the other guys in the band decided none of them would talk at all, not even respond to anything Len might say, just to see how long he'd babble on. They timed him with a stopwatch and found he talked without interruption for twenty-two minutes and twenty-five miles.

"Look out!" he'd cry every time we'd pass a side road. "That car's gonna pull out in front of us and we're gonna be snuffed out!" And then he'd pick up his drumsticks, which I could never talk him into putting in a stick bag and stashing in the trunk of the car, and he'd beat nervous rhythms on the back of the front seat. I'd tell him to cool it, but in thirty seconds he'd be turned around doing the same thing up behind the backseat. All the time yelling every time we'd meet a car or truck, "We're gonna be snuffed out, I just know it! Snuffed out!"

I finally backed off the accelerator driving somewhere through the Dakotas late one night, turned around, and told him, "Len, I am sick and tired of hearing you run your mouth. And I'm telling you if you say 'snuffed out' one more time I'm gonna dock your paycheck. And that's not all. I'm gonna introduce you on stage tomorrow night as 'Snuff' Miller!" Sure enough, he did, sure enough, I did, and nobody has ever called him Len Miller since.

"Snuff" soon became "Snuffy," and the heretofore shy, pudgy little drummer quickly began to take on a whole new extroverted personality to match his colorful new nickname. He used this new persona as the basis from which to launch a fresh, spontaneous comedy act that he and I developed together. I ended up playing the part of Snuffy's straight man for more than six years.

We built our stage routines around his constantly agitating me, which was typecasting at its finest. Snuffy was marvelous at getting under my skin both on the stage and off. At certain points in the show he would deliberately goof up playing the drums and I'd light into him. From then on he was liable to do anything to me and I was liable to say anything to him. And the more we fought, the funnier it usually became, and the more the audiences loved it.

He'd sit behind me at the drums and mimic my facial expressions while I was singing. He'd hide a pair of custom-made drumsticks about the size of baseball bats behind his stool, and when I'd stop and accuse him of not playing right, he'd wait until I had turned back to face the audience, pick up the sticks, and act as though he were going to bring them crashing down across my head. After a while our timing became impeccable and the act which started quite by accident became a highlight of our stage show.

We eventually found certain routines that worked so well they became a permanent part of the show, but everything Snuffy and I did in the beginning was strictly ad-lib. I never knew what he might do next, he never knew how I might respond, and that was a big part of what made it funny.

The routine we became best known for occurred near the end of our show when Snuffy would say to me in mock disgust, "Whisper, you're just not with it tonight. I've been watching you real close and you're just not putting enough feeling into your songs. Let me come up there and show you how to do it." He'd unhook his snare drum and, before I could stop him, he'd be standing center stage. "Now, this is how you're supposed to do it," he'd say, and the band would break into "Still." Snuffy would stand there, kick his right leg back behind him like I used to do when I played guitar and sang, and with an exaggerated whisper in his voice he'd make fun of the way I recited the second verse of my biggest hit song:

> This flame in my heart is like an eternal fire
> For every day it burns hotter and every day it burns higher.
> And if this flame burns any hotter or any higher
> You'll come home and find that I've made an ash of myself!

And the audience would roar. Later, when Jan Howard joined our show as the featured female vocalist and my duet partner, Snuffy would tie a ladies' scarf around his head, come up front with the two of us, and play the role of "the other woman" in a song about a three-sided love affair called "The Game of Triangles." He could be hilarious and the crowds at our shows loved him. Even one of the major newspaper critics in hard-to-please New York City once reviewed our show at the Taft Hotel in Manhattan and called our routines "cornball humor done well." The "done well" part is underlined in red ink in my scrapbook.

Snuffy could be funny in ways the audience never saw or heard too. On a night when I might be having trouble getting the crowd warmed up and into the flow of the show, he'd call out encouragement from his perch back on the drums: "Hang in there, Willy, you'll get 'em. Just rare back and whisper!"

In addition to his being a pretty fair country drummer (he was good enough that Owen Bradley hired him to play on most of my recording sessions) and a crowd-pleasing comedian, Snuffy was also not a bad singer at all. I'd try to let him sing on our concert dates when time permitted, he sang frequently on our syndicated television shows, and he sang at least one solo on each of the record albums the Po' Boys cut in the late sixties. He enjoyed the center spotlight and decided one day in the early seventies that he wanted to get serious about perhaps launching a full-time singing career. His voice was good enough that Pete Drake, the great steel guitarist and record producer, signed him to his label, Stop Records. I wrote what I thought was a solid, commercial song for him to record, called "I Sure Do Enjoy Loving You," encouraged him to sing it on stage, and smiled when the fans applauded and told him how much they liked it. But with each round of applause, each bit of critical acclaim, Snuffy the funny man, the comedian, the goofy-acting drummer that everybody loved, began to take himself more and more seriously.

He went from being comical and lovable to being uptight and difficult to deal with at times. He seemed to lose all interest in playing the drums and in playing comedy. He wanted to be a star, and he started acting like one. One Saturday night in Tulsa, he laid the crowd in the aisles with his antics and his singing, so much so that he decided it would be all right if he rested up for the next night's performance in Oklahoma City by sleeping through the Sunday afternoon matinee. I had to go to Merle Haggard, who was working the dates with us, and ask him if he'd let his drummer, Biff Adams, back me up that afternoon, which he graciously did. When Snuffy showed up for the night show all fresh and ready to go, I took him out to the bus and told him I thought it might be best from that point on if we went our separate ways.

It was really a hard thing for me to do because deep down inside I've always loved ole Snuffy, and he had become an important part of my act.

For the first few months after he was gone, in fact, I felt like a lost little puppy out on stage without him.

Snuffy's singing career lasted only a short while. He played drums briefly for Dottie West and later for Nat Stuckey, then finally decided to get off the road entirely and pursue other interests.

Later, Snuffy produced albums for comedian Jerry Clower, and in the summer he sometimes drove the bus for the Nashville Sounds Triple-A baseball team. I just hope he didn't sit up under the wheel late at night and keep the players awake yelling, "Help! . . . we're gonna be snuffed out!"

Snuffy died in 2008. Another true country character, gone.

In the beginning, I never quite believed I could hire Jimmy Gateley to be a part of my group. After all, he'd been in the music business for years in and around his hometown of Springfield, Missouri, and along with his duet partner, Harold Morrison, had been a big part of the cast on the Red Foley shows on ABC television in the early fifties. I just couldn't imagine anybody with that kind of background wanting to play bass in my fledgling band.

But he did, and it was my lucky day when I hired him. He had moved to Nashville from Springfield after the *Ozark Jubilee* had folded, and in the beginning he was primarily interested in working as a songwriter. He'd written a couple of pretty fair country hits, "The Minute You're Gone" for Sonny James and "Alla My Love" for Webb Pierce, and from all outward appearances his career was in good shape. But he missed the excitement of performing live, and I just happened to be in the right place at the right time. He heard I was looking for a bass player, gave me a call, and joined the Po' Boys in April 1964. He stayed with me for thirteen years.

Jimmy (we all called him "Gate" or "J.G.") wasn't a great bass player, and as soon as I could afford to expand the band to five members I let him out of that job. What I primarily wanted him to do onstage was to open our shows, welcome the people, relax them, sing a song or two and get them in a good receptive mood for the rest of the evening. And he was great at that.

When the curtain would go up, he'd come out and get things moving by singing a good peppy song, then slow it down with a· pretty ballad or two, tell a couple of funny stories, and finally he'd tear into his rousing version of "Orange Blossom Special" on the fiddle. And Jimmy was an excellent fiddle player. Much better than he was on the bass, though the bass is generally considered a much easier instrument to play than the fiddle. Go figure.

I heard him play "The Blossom" so many times over the years that sometimes I can close my eyes and almost hear him … dragging that big, rosined
bow across the finely tuned, tightly stretched strings; filling the night with
the sound of the whistle of an onrushing steam locomotive; plucking a couple of the open strings with his fingernail to emulate the sound of a ringing
cowbell; daring Snuffy and the rest of the band to play fast enough to keep
up. Even if nothing else in the show had clicked up to this point, by the time
that old train sped around the last bend and headed for home, Jimmy had
the crowd in the palm of his hand. While they were still applauding him,
he would introduce me. All I had to do was hit the stage running. Gate had
already made sure the audience was on my side.

During my part of the show, he would step quietly to the rear and
play either rhythm guitar or fiddle behind me, depending on which song
I was singing. And he'd sing harmony with me. And we'd check out the
good-looking ladies in the audience and laugh and have a ball.

Jimmy Gateley meant a lot to me onstage, later on records, and then on
television for several years, but it was offstage where he came to mean the
most. He was the only band member I've ever had who was older than I. In
those days I was not only young, but I could also sometimes be extremely
impatient and moody. Occasionally I'd become so intense that I'd let my
feelings overrule my better judgment. I know now that I just had a very
large case of insecurity. I was afraid I'd wake up one morning and find this
had all been just a dream and I was back in Georgia somewhere picking
peaches.

But Jimmy Gateley, more times than I could ever begin to count, was the
calming force that cooled me down. He never seemed to get upset himself, and he always seemed to know just what to say to me and how to say
it when I'd let my emotions get the upper hand. He could smile his way
through any situation and was one of the funniest people offstage that I've
ever been around.

His humor didn't run to the side-splitting, rib-tickling style of a comedian but was rather the heartfelt, soft-spoken wisdom of someone who'd
been down a few roads and learned a few lessons along the way. I'll never
forget how he'd stop right in the middle of something he was doing and,
with a serious, almost pained expression on his face, say to me, "Willy, I'm
really worried."

I'd fall for it every time and take him seriously. "What's the matter, Gate?"
I'd always ask, truly concerned. "It's nothing really," he'd reply. "I'm just

worried. I'm afraid I won't ever be this happy again!" And I'd crack up.

On the rare occasions when we were able to eat a big meal in a nice restaurant out on the road, he'd inevitably lean back in his chair after dinner, pat himself on his full, round belly and sigh, "Boys, I'm sufferin' in comfort!" Or he'd smile and say, "I wonder what the po' folks are doin'? I know," he'd reply to his own question. "They're playin' rock 'n' roll!"

And he'd tell stories about the country people he grew up around in rural Missouri, like the ole boy who thought the shiny metal inlay on the front of his car was called the "hood ointment," and the farmer who wandered into the local radio station one morning while Jimmy and Harold were taking a break from their show and a newscast was on the air. Peering into the studio through the glass-enclosed partition in the hallway, the farmer became very upset and called Jimmy over. "Hey," he said indignantly, pointing to the newscaster on the other side of the glass. "That news teller is *readin'* that news!"

But my favorite story Jimmy used to tell concerned an elderly, almost blind musician who once toured with the Foley show and was constantly begging someone in the group to let him drive the car. "We can't let you drive," Gate told him. "You can't see well enough."

"Sure I can," the old man answered. "Just give me a chance."

Finally one night when he'd stayed awake driving about as long as he could, Jimmy relented and let the old fellow under the wheel. Jimmy slid over by the window and immediately fell asleep. He woke up suddenly just before dawn when he realized the car was stopped. He sat up with a start just in time to see the old man roll down the window, lean out, and ask directions from a mail box.

Jimmy Gateley and I had more than an employer-employee relationship. We had to for it to last almost thirteen years. Most musicians are gypsies at heart and not many are willing to stay in one job for that long. And, quite frankly, not many employers want people around that long. But Jimmy was special. We wrote songs together, the most well-known of which I still use as my theme song at the Grand Ole Opry, "Bright Lights and Country Music."

The last conversation we had was on the telephone in early 1985. Jimmy had just returned home from a stay in the hospital, and I was confined to my bed with back pain. We must have spent an hour one Sunday night lying flat on our backs, laughing and talking about old times. His heart had been causing him some problems, but he felt sure the doctors had everything under control. He sounded happy to be back with his family and assured' me that he'd be up and around again in no time. Less than two weeks later Mary Lou Turner called and told me Jimmy had died. I cried like a baby. Three decades later, I'm still sad about it.

The country music business creates stars, sometimes even legends. I've been privileged to be around many of those legends, and I value every moment I spent around Johnny Cash, Roy Acuff, Patsy Cline, and so many others. But their music wouldn't get played without the Jimmy Gateleys of the world. Jimmy Gateley worked just as hard as I did to entertain the fans. He traveled the same miles and made those miles so much easier and more pleasurable. You may have never heard of him before. Now, you have.

Gateley and Snuffy Miller were probably the two people more responsible than anyone for getting the Po' Boys out of the car we traveled in and into our first bus. Looking back, I don't know if I should have thanked them or blamed them.

The trip that convinced me there surely must be a better way to travel than by car was when we had to drive and pull our trailer all the way from Prince George, British Columbia, Canada, about four hundred miles north of Vancouver, to New York City in slightly over three days. It was the most brutal trip imaginable. When the guys came to me a few days later and told me they'd located an old bus for sale in Mansfield, Ohio—"Cheap!"—I listened.

Actually, they made me an offer I couldn't refuse: "Willy, if you'll get us a bus, we promise you'll never have to drive on the road ever again!" Up to that time I had been driving a regular shift in the car just like everybody else. We'd each get under the wheel for three hours at a time and then we'd rotate our sitting places in the car. The worst spot of all to ride was in the middle of the backseat. Right over the hump, with somebody sitting next to you on each side. There was no place to stretch your legs and very little padding beneath your bottom. We affectionately nicknamed that most miserable of all saddles "Big Sid."

"And you'll never have to ride 'Big Sid' again, either. We promise! If you'll get a bus we'll do all the driving. We'll clean it, we'll take care of it, everything. Please!" I should have made them put it all down in writing. In blood.

But for something like forty-five hundred dollars, they finally convinced me to purchase what was left of an old GMC Silversides, the bus

Greyhound ran on the road for years, the one that had the picture of the big leaping dog down the side. That particular model was also referred to by many as "Ole Frog Eyes" because of the weird appearance of the two small rear windows above the engine. Before I was through with my particular Silversides, however, I called it a lot worse things than "Frog Eyes."

Not many country stars were traveling in buses back then. The larger bands, like Hank Thompson's and Ernest Tubb's, were in them, and I think maybe Johnny Wright and his wife, Kitty Wells, transported their large family entourage via bus, but basically it was still a relatively new way for entertainers to travel. There weren't, therefore, many companies experienced in converting buses from coaches full of seats to traveling houses on wheels complete with beds, baths, and many of the conveniences of home. We found a carpenter to strip out the seats, nail together a few bunks, put in a toilet and a door or two and that was about it. It couldn't go as fast as a car, but at least we could get up, stretch our legs, and not have to stop as often at rest areas.

The people who sold me the bus had said, "Sure, she has heat and air conditioning!" And she did. Lots of heat in the summer and plenty of cold air in the winter. Once, right after I bought her, we had to take her up east for a couple of days. It was in January and during the time after the bus seats had been taken out but before the bunks had been put in. Everybody had agreed it would be no problem, we'd just bring sleeping bags and pillows and sleep on the floor. Kinda like a rolling, hillbilly Boy Scout campout.

Well, we should have brought some sticks to rub together. The morning we headed back to Nashville I woke up frozen to the floor. There was a sheet of ice about a half-inch thick covering the entire floor of the bus. It's a good thing I didn't have any matches. I'd have probably tried to start a bonfire right then and there and blown Ole Frog Eyes to bits.

Because of the color the bus was painted when I bought it, we immediately nicknamed her "the Green Goose." Actually the green-and-white paint job didn't look too bad, but when Snuffy decided to surprise me one day by having "The Bill Anderson Show" painted down the sides in brilliant red lettering, the ole Goose lost a bit of her charm. I never wanted to choke anybody as bad in my life as I did Snuffy when I first saw the paint job. And to make matters worse, he had the sign painter send me the bill.

Buses today are a far cry from the old Green Goose. I've owned four of them in my lifetime and had a couple of them outfitted pretty fancy. But still it's hard to explain to someone who's never been inside an entertainer's bus exactly what they're like.

And I guess there really is something that just doesn't sound romantic about saying you travel in a bus. I remember the crusty old man in overalls who knocked at the door of our bus one time when we were parked behind the stage at a fairgrounds in North Carolina.

"You boys come over here in that thang?" he asked.

Fighting the temptation to say, "No, we stopped by the rent-all and picked it up after we got here," I answered, "Yes, sir."

"Ernest Tubb was here a few weeks ago, and he come in a Cadillac."

"Is that right?"

"Yep, a gold Cadillac. I thought you was doin' at least as good as Ernest Tubb. Why ain't you got a Cadillac?"

"I do," I answered, "But it's at home. Besides, you can buy a dozen Cadillacs for what it cost to buy this bus."

"Yeah, but I thought you'd a-come in a Cadillac."

"Well," and I was getting a bit testy by this time, "we prefer to travel by bus."

"Hell," the old man said as he spit the juice from his plug of chewing tobacco at my right front tire. "Stars are supposed to ride in Cadillacs. I can ride in a bus!"

My introduction to Bill Anderson came through a 1978 book penned by Frye Gaillard, one called Watermelon Wine: The Spirit of Country Music. *It's a great book. Maybe find a copy and read it, once you get done with this book. In one chapter, Gaillard interviews Anderson about the significant hubbub, both positive and negative, that surrounded his 1970 hit "Where Have All Our Heroes Gone?" Not long removed from that controversy, Anderson admitted to something that few people will cop to: a shift in focus and perspective. A softening of sorts.*

"I guess I feel sort of like Johnny Cash, who says he's 'born a little every day,' and that once he stops learning and changing he starts dying," Anderson said.

Later, Anderson would write about learning and changing in a song called "A Lot of Things Different," a 2002 hit for Kenny Chesney. In this chapter, he writes about such things, as well as about the pleasures and dangers of travel in a world that has somehow both grown and shrunk since his birth in 1937.

Robert Shelton of the *New York Times* once wrote, "Vaudeville never died, it just moved to Nashville." In a way, I guess he was right, because those of us in the country music business do keep a lifestyle similar to that of the old vaudevillians of the early 1900s. We pack and unpack a lot of suitcases, eat meals at places we probably wouldn't be caught dead in if we were at home, sleep everywhere except in the comfort of our own beds, and ply our craft in far-flung places with strange names like Ottumwa, Oshkosh, Oneonta, Oneida, and Opelika. We are gypsies of a sort and not everybody understands. Many's the time I've been asked, "Why do you work the road? Why don't you just stay home and write songs?"

Sometimes I'm not too sure of the answers myself, but the bottom line is probably that in spite of all the hardships and inconveniences of such an existence, I still love it. Even now, in my seventies, I love it. I don't know of anything else I could be doing that I would enjoy as much. And any entertainer will tell you the same thing: There's no feeling in the world quite like the feeling you get when you're up on that stage performing for an audience. Nobody applauds when I write a song. The great singer and songwriter Tom T. Hall said that there are a few afflictions common to show business people: fame, booze, sex, drugs, and applause. And applause, Tom T. said, is the only one that's incurable.

If I'm going to make music, appear on television, and have a career in show business, then the unwritten portion of the contract I make with the world says that I will also make myself available to people. That I won't go hide in a closet, but rather I'll ride up and down the highways and byways thanking my fans for their support and singing personally for them the songs they've heard me sing on the radio and on TV. It's not much to ask, and fortunately for me I've built up a long and varied list of songs over the years that people have wanted to hear.

Following the success of "8 × 10" in 1964, my next hit was a sad, somewhat prophetic song about the inspiration a father received from his child following the death of his wife, called "Five Little Fingers." We knew when we cut it that this song didn't have the crossover potential of a "Still" or an "8 × 10," but it was a solid country success just the same. Next came a couple of even more traditional country offerings, "Three A.M." and "Bright Lights and Country Music," followed by another crossover success, "I Love You Drops." The flip side of "I Love You Drops" was also a top-ten country hit, the poignant "Golden Guitar." Written by a young Texan named Curtis Leach, "Golden Guitar" was my first hit recording of a song I didn't write.

The first up-tempo record I ever had to go to number one, "I Get the Fever," came in 1967 and was the first in a chain of hits I wrote and set to a musical beat that was quite different for that day and time. Musicians around town called it "the Fever beat" or "the Bill Anderson beat" for years, but it was simply music played four beats to the measure with equal emphasis given to both the downbeat and the upbeat. In effect, that made it sound like eight beats to the measure.

Today it's commonly called "straight eights," and it's a rhythm pattern used on both up-tempo songs and ballads as well. I used straight eights or some variation thereof on subsequent hits like "Get While the Gettin's Good," "Wild Weekend," and my country version of the First Edition's "But You Know I Love You." For a while this unusual rhythm pattern became almost as much a part of the Bill Anderson signature as the soft-sell talking and singing sound that preceded it. "The Bill Anderson beat" added thump to the whisper.

By the late sixties and early seventies I had had hit records of several different types and began feeling secure enough as an artist to begin experimenting musically and reaching out a bit. In 1969 I got caught up in the emotion and turmoil of my personal life, and in answer to my wife's charges that I'd be throwing away my life if I allowed our marriage to dissolve, I wrote the biting "My Life (Throw It Away If I Want To)," the humor and poignancy of which was totally lost on both her and her divorce lawyer. *Billboard* magazine liked it, however, enough to name it the number one country record of the year. In a 180-degree turnaround just one year later, I stirred up nationwide feelings of both patriotism and anger when I coauthored and recorded "Where Have All Our Heroes Gone?"—interpreted as a flag-waving anthem by some but in my mind, at the outset, simply the posing of a social question.

The song was born quite innocently. I was sharing the concert bill with Merle Haggard one Sunday afternoon at mammoth Cobo Hall in Detroit when his "Okie from Muskogee" was at the height of its popularity. The huge auditorium was packed to the rafters, and when Merle broke into the opening line, "We don't smoke marijuana in Muskogee," the place nearly came apart. Spotlights danced across the gigantic American flags draping down from the ceiling, eighteen thousand people leaped to their feet screaming and applauding their approval, and tears of patriotic pride welled up in every eye in the house. We were in the heart of a city, remember, that had only a few months before been racked by dissension and strife, fire and bloody riots in the streets, and Merle's politically conservative message was exactly what the white, blue-collar Detroiter wanted to hear.

I was standing off to the right-hand side of the stage visiting with a Detroit newspaperman named Bob Talbert when the eruption took place. Bob was originally from Columbia, South Carolina, as I am. He watched Merle, then turned to me and said, "Boy, this is exactly what these people need right now—a real hero. Look at that . . . Merle is their hero. Where have all our heroes gone, anyhow?"

We started talking about the people we admired and looked up to when we were kids going to the movies and to ball games and listening to the radio back in South Carolina. Bob started rattling off names like Joe DiMaggio, Stan Musial, Roy Rogers, Gene Autry, Eisenhower, MacArthur, and I said, "Whoa! Wait a minute! You're going too fast. But this is a great idea for a song. Take all that you're saying, put it down on paper, and send it to me in a letter. I believe I could sort it out and make a song out of it."

Bob liked the idea and went right to work on it. In just a few days I received from him sheet after sheet of single-spaced typewritten thoughts at random about America's heroes of the past, our lack of modern-day heroes, and even the presence of the antihero in our current society. Within a few weeks I had condensed Bob's rambling thoughts into a narrative for a song, written a melody and sing-along chorus, and prepared a speech designed to convince Owen Bradley that I should record it. Owen didn't even put up a fight. I sang it for him one time, and we cut it immediately.

I have never, before or since, released a song that created the impact of "Where Have All Our Heroes Gone?" Radio stations started playing it the day the record came in. When people heard it, they jammed the phone lines at stations all over the country wanting to hear it again. Record stores couldn't get copies in stock quick enough to meet the demand.

The story of the song was built around a man who overheard a group of young boys talking about the contents of a magazine they were reading one day while out on the playground. Supposedly the youngsters were enamored by the pictures and stories of the longhaired, headline-grabbing anti-heroes that our society seemed to be producing in abundance back in those days. As the man listened to the boys' comments and heard their professed adulation for the people whose behavior he abhorred, he was shocked into wondering out loud how our society had managed to sink to such depths. "Are these the people these young boys look up to?" he asked. "Are these their idols? Are these the heroes of the 'now' generation?"

To me, my thoughts and musings weren't anything all that shocking. I had read numerous newspaper and magazine articles that said virtually the same thing I was saying. Youth leaders all across the country were voicing similar concerns. So were ministers and teachers and guidance counselors. Everybody was wondering where the admirable people in our society had wandered off to. All I had done, to my way of thinking, was condense their thoughts into a narrative and put some music behind it. For that reason, I was totally unprepared for the reaction my record received.

I was called to be on the *Today* show, and all the other talk shows wanted me, too. Suddenly my political views were being sought out, people were labeling me everything from "super patriot" to "super idiot," and most of America was missing the entire point of what Bob and I had been trying to say. It was such a time of polarization in this country—the Vietnam War, the riots in the streets, the emerging drug culture—that people saw themselves and others as either liberal or conservative, either right or left, black or white. There was very little patience with anything gray. We hadn't been trying to make a political statement but rather a social statement. Kids were looking up to the free-living Joe Namaths, the rebellious Joan Baezes, the angry Huey Newtons, and we were simply saying, "Hey, where are the John Waynes and Gary Coopers and Lou Gehrigs when we need them?"

You know, maybe I'm just still irritated at Joan Baez because she kept Bob Dylan from singing a song of mine in a movie. In the documentary *Don't Look Back*, Dylan and Baez are seen singing songs in a room, when Dylan asks Baez if she has heard my song "Three A.M." He says, "Bill Anderson." Then Baez cuts him off and starts singing another song.

Okay, enough about Joan Baez. Back to "Where Have All Our Heroes Gone?" which was strictly a love-hate record. Fortunately, most of my fans loved it. We started selling out concert appearances everywhere we went and receiving standing ovations every time we performed the song. Promoters were bringing American flags into the coliseums and theaters where we were performing, and while I was singing they'd have the spotlight operators focus one pin-spot on me and the other one on the flag. The crowds would go into a frenzy. I had never seen anything like it.

But on the other side of the coin, the program director of a radio station in Aspen, Colorado, wrote MCA Records and said, "Don't ever send us another MCA Record and expect us to play it. Any company who would release such a piece of maligning bullshit as Bill Anderson's 'Where Have All Our Heroes Gone?' doesn't deserve our support." At the same time a right-wing organization from Florida petitioned me to go back into the studio and overdub my voice on the record to include the name of Lieutenant William Calley, of My Lai massacre fame, among my list of heroes. I couldn't win for losing.

A friend of mine helped me put it all in perspective, though, one Saturday night backstage at the Opry. I started telling him how unsettling it was to be written about in the press nearly every day, how hard it was to have to listen to all the criticism that was being dished out, even though I could also hear the cheers ringing in the background. "Are they spelling your name right?" he asked. I said they were. He reached out his hand and touched my arm. "Then don't worry about it," he smiled. And from then on I didn't.

With hindsight, though, I did begin to understand some of the negative responses to the song. I still think America needs heroes, but some of the lyrics in "Heroes" generalized about long hair and put down some people a little too hard. In the wake of "Where Have All Our Heroes Gone?" I recorded another song, written by a New England songwriter named Jud Strunk, called "My Country." It is, perhaps, a more complex, balanced take on things, with references to war, poverty, and political assassination.

"I may not stand for everything my country's about," it says. "But I do stand for my country."

In my opinion, that's as patriotic a stance as the ones taken in "Where Have All Our Heroes Gone?" And Joan Baez is a pretty good singer. And Joe Namath was a great quarterback, too. See, friends, I've mellowed.

After "Heroes," I thought it best to return to more traditional themes for the subject matter of my songs. I warbled such noncontroversial lines as, "Always remember I love you," "Don't she look good in the new dress I bought her," and "We called it magic . . . then we called it tragic . . . finally we called it quits." The *Today* show wasn't calling, but I wasn't getting any hate mail either. And I was working the road to the tune of some two hundred dates nearly every year.

When people realize how much I've traveled and the places my travels have taken me, their first reaction is, "Boy, I wish I had a job like yours. You get to go to so many exciting places and see so many interesting things. That must be the greatest life in the world." In a lot of ways they are right, but two hundred days a year is hard work. That's two hundred working days, so you add in at least another fifty to seventy-five days or part-days for travel. That's more than 75 percent of a year spent away from home. And on the days at home, an entertainer doesn't exactly get to loaf. If he did, when would records get cut, publicity photos be taken, television appearances be taped, and all the other thousand-and-one things that go to make up an artist's career get accomplished? But the travel can be enjoyable, particularly if you look at it as part of the overall learning experience. That's how I've tried to approach it over the years, particularly the times I've had the opportunity to travel outside the United States.

Some entertainers don't like to travel overseas. It's tiring and often difficult to adjust to the time change, the food is different, the hotels aren't what they are at home, there's no twenty-four-hour room service, no McDonald's right outside the window. But I've enjoyed seeing other countries, other lifestyles. Had it not been for the music business, I'd probably still think the world started and stopped at the city limits of Commerce, Georgia.

I've had the opportunity during my career to perform in Germany, England, Ireland, Scotland, Holland, Norway, and Sweden, as well as every state in the union and every province of Canada. I've found in my travels that people are people wherever you go and that music is an international language. It can cross a lot of boundaries.

People might not always understand the words you say to them, but they can always feel the music you sing and play for them. For example, once in the early seventies I was touring Europe with Conway Twitty and Loretta Lynn, and we ventured north into Scandinavia where none of us had ever been before. It was our opening night in Bergen, Norway, which is probably the most beautiful place I have ever been, and our concert was being tele-vised live all across the country. I was the first act to go on stage. After my opening medley of songs, the audience applauded generously. Then with no warning at all their applause turned into a loud, rhythmic foot stomp-ing. It began softly at first . . . and slowly . . . then it became more staccato . . . then louder . . . and louder . . . until all I could think of was pictures I'd seen of German soldiers in World War II marching in that high-kicking, goose-step motion. I didn't know if the audience was organizing into a mob about to storm the stage and lynch me or not. They just kept on stomping and clapping louder and louder.

Finally, I held up my hand for quiet and I said to these people in my slowest and most deliberate English, "I . . . do not . . . understand. What . . . does . . . this . . . mean?" The auditorium grew strangely still and quiet. Then a young man seated by the aisle about halfway back in the house stood up and said in halting English, "It means . . . we love you!"

With that, I turned to the band and motioned for them to join me, and we started clapping and stomping our feet right back at the audience. "We love you too," I shouted, and the crowd went berserk. I don't know of another single moment in my career when I've felt so much love fill one hall. And it was all because of the music. The music spoke to everyone there regardless of their nationality or their native tongue. There has been only one other night in my career that could possibly have matched that one for me emotionally. That came several years later in Belfast, Northern Ireland.

Things were so bad between the Catholics and the Protestants on my first trip to Belfast that our tour promoters wouldn't even let us stay at a hotel in town. They feared for our safety. They put us up in a little inn way out in the country where they said we'd be less likely to have any trouble. As soon as we checked in, I went to the room and sacked out, but my wife, Becky, wasn't tired at all. She took a shower, got dressed, and went down to the restaurant to get a bite to eat. When I woke up she told me, "Boy, this sure is a nice hotel. Everybody downstairs was dressed so nice."

"What do you mean?" I asked.

"Well, when I was down there eating, there were all these men sitting around the lobby in three-piece suits reading newspapers. Several others were in the dining room, and they were all dressed real nice, too. Even the men walking outside in the garden were all dressed up."

I pulled the curtains back and looked out the hotel window. Sure enough, Becky was right. Well-dressed men were walking around everywhere, but I knew immediately what they were. "Those aren't just hotel guests," I told her. "Those guys are detectives or policemen or something like that. Lord, I hope they're on our side!" Turned out that's exactly who they were and what they were. They were there to protect us, to make sure no incidents took place while we were there. It was scary.

On my second trip to Northern Ireland, we stayed right in downtown Belfast, but our hotel was completely surrounded by barbed wire and was staked out twenty-four hours a day by uniformed, armed security guards. A week after we left, I read in the paper where that very hotel had been bombed. I don't know about anybody else, but the night we were there I slept with one eye open.

The emotional part came at the show itself. You see, they didn't get much entertainment there at the time, and people came from everywhere to see our show. They walked, they rode bicycles, they came any way they could just to be there. There was a curfew on how late they could be on the streets in their cars, so most people just left their cars at home. The concert hall was packed, and I didn't find out until long after the show was over that in addition to all the fans, there had been over sixty armed guards, plain-clothesmen wearing bulletproof vests, scattered throughout the audience. They, too, had been there, we were told, for our protection "just in case." Fortunately, everything came off without incident.

It was the opening night of our tour and the promoter, Jeffrey Kruger, was anxious to see our show and to time the individual segments. This was because there were to be future dates on the tour where the amount of time we'd spend on stage would be critical. Some of the theaters we were to play were only in the two- to three-thousand-seat range, and in order to accommodate the crowds there would have to be both an early and a late show the same evening. So on this particular night in Belfast he sat in the audience with a stopwatch to clock our numbers.

As we were told to do, we stayed on stage for exactly sixty minutes. I sang a variety of the songs I figured they'd heard over the years—a few of the fast ones, a few of the slow—and the reaction was incredible. When we came off, I met Jeffrey in the hallway backstage. He was staring at his stopwatch as if he didn't believe what it was telling him. "Do you know that ten minutes and thirty-seven seconds of your sixty minutes was taken up by applause?" he asked. "I've never seen such response in my life. Go back out there and sing them a few more songs," and we did.

Again the applause was deafening.

I came offstage the second time emotionally drained and out of breath. And then I learned why they had accepted us so warmly. "Most entertainers won't even come here," an elderly man said to me softly as he stopped me outside my dressing room, deep lines creasing his brow. "We're so thankful you came," and I noticed a tear beginning to form in the corner of his eye. He reached out his burly arms and gave me a big bear hug. "Thank you," he said. "Thank you for helping us forget our troubles for a while. May God bless you and keep you safe," and then he broke down sobbing. Many of the other fans followed suit, coming up to embrace us, shaking our hands warmly, and begging us to "Please come again!" I was very touched to think that all I had done was something that I loved to do—play and sing my music—and in the process I had made so many people so very happy.

The ladies who cooked in the kitchen of the little country inn where we were staying baked us a rich layer cake and a fresh fruit pie to take with us on the return flight to London the following morning. "You must come again," one of them said to me, "when things are better." I thanked her and assured her that we would. But the look in her eye told me she expected that to be a long, long time.

In the following chapter, Bill brings us soap on the bow of a fiddle, and beans and ham with the First Couple of Country Music. He brings us Grandpa Jones and the generator, and we get an umpiring lesson from Ronnie Milsap. And we meet one fan who liked Bill back when he used to be popular. All in a life on the road.

Traveling musicians form something of an unspoken fraternal bond among themselves, sort of a modern code of the Old West. They do for each other . . . and they often do to each other as well. Guys who share bumpy bus rides, lousy restaurants, crummy motels, long hours, days, weeks, and months together away from their families sometimes become closer than brothers. And brothers, as you know, often have no mercy on one another.

One night in Wichita, Kansas, for reasons that will forever go unknown, Snuffy Miller decided he'd put some soap on Jimmy Gateley's fiddle bow. He knew if he put enough of the waxy substance on the hairs of the bow they couldn't rub against the strings of the fiddle and the fiddle couldn't make a sound. He also knew I'd had a hot record in Wichita with "Bright Lights and Country Music" and that it had a fiddle intro. And he knew I'd be awfully upset if Jimmy stepped up to the microphone to kick off that song and no sound came out of his instrument.

Which is exactly what happened. I gave the song a powerful introduction . . . "Folks, here's a song you made a big hit here in Wichita. I hope you remember it, and I hope you like it." Jimmy strode into the spotlight at center stage, placed his fiddle under his chin, and dramatically raised the bow. He brought it crashing down against the strings and . . . dead silence. He tried it again. Again no sound. Believing the third time to be the charm, he went through the whole exercise again and still nothing happened. I looked at Jimmy, not understanding exactly what had happened myself, and there was a horrified look on his face. Suddenly he took his fiddle out of his left hand and switched it over into his right. He began pounding his left ear with the palm of his hand. It never occurred to him that his bow had been tampered with. The poor guy thought he had gone deaf.

Everybody laughed like the dickens. That is, everybody but Gate. He was too bent on revenge. He got it, too, in short order. I had used a trumpet to play the introduction to my recorded version of "But You Know I Love You," and on stage Snuffy had become quite proficient at playing his snare drum with one hand and the intro on a trumpet with the other. Never quite forgetting or forgiving Snuffy for the soap-on-the-bow incident, Jimmy decided to stuff the horn of Snuffy's trumpet with Kleenex. The effect was the same as with the fiddle. No sound could come out. In fact, no air could pass through the instrument at all. This time when I cued the intro for my song, Snuffy took a big deep breath, raised the trumpet to his lips, and nearly blew his brains out.

Fun on the road comes in all shapes and sizes. I once organized a softball team among the members of my group, and for a while we almost forgot we were traveling musicians. We'd get ourselves booked into a town for an evening's concert and then arrange an afternoon softball game pitting our band against a team of local disc jockeys, musicians, or the local chapter of Little Sisters of the Poor. We weren't too choosy about our competition. We just wanted to play.

We'd come bounding off our bus at the local ball field, sometimes with several thousand people in attendance, wearing our black-and-white soft-ball uniforms trimmed in gold, trying our best to hold our stomachs in and let our athletic prowess hang out. The games were always played for a local charity, so in addition to finding an outlet for our pent-up energies, we raised a lot of money over the years for a lot of worthwhile causes.

Once in Hattiesburg, Mississippi, the immortal Dizzy Dean served as our umpire. And Ronnie Milsap, the great blind singer and musician, snuck up behind me without my knowing it at a game in Nashville dressed in full umpire's regalia. I was at bat, and the pitcher threw a pitch that sailed at least five feet over my head. I heard the ump yell, "Strike one!" The crowd roared, and I turned around to jump all over the umpire. When I saw Ronnie standing there in his umpire's uniform and wraparound dark glasses, I yelled "Hey, what's going on?"

"Don't you scream at me," he barked, "I calls 'em like I sees 'em!"

Ball playing at our ages was sometimes more dangerous than I had real-ized. Prior to a game one night, I was hitting some fly balls to our outfield-ers when my piano player, Monty Parkey, walked right in front of a blister-ing line drive hot off my bat. It hit him square in the face and blood came gushing from everywhere. It scared me to death. I thought I had killed him. I rushed him to the hospital, and he ended up missing several concert engagements suffering from a broken nose.

Rounding third base at Tim McCarver Stadium in Memphis one night, I got tangled up in my own feet and did a triple somersault right across home plate. I lay there in the dust and the dirt afraid to move, frightened that I might have separated the shin bone connected to the ankle bone. The crowd was evidently afraid that something much worse had happened, for they grew quiet as a mouse. When I caught my breath and realized I was all right, I jumped to my feet, dusted off my uniform, and trotted to the dugout to the tune of a standing ovation. I politely tipped my cap just like I'd seen the big boys do on TV.

I not only played softball, but once I even got back into playing baseball for a while. A group of country music stars, musicians, songwriters, and others who worked in our industry decided in the midseventies to form a team. They called it the Nashville Pickers and rounded up some sponsors to furnish uniforms, others to furnish equipment, and an ex–major league player, Dick Sisler, who lived in Nashville, to serve as manager. They came up with a unique way to promote and market the team and at the same time have a lot of fun.

They would sign contracts each season to bring the ball team to a half-dozen or so major league cities on the day of a regularly scheduled game. An hour or so before the big league game, the Pickers, many of whom were well-known country stars (Charley Pride, Roy Clark, Johnny Duncan, Bob Luman, and Charlie McCoy among them), would challenge a team made up of local radio, television, and newspaper personalities to a baseball game. They'd play three or four innings, or as much as time would allow, then turn things over to the real ballplayers. After the major league game, the stars would come back out and give an hour-long concert.

It was a tremendous concept, and there were very few big league clubs who weren't receptive to the idea. Some of the larger cities with minor league clubs went for the idea as well. Over the years, there weren't many baseball parks of any size around the country that didn't receive at least one visit from the Nashville Pickers. When the team was first organized, I was working so many dates on the road every summer that, even though I wanted badly to be part of it, I just couldn't fit it into my schedule. Finally one year things eased up a bit, and I made it to a few of the games.

I'll never forget the Sunday afternoon I got to play first base in the Astrodome in Houston. The Montreal Expos were in town for a game with the Astros, and I was like a kid at the circus. I guess I might have been a bit too nervous because I came to bat twice in the game and both times hit weak little rollers back to the pitcher. I was thrown out at first base by twenty yards each time.

When the game was over, my longtime friend Tommy Helms, who had played for years with the Cincinnati Reds and was finishing out the last days of his career as a member of the Astros, called me over to the Houston dugout and gave me one of his custom crafted Louisville Slugger baseball bats. I guess he figured I needed something to help me hit the ball better than I had done that afternoon. I was thrilled with the bat and could hardly wait to get it back to Nashville and show it off.

But there was one rather pertinent question: How was I going to get the bat home? It was too big to fit in my suitcase, I'd have felt like a fool carrying it on my shoulder through the Houston airport, and besides I figured they wouldn't let me on an airplane carrying a ball bat anyhow. What was I going to do?

Finally, I hit on a solution. I was carrying my stage costume in a leather hang-up garment bag. Why couldn't I just slide the bat down into the garment bag and carry it on the plane with me? Sounded like a good idea to me.

The next morning Johnny Duncan and I caught a cab to the airport, and I told him what I was doing. "I'll bet they stop me at security, though," I said. "They'll think I'm gonna use the bat to hit the pilot over the head and hijack the plane or something." But, surprise, when I put my bag on the conveyor belt to be x-rayed the security guard let it pass right on through.

I picked up my bag as it came off the far side of the belt and was about to walk on to my gate when the guard tapped me on the shoulder. "I'd like to take a look inside your bag, please, sir," he said.

"Uh oh, here it comes," I thought. "He'll never let me take this bat on board. Guess I'll have to leave it in Houston."

The guard never said a word. He unzipped my bag, reached in behind my clothes, and pulled out the shiny Louisville Slugger. He looked at it carefully, rolled it around in his hands once or twice, then put it back in the bag and zipped it up again. Then he handed the garment bag to me.

"Aren't you going to confiscate my bat?" I asked him, puzzled by his actions. "I could use it to hit the pilot over the head, you know."

He looked at me and never changed his expression. "I saw your game at the Dome yesterday," he said softly. "I'm not worried. In your hands that bat is no weapon."

I got so serious about playing ball there for a while that it began to affect my business. I signed our team up to play in a city league in Nashville and found myself canceling and moving show dates around so we could play softball every Wednesday night. In a double-header league no less. One night it dawned on me that while I was having tons of fun playing ball, I was really starting to neglect my career. I had chosen years ago to be an entertainer, not a ballplayer. I began to rethink my priorities and decided I'd best put my bat and ball back in the closet and get back in the music business where I belonged.

I've never been much of a card player, but there didn't used to be a band in the business that didn't play a lot of poker or other card games while riding down the highway looking for a way to pass the time. I once had three or four extremely serious poker players in my group who would break out the cards the minute the bus was loaded after a show ("You wanta look at a few?" was their byword invitation to one another) and still be playing when we'd pull into the next town the following morning. I don't think the stakes were ever very high, but evidently they were high enough to attract poker players from some of the other bands we'd be touring with. I remember one tour when Del Reeves, Jack Greene, and Kenny Price rode more miles on my bus than they did on their own just to play cards with my band.

I miss the old package show tours where several artists would travel together for long periods of time. It was always fun to have other singers and musicians climb on our bus, and I'd often ride with them on theirs. In later days, I might work a show with two or three other artists and never even get a chance to speak with them. They'd come into town from one direction, we'd come in from another. They'd check into one motel, we'd check into another. They'd then stay secluded on their bus until show time, and our paths never crossed. I didn't like that. We were all missing out on a lot of fun.

I especially used to love to work in the Sunday package shows with George Jones and Tammy Wynette when they were married. Tammy would put a pot of beans on the stove in their bus and a ham in the oven prior to the matinee performance and let them cook slowly while she and George were on stage singing. Between the matinee and the night show, she'd mix up a pan of cornbread and invite the other entertainers on the show over for dinner. I used to tease and tell them their bus was one of the best truck stops on the circuit.

Some of the best socializing among entertainers can take place on the tour buses. Grandpa Jones, one of my favorite people in the world and one of our business's greatest characters, was once visiting on my bus at a little county fair. We were sitting around swapping stories, waiting for the time for us to go onstage. The bus was parked directly behind the stage, and when the local band opened the show and began to play, the noise from the power generator running the lights and air-conditioning on our bus began drowning them out. They turned to the promoter of the show, who was standing off in the wings, and asked him to ask us if we'd either turn the generator off or move the bus a few feet away from the stage.

Since the day was a scorcher and we didn't want to sit there with no air-conditioning, we decided on the latter. Our driver cranked up the big diesel engine and backed up a good hundred yards from the stage. In about ten minutes here came the promoter again telling us the generator was still too loud on stage. So we backed up another hundred yards or so. Believe it or not, this still did not satisfy the musicians, who must have had supersonic hearing, so for the third time we were asked to back the bus up even farther. All this time Grandpa hadn't said a word. He'd just sat there watching and listening.

Finally we had moved the bus as far away from the other band as possible without leaving the fairgrounds. Grandpa looked out the front window at the other performers, who were now just a small spot on the horizon. "Well," he said in his patented nasal tone, pronouncing "well" as if it rhymed with "pail," "we'll have to book a date between here and the stage."

For several years in the late seventies and early eighties, I placed in back of me and the band on stage a backdrop comprised of three large movie screens, behind which we mounted up to as many as nine computerized slide projectors, and at various times throughout my concerts I would show pictures on the screens to illustrate the music the band and I were performing live. These days, the big singers carry incredibly involved audio visual equipment and play in front of enormous, high-definition video screens. But at that time my slide show was something quite innovative. As you might suspect, in those days there was still a lot of room for improvement in the equipment.

When our slide show worked right, it was one of the most effective and stunning presentations imaginable. But when it didn't, it could be disastrous.

I used it only at certain strategic points in the show, one of which was when I sang a medley of songs from the sixties. I would pull out one of my old custom-made rhinestone suits from that era and put on the jacket, talk about the sixties, and ask the audience to remember the music that went with the times. As we played and sang our songs, slides would appear illustrating the current events of the decade. Later in the show I did a tribute to the history and the roots of country music with a different set of slides. My opening line was, "In the beginning, there was just a man and a guitar," and an old black-and-white picture of a farmer sitting on the front porch of a little log cabin picking his guitar would slowly fade up on the screen. It was quite dramatic. As the slide slowly eased into focus, the guitar player in my band would begin picking out the melody to "Wildwood Flower" on his acoustic guitar.

We were working at a big fair up in New England and I was about to close the show with the country music medley, when somehow the computer and the slide projectors got their signals all crisscrossed. The lights went down, and I began talking about how country music began, saying slowly and dramatically, "In the beginning, there was just a man and a guitar." The guitar player went into his soft, emotional version of "Wildwood Flower." But suddenly I noticed the audience shifting nervously in their seats. A couple of them were looking at the screen with puzzled looks on their faces. One or two were even snickering.

I turned to look at the screen behind me. Instead of seeing the picture of the old farmer quietly strumming his guitar, I found myself looking directly into an eight-foot-high picture of the sneering face of Spiro Agnew. It was no doubt the only time in history that the former vice president of the United States had ever been credited with founding country music.

My audiovisual show was such a hit with audiences all over the country, though, that I was once invited to showcase it before one of the most influential and prestigious groups of all, the National Association of Fair Buyers at their annual convention in Las Vegas. These were the ladies and gentlemen responsible for booking most of the acts into the biggest fairs around the country, and it was an honor to be asked to appear before them. I knew if we did a good job we'd get booked at a large number of major fairs the following season.

The showcase was set for the large auditorium inside the beautiful Aladdin Hotel. We got to town the day before the showcase, and our technical crew spent all the next day making sure everything was in perfect working order. But, alas, when I went to wrap up my performance with "In the beginning, there was just a man and a guitar," a field of beautiful yellow flowers appeared behind me on the screen.

I stopped and told the fair buyers that something had malfunctioned, and we started over again. This time, the "man and his guitar" turned out to be the silhouette of two lovers rubbing noses in the twilight. The buyers roared. They had all been through the experience of a Ferris wheel breaking down or a merry-go-round that wouldn't work at their fairs. They knew what I was going through, and they were laughing because this time it was me suffering instead of them. When on my third attempt at getting it right still another wrong slide appeared on the screen, I turned to the audience and said, "Aw, to hell with it. If you want to see this thing work right, you'll just have to book me." And I walked off the stage to a standing ovation.

I've had the opportunity to meet many people, see many places, and witness many special events in my lifetime that I'd never have gotten the opportunity to be a part of were it not for the fact I was an entertainer traveling the road. I've been invited to the White House, I've been to two Super Bowls, to the World Series, to the bottom of the Grand Canyon, and to the top of Pike's Peak. I've been able to go on Caribbean and Alaskan cruises, and I've taken my band members and their spouses with me. We've seen shows on Broadway, been to both the baseball and the pro football halls of fame, watched them make beer at a brewery in Wisconsin, manufacture maple syrup in Vermont, make cereal in Battle Creek, and build guitars in Kalamazoo. I've had fans take my picture, ask for my autograph, and pay their hard-earned money to sit in the audience and applaud my music and laugh at my jokes. One night at Memorial Hall in downtown Dayton, Ohio, a lady dressed in a full-length dress and a mink coat walked up on stage in front of several thousand people while I was singing "Still" and started taking off her clothes. And I've had people say to me just about every conceivable thing imaginable. Like the lady who told me after a concert just recently, "I would have been at your show the last time you were in town, but I had something else to do." And another one who said, "Oh, Bill Anderson, it's such a thrill to meet you. I've liked you ever since back when you used to be popular."

In the late 1980s, I was driving a new four-wheel-drive vehicle I had just bought in Florida back to Nashville and had to stop and check into a motel in northern Alabama to avoid an oncoming ice and snow storm. (I bought the car to help me navigate the icy, snowy hills in the section of Nashville where I live, then I couldn't even get it home because of an ice and snow storm.) I signed the guest register at the motel and handed the lady behind the counter my credit card. She looked at my card, looked down at the name I'd just written, glanced back at my card, then looked up at me.

"Bill Anderson," she said slowly, as if trying to remember where she'd heard that name before. "Bill . . . Anderson. Bill . . . ? Say, didn't there used to be somebody famous named Bill Anderson?"

I looked at her and smiled. "Yeah, I think there did," I said. "But it was a long time ago."

"Really? What did he do?" she asked seriously.

I just laughed. "I don't know, but I bet he had a lot of fun doing it, don't you?" She stared at me blankly.

Bill Anderson, a twenty-first-century man who texts and e-mails and does the things that the rest of us do, was both alive and prominent at a time when a television producer could, with warped but commonly held consideration, scream that a black man could absolutely, positively not appear on a syndicated television show. This was 1966, and it was Bill Anderson's show, and the African American in question was a future Country Music Hall of Famer named Charley Pride. Overruling the producer, Bill offered Pride his first-ever televised introduction to country music fans. That story is here, as are tales of Bill's prominent duet partners and an explication of how another future Hall of Famer, Connie Smith, came to grace Nashville stages and to make enduring country music. Oh, and there's a good Grandpa Jones funny here, too.

After he'd hired a band, bought a bus, and outfitted all the band members in the most ornate costumes imaginable, the next thing any self-respecting touring country music star would do back in the sixties was add what was then called a "girl singer" to his entourage. I was no exception.

By the end of the decade, I was playing more and more places where the promoters of my concerts expected me to provide the entire evening's entertainment, and there was no way to please everybody in the audience all night long (especially the men) by giving them nothing but a half-dozen hairy-legged ole boys to stare at the whole time. Porter Wagoner faced the same problem and hired "Pretty Miss Norma Jean" to tour with him. The Wilburn Brothers introduced to the world a young girl from the coal-mining regions of Kentucky named Loretta Lynn. And thanks to an unusual sequence of events, my female counterpart became a talented but feisty little redhead from West Plains, Missouri, named Jan Howard.

I had started a weekly syndicated television show in early 1965 called, oddly enough, *The Bill Anderson Show*. The original cast consisted of myself, the Po' Boys band, singer-comedian Grandpa Jones (this was a couple of years before *Hee Haw* came along), and country songstress Jean Shepard. Our show was videotaped in Charlotte, North Carolina, at the facilities of Jefferson Productions, where we'd gather once a month to crank out four thirty-minute programs. "Syndicated" meant our show was sold to television stations all across the country on a station-by-station basis rather than being offered to them as part of a network. It was my first regular television exposure to a nationwide audience, so in spite of the hardships of having to tape the shows five hundred miles from Nashville, I was thankful for the opportunity of doing the show, period.

Jean and Grandpa, however, weren't exactly as thrilled about recording it in North Carolina as I was. Jean was consistently in the country charts with her recordings in those days and could work all the personal appearance dates she wanted to with or without the exposure from the TV show. Grandpa had always been an outstanding act on any country show, especially at the fairs and the outdoor festivals, and while I think he enjoyed television, those dreary ten-hour rides from Nashville across the mountains to Charlotte (no interstates then, remember?) seemed to get longer and longer each time. Jean and Grandpa made the trips for a year with no complaints, but when their paychecks from the producers began taking longer and longer to come in, they began to grow more and more unhappy. Finally, when the checks stopped coming in at all, they each decided that there had to be a better way for them to spend their time. In January 1966, they somewhat angrily quit the show.

Grandpa, in particular, had a short fuse back in those days, and I'll never forget one of his last taping sessions with us when he was getting fed up with the whole situation. My band was attempting to play an instrumental following a song Grandpa had just sung, and they couldn't get it right for anything. At that time there was no such thing as editing videotape, so every time the band would make a mistake, the director would yell, "Cut!" and stop the tape. This meant we had to go back to the point of the last commercial break and start over. So Grandpa, who'd sung his song perfectly every time, had to come back on the set and sing his song again. And again. And again and again. I thought if I heard "Methodist Pie" one more time I was going to change my religion, or give it up altogether.

And if you think I was upset, you should have seen Grandpa. Finally, after at least a half-dozen attempts, the band played their song well enough for the director to be pleased. But then the guitar player said he didn't like his part and asked if he could play it "just one more time." Whereupon I looked over into the corner of the studio and spotted Grandpa. He had shoved his banjo down in its case and had picked up a broom from back in the prop room. And he was moving like a madman ninety-to-nothing across the studio floor with that broom.

"What in the world are you doing, Paw?" I asked.

He shot back, "I'm a-sweepin' me off a place to have a fit!"

I wasn't getting my paycheck most of the time either, but the exposure from being on a hundred or more television stations all across the country each week was helping me in a lot of ways that veteran performers like Jean and Grandpa didn't necessarily need. The show was helping country fans to put a face and a personality with my name. People who had only heard me sing on the radio or jukeboxes up until then could now invite me right into their homes and watch me as well. And I learned real fast that no medium in the world creates closeness between performer and audience like television.

During the year we had been taping in Charlotte, Jan Howard had appeared on our show two or three times as a special guest. The producer liked her singing and her personally, so when he got wind of Jean's planning not to return, he offered the permanent female singer's job to Jan. She asked me what I thought about it, and I told her not to plan on spending all the money she'd be making in one place. She got the message. But at the same time she had made a new commitment to her career and was as anxious as I was to add to her exposure. She accepted the job eagerly. Funny man Don Bowman, who had just begun recording a series of comedy albums for RCA, signed on in Grandpa's place.

With our new cast and new look, we continued to tape our programs in Charlotte until the fall of 1966. Quite a few new stations began to carry our show, and more and more artists with records to promote began asking me if they could come to Charlotte and tape guest appearances with us. I was always glad to welcome my friends to the show, but I invited one artist that, had his appearance not been a smashing success, could have cost me my job.

Charley Pride was new on RCA Victor records and had just begun to promote his songs and work on his career. There weren't many people who had even heard of him at this point, and I doubt the ones who had had the slightest idea that he was black. At that time there had never been a black singer in the field of country music. And in the mid-1960s, segregation was still a reality in the South. This was a time of marches, sit-ins, violence, and assassinations.

But Charley Pride was a whale of a country singer, and he had also never been on television. When I realized I had a chance to be the first person in the country to present him to a TV audience and found out how badly he wanted to come guest on my show, I extended him an invitation. And he accepted. Only trouble was I didn't tell the producers he was coming.

The morning of the taping I figured I'd best tell somebody that I was about to have the first black country singer in history on my show, so I went upstairs to the Jefferson Production offices and decided I'd go right to the head man. No use beating around the bush with the peons. I told him everything.

"You've done what?" I can still hear him yell. "You can't have a black man on your show! We just went on the air in Meridian, Mississippi . . . Jackson, Mississippi . . . Alexandria, Louisiana . . . for God's sake! We'll lose all those stations, don't you know that? You just tell him you're sorry, that you made a mistake. But you can't put him on. It'll be the end of your show!"

"No, sir, I'm not going to tell him that," I answered. "You'll have to tell him. But I don't think it'll hurt the show at all. In fact, I think it will help it. He's never been on TV. We've got a chance to have him first. Don't you think that's worth taking a chance for?"

Mr. Boss Man didn't like it one bit, but after giving me all of his reasons and listening to all of mine, he finally gave in. After all, Charley was already in the dressing room downstairs and getting ready to go onto the set and rehearse with the band. When the tape started to roll early that afternoon and Charley Pride walked on camera to sing his first song, everything in that entire building came to a standstill. Every executive, every secretary, every person who could crowd into the little viewing room high above the studio was there, looking down through the thick plate glass, watching something they didn't understand and could scarcely believe—a black man singing country music. And Bill Anderson committing professional suicide.

Fortunately, Charley never knew until I told him years later that anything out of the ordinary was going on. He was nervous enough just standing in front of the camera. He certainly didn't need anything else to worry about. He sang both sides of his first release, "The Snakes Crawl at Night" and "The Atlantic Coastal Line." And he sang them well, even though he told me many times later that he was scared to death.

The show began to air on stations around the country about three weeks after we taped it, and the reaction from our viewers was unbelievable. Whereas in a normal week our show might have generated a couple of hundred letters nationwide, this week they brought mail to me in a bushel basket. Hundreds upon hundreds of cards and letters, all with something to say about that new singer, Charley Pride. They loved him. Mississippi loved him, Louisiana loved him, every single letter but two said, in effect, that they thought Charley Pride was fantastic. We didn't lose one station or one single viewer that I ever knew of. The only negative letters I received were one postmarked Chicago and another from Milwaukee. I threw them both in the trash.

For his part, Charley Pride went on to have a remarkable and storied career in country music. Now, if you visit the Country Music Hall of Fame and Museum in downtown Nashville, you can see a plaque in the Hall of Fame Rotunda signifying his spot as one of country music's all-time greats. There's also a plaque up for DeFord Bailey, who was actually the first African American star in country music: Bailey played harmonica on the Grand Ole Opry beginning in the 1920s, but he was fired from the Opry in a racially motivated incident in 1941. It was a different time, and not necessarily a better one.

It had nothing at all to do with Charley Pride's appearance on our show, but before the year was out we left Charlotte and moved the production of our show to the studios of CKLW-TV in Windsor, Ontario, Canada, just across the river from Detroit. We had a new producer and new syndicators by this time, and the new folks had promised us if we'd make this move they could get our show onto stations all across Canada as well as keeping us on all the stations that were already carrying the show throughout the United States. It sounded like a good idea to me. Besides, we could get to Windsor about as easily as we could get to Charlotte, and CKLW-TV saturated the metropolitan Detroit market on channel 9. Plus, they wanted us to add another ninety minutes of prime-time programming every week in the nation's fifth-largest market to the coverage we already had for our weekly half-hour in the rest of the country. That meant we'd have two hours of TV exposure every week in Detroit alone as well as the exposure across Canada. I figured we couldn't lose on a deal like that, and even though the Canadian part never fully materialized, I was right. In addition, once or twice we even got paid!

About the same time Jan Howard was asked if she'd like to join our television show, she was in the process of dissolving her recording affiliation with Capitol Records and had begun negotiating a move to the label where I was recording, Decca Records. As soon as she came with us on TV, it seemed like the natural thing for us to begin singing duets together. Our voices had a unique blend, and we began to receive a lot of extremely favorable mail from our viewers. The next thing I knew Jan had signed her contract to record for Decca, and we were badgering producer Owen Bradley to let us record together. He agreed that it might work, it did, and a whole new career was born for both of us.

Jan's and my first duet release was a remake of the old Reno and Smiley classic "I Know You're Married (But I Love You Still)," and as soon as people heard it they began to whisper that some kind of wild offstage romance must be going on between us. Otherwise, why would we be singing a song like that? Then when our second release, "For Loving You," turned out to be an even mushier, gushier ballad, the tongues really started to wag. Especially when we'd perform the song live and I'd say to Jan:

> For loving you . . . My life is so much richer.
> You've given me so much to live for
> And I never really lived before . . . Before loving you.

And in return she'd say to me:

> And for loving you . . . My faith is a little stronger.
> For a world that could give you to me
> Couldn't be as bad as it's made out to be.
> There was good there I just could never see
> Before loving you.

Neither one of us composed those words, but when we recorded them and our record started racing up the charts toward number one many people began to assume we were actually living all the things we were saying and singing. Nothing could have been further from the truth.

I first met Jan in the early days of my career when she and her songwriting husband, Harlan Howard, lived in a modest little house in Gardena, California, long before they ever moved to Nashville. At the time my impression was that Jan was much more interested in being a good wife and a good mother to her three sons than she was in becoming a singing star. I had gone to California early in 1960 to work a few club dates, a few radio and television shows, and to try and get my name known a bit on the west coast. I had come to know and admire Harlan through his terrific songwriting and a few phone conversations I'd had with him from Nashville, but we'd never met face-to-face. He'd already written such hits as "Pick Me Up on Your Way Down," "The Key's in the Mailbox," and "Mommy for a Day," and I wanted badly to meet this man whose work I admired.

Jan had made a couple of records at the time, including a hit called "The One You Slip around With" and a successful duet with Wynn Stewart titled "Yankee Go Home," records I had played on my radio shows back in Georgia. She primarily looked upon herself, though, as someone to help Harlan make demonstration tapes of the songs he had written and someone to cook supper for him and the boys when they got home. When Harlan would write a song he thought would be right for a female singer to record, he'd teach it to Jan, and she'd sing it on the demo session, but I honestly don't think at that point Jan cared one iota about being an entertainer herself.

I was a couple of thousand miles away from home and living alone in a small motel in what were then the far reaches of the San Fernando Valley when Jan and Harlan called one day and asked me if I'd like to join them for dinner at their home the following Sunday afternoon. I told them I'd love to come, and I drove out in my rented car.

Harlan and I hit it off immediately, and after dinner we sat up until the wee hours of the morning passing his guitar back and forth, bouncing our newest song creations off one another, and swapping lies. I ended up spending the night in a small bedroom in their home, sharing bunk beds with their three boys. It was a happy and innocent time.

The professional coming together of Bill Anderson and Jan Howard in the late sixties provided me with some of my most memorable times in this business. Good friends or not, we had ups and downs like anybody would have living and working so closely together all the time, but I've always figured if Jan hadn't liked me a little bit she wouldn't have saved my life one night on the bus in Fort Worth, Texas.

We were working a Saturday night gig at the infamous Panther Hall in Cowtown, and I was alone on our parked bus in back of the building a few minutes before show time. Jan had gone inside with the rest of the group to get ready. I was brushing my teeth when somehow I became choked on the toothpaste. I could not catch my breath.

I tried raising both my arms over my head, then dropping one arm and pounding myself on the back with it as hard as I could, but nothing would unclog my windpipe. I was becoming frantic and began stumbling toward the front of the bus to try and go for help when, for some reason, Jan just happened to walk back on board. She immediately sensed my problem and came running toward me, hitting my back with her fist. She liked to have beat the living daylights out of me, but whatever was stuck in my throat soon dislodged and I caught my breath. I doubt that I could have made it up the tall stairs and inside Panther Hall before passing out had Jan not come along. I might have become the late and not-so-great Whisperin' Bill.

One of the things that made Jan and me different from the other male-female duets of the day was the fact that when we performed our songs onstage or on television we'd always look directly at one another rather than looking out into the audience or staring head on into the TV camera. Much of our material was the intimate boy-talks-to-girl, girl-talks-to-boy type, and somehow it always bothered me to perform it staring away from the person I was supposed to be communicating with. But more times than not, it was extremely difficult for me to look directly into Jan's eyes and keep a straight face while reciting or singing those highly personal songs. I'd always think about something that had happened on the bus on the way to the show or some goofy thing we had been talking about backstage, and I'd start laughing. Jan was just too much of a buddy for me to be very serious with her. Finally, after far too many times of my cracking up and laughing in the middle of our serious songs, I hit upon what I thought would be the perfect solution. I'd pick out a spot on Jan's forehead and stare at it rather than trying to look her directly in the eyes when we sang. It was the only way I knew to act serious and not break into uncontrollable laughter.

From the audience no one could tell I wasn't looking Jan directly in the eyes, but she could tell it. Try sometime talking to a person just a few feet away and look at their forehead instead of into their eyes while you're speaking to them. It'll drive them crazy. She'd beg me every night, "Please look me in the eyes," but I couldn't do it.

Finally, on the last day of a long Canadian tour, she couldn't take it any longer. She went out that afternoon and bought a copy of *Mad* magazine and found a picture of the most repulsive, disgusting bloodshot eye you could ever imagine. And in her dressing room before the show she cut the eye out of the magazine and glued it to the spot on her forehead where I usually stared. Then she combed her hair down over the paper eye, and I never knew it was there.

About halfway through our closing song, "For Loving You," when I was staring at her forehead and reciting the part about how much I loved her and how much I needed her, she slowly started to move her hand up to her face and gently began sweeping her hair off to one side. And then in a soft whisper that only I could hear she said slowly, "I said, 'Look me in the eye, dammit!'"

Well, I totally lost it. There I stood staring into the most hideous picture of an eye I had ever seen. Right in the middle of Jan's forehead! I knew immediately what she had done and why, and I went into convulsions right there on the stage. The audience, of course, hadn't noticed a thing, and they were totally stunned to see this long-legged hillbilly all of a sudden begin to flop and fall all over the stage. But I honestly could not help it.

I finally began to gather my composure enough to explain to the silent crowd what had happened. Once they understood, they laughed as hard as I did. Jan had made her point. From that moment on I was afraid not to look her in the eyes ever again.

Following the success of "For Loving You," we had several more hit duets together, including "If It's All the Same to You," a country version of the Supremes' "Someday We'll Be Together," and a song we co-wrote with her son Corky called "Dissatisfied." We even recorded the original version of "Satin Sheets" as a duet long before Jeanne Pruett hit big with it as a solo, but we didn't have enough sense to release it anywhere except in an album. We recorded a gospel album together, and our TV show grew to become one of the most widely seen of all the country shows in syndication. On several occasions the various country music fan magazines and trade publications around the country named us country music's Duet of the Year.

Jan and I split after the death of our manager, Hubert Long, in 1972. We disagreed deeply over who should handle our careers at that point, and it turned into something we simply could not resolve. I felt strongly one way, and she apparently felt equally strongly another way. We decided it was best to part professionally while we could still be friends. It was a good decision because I haven't had a better friend in the world than Jan Howard.

In many respects I didn't want to try and find a replacement for Jan after we split. I wanted to tour with just the band for a while. But the promoters of our concert dates had become so used to my show's being a complete package that my agent was afraid if I didn't continue with myself, the band, Jimmy Gateley (who had become a featured act himself), and a "girl singer," it would hurt our bookings. Plus I did need to add a new woman to the TV shows. So I launched a nationwide talent search, complete with tons of publicity, to try and locate the best female artist available.

As soon as the word got out that I was looking for a singer, hundreds upon hundreds of applications began pouring in from female singers all over the world. I sifted through every single one of them, but I ended up hiring someone who didn't even know the search was going on.

Mary Lou Turner was performing in relative obscurity on the *Jamboree USA* show in Wheeling, West Virginia, when I saw an album review of her newest release in *Cashbox* magazine. The review, which was superb, reminded me that I had seen and heard Mary Lou on several occasions when I had appeared as a guest in Wheeling and that I had been impressed with her talent. I phoned Glenn Reeves, talent director at the *Jamboree*, and asked if he'd mind my talking to her about the job. He said no, even gave me her telephone number, and I gave her a call.

"Why haven't you applied for the job?" I asked when I got her on the line.

"What job?" she replied.

I explained that Jan and I had decided to go our separate ways, and I told her I was looking for someone to take Jan's place. We'd be working a show in Vero Beach, Florida, in a few days, I explained, and if she'd like to go along and sing a few songs and let me listen to her, I'd be glad to let that serve as her audition. That is, I said, if she were interested in working with me at all.

She said she was most definitely interested and took me up on my offer. She came to Nashville, had dinner with Becky and me in our home, asked a million questions about the job and all it might involve, then rode to Florida with me and the band on the bus. When we got to the show in Vero Beach, however, she walked out on stage and promptly forgot the words to the song she'd come all that distance to sing. She thought for sure she'd blown her big chance, but I thought she covered it up so well and handled the situation in such a professional manner that I hired her right on the spot.

Mary Lou stayed with our show for six years. She was a delightful lady to work with, pleasant to be around, and my fans liked her a lot. When I first hired her, I envisioned her singing only on the television shows and touring with us on the road. I hadn't intended for us to make records together, thinking it might not be fair to all concerned for her to come along so close on the heels of my recording career with Jan. ("Mary Lou broke you and Jan up, didn't she?" was a comment I'd already heard more than once during those days.) But I wrote a song while we were on tour in England in

1975 that I knew was a smash. It was one of those songs that didn't care who sang it, it was going to be a hit anyhow. I figured Mary Lou and I might as well have the hit as anybody, so when we got home we cut it. I was right. The song was called "Sometimes."

In the lyrics I would say to her: "Hello beautiful . . . Are you married?" And she would reply, "Sometimes . . ."

The plot thickened from there. Not only did the song go to number one on the charts in 1975, it put a lot of Bill-and-Jan rumors to rest for good.

Mary Lou and I followed "Sometimes" with another hit duet called "That's What Made Me Love You," a song that nobody remembers by that title. Everybody calls it "Champagne in a Dixie Cup" or "Motel in Dallas," two of the key phrases from the lyrics of the song. Later, we had some chart success with "Where Are You Going, Billy Boy?" and after that with "I'm Way Ahead of You," a clever song in the same vein as "Sometimes," but one where we each anticipated and interrupted what the other had to say.

There came a time when she finally began to wonder, as Jan had sometimes wondered before her, if being primarily known as "Bill Anderson's girl singer" wasn't more of a detriment to her than it was an aid. Eventually she decided that if she were ever going to make it on her own in a solo career she needed to give it a try while the opportunities gleaned from our years together were still there. She left me in 1979 and went out on her own. She recorded some good records, but they never were quite commercial enough to help her turn the corner.

I've had a couple of other interesting experiences with female singers in my lifetime.

In August 1963, when "Still" was at its peak and people figured anybody with a record that big must know the answer to everything, I was asked to help judge a talent contest at a country music park called Frontier Ranch just east of Columbus, Ohio. The deal was that I'd appear on the show myself that afternoon, sing a few songs, and then take a seat alongside two or three local dignitaries out in the audience and help them decide who among the area's hopeful young artists was the most talented. The winner would then be invited back to sing on our night show and would be richer for his or her efforts. The promoters of the contest spared no expense. First prize was five shiny silver dollars.

But it turned out to be no contest at all, not after a tiny young lady with long blonde hair and sparkling blue eyes walked out onstage wearing a white-fringed homemade cowgirl outfit and white boots, playing a guitar almost as big as she was, and singing like nothing that I or any of the other judges had ever heard before. Three notes into her song, the five silver dollars had a home.

The song she sang was one Jean Shepard had made popular called "I Thought of You," but it was the singer and not the song that turned all the heads. None of us could believe such a big voice was coming out of such a petite lady. I actually wondered for a minute if she were pantomiming somebody else's record. She sounded that good.

Her name was Connie Smith. Constance June Meador Smith, to be exact, and I told her backstage after the contest was over that if she ever wanted to come to Nashville and try to make it in the music business I'd be there to try and help her. I knew instantly she had the talent it took to be successful, and I told her so.

But no, she said, she didn't think that was what she wanted to do right then. She hadn't been married very long, she had a new baby boy, and she was happy just being a housewife and a mother. She traveled once a week or so over to West Virginia to sing on a television show, and that was about all she cared to involve herself with right now, thank you very much. And I told her if she ever changed her mind to let me know.

I didn't even see her again until one Sunday afternoon in January of the following year. I was performing at the Municipal Auditorium in Canton, Ohio, and she and her husband, Jerry, drove through a blinding snowstorm from their home in Warner, Ohio, to come see me. They had been thinking more and more about my offer to help Connie launch a singing career, and they wanted to talk with me about it. That is, if I were still interested. I assured them that I was, and the three of us sloshed our way through the snow to a small nearby restaurant between the matinee and evening performances to have dinner and continue our discussion. Connie confessed that she'd been thinking a lot about my offer, and if it were still open, then maybe now was the right time for her to give the music business a full-time shot. I told her it wasn't going to be easy, but I was game if she was. We trudged back to the auditorium through more snow, making plans for her and Jerry to come to Nashville in the spring.

I've often thought it was a curious coincidence that Connie and I reached our decision where we did and when we did. The auditorium I was working that day was the same one Hank Williams had been en route to on New Year's Eve 1952, when he'd died in the backseat of his car near Oak Hill, West Virginia. And the very same day Connie Smith came to Canton to see me, a group of four young singers calling themselves the Kingsmen had driven up from Virginia through that same snowstorm to audition as background singers for Johnny Cash. When Connie and I got back to the auditorium after dinner, we stood in the wings and watched these four young men tear the audience apart with their unique vocal harmonies and hilarious comedy routines. Johnny hired them right there. Later, the Kingsmen became known as the Statler Brothers.

I left Canton and went back to Nashville to begin concentrating on writing some songs for this new female discovery of mine to sing. My first step had to be to find her a recording contract, and I knew that her having good songs would be the key. I came up with three new ones that I believed in and went to talk with Owen Bradley about the possibility of his recording her for Decca.

"She sings great, Bill," Owen said after listening to the demo tapes she'd made, "But I've just signed this new girl the Wilburns brought me named Loretta Lynn, and I think I need to concentrate on her right now."

"Well, I just wanted to give you the first chance at her," I replied, "and I hope you won't mind if I take her to somebody else." Owen assured me that he didn't mind at all and thanked me for my loyalty. The next move was already calculated in my mind. I wanted Chet Atkins to listen to her at RCA.

There was no way Chet could not have been impressed when he heard Connie sing, but after my manager and I played him the tapes he expressed concern about her ongoing supply of good song material.

"We've got more girl singers already than we've got good songs for them to sing," he said. "Our people are constantly looking for songs for Skeeter Davis and Norma Jean and Dottie West. If this girl hits, where are the rest of her songs going to come from? I don't have time to go looking for them."

I assured Chet that I could write hits for Connie, and those I couldn't write I'd help to find. It wasn't like me to make rash promises, but I believed in her that much and I believed in myself. I felt like the two of us were a winning combination. Chet agreed to let me give it a whirl.

We began to lay the foundation. Connie took her first airplane trip and flew to Nashville in March to appear on the *Ernest Tubb Midnight Jamboree*. In May she came back to town to record some demos, in June she returned to sign her RCA contract, and in July she came to sing.

Connie's first recording session for RCA Victor Records took place July 16, 1964, not even one full year after the talent contest at Frontier Ranch. True to my word, I provided three of the first four songs she recorded: "I'm Ashamed of You," "The Threshold," (co-written with my friend Chuck Goddard), and "Once a Day." She cut them in that order. The fourth song, written by Willie Nelson and Hank Cochran, was called "Darling Are You Ever Coming Home?"

Weldon Myrick, Jimmy Lance, and Snuffy Miller from my band all played on the session. The producer, Bob Ferguson, was on staff at RCA, but he said since I knew Connie better than he did at the time and since the songs she'd be singing were mostly mine anyhow, he'd allow me to have a good deal of input into what went onto the tape if I wanted to. It turned out to be a collaborative effort on everybody's part. We all got excited and pitched in. Then when the session was over and the tapes began to circulate among the RCA executives over the next few days, the whole company started to grow as excited as we were about the future of the little girl with the big voice.

There was no doubt in any of our minds but that the most commercial record we'd made was "Once a Day." RCA agreed, coupled it with "The Threshold," and released it to the disc jockeys in late August. Most of them loved it and put it on the air immediately. Listeners started calling in and asking to hear it again. It began to play like crazy on jukeboxes, and it was making cash registers ring at record shops all across the country. It raced up the charts like wildfire, and the week of the annual DJ Convention and Grand Ole Opry Birthday Celebration in November, "Once a Day" became the number one song in the nation. And Connie Smith was suddenly the hottest new act in country music.

From that point on things broke fast and furious. I signed Connie to a management contract and arranged for the Wil-Helm Agency to handle her concert bookings, and the career that she hadn't even been sure she'd wanted only a few months before shifted into high gear.

I guess a lot of it happened too fast. One day this immensely gifted, beautiful young lady is a wife and a new mother and in less than a year she's got the number one record in the country and people are saying she's the greatest thing since sliced bread. George Jones, who had always been Connie's idol as a singer, was going around saying Connie Smith was his favorite singer. It often became more than the shy little housewife could cope with.

Connie says now that she never had time to learn, never had time to build her career one brick, one step at a time like most artists do. She had hit the ground running before she even knew what track she was on.

"I didn't have any idea what was happening," she confessed to me one night in the 1980s, sitting in my dressing room backstage at the Opry. "I even started feeling guilty because I felt like here I was having all this success and I hadn't earned it. I hadn't paid any dues. It really messed my head up, too. I'd go onstage and see somebody like Loretta Lynn standing over in the wings watching me, and I'd forget the words to songs I had sung a thousand times. Then I'd start to withdraw, to hide, because I felt guilty and I was so insecure. People started thinking I was stuck up but really I was just scared."

I helped to get her guest spots on the Grand Ole Opry and eventually an invitation to join the cast as a regular. She began to appear on national television, starred on the *Jimmy Dean Show* when it was the hottest country program on television, and flew to California several times to appear as a guest on *The Lawrence Welk Show*. She was once even offered the chance to become a regular member of the Welk cast but turned it down. I had trouble understanding why.

"The show's not country enough," was her answer at the time, "and they make me sing standing too far away from the band. I can't hear." I thought she was making a mistake and told her so. It was years before she finally admitted the real reason she didn't take the job was because it nearly killed her to leave her young son and fly all the way to California.

She began to tour, taking her husband and her boy with her whenever she could, but often having to leave them behind for days, weeks, even months at a time. This was a part of the business she hadn't counted on, and she didn't like it at all. Even as the world was beating a path to her doorstep and calling hers the Cinderella story of the decade, Cinderella herself was slowly beginning to grow very confused and very unhappy.

From the beginning I liked Connie a lot personally and tried to help her, to talk with her, to explain this crazy business to both her and her husband as best as I could, but I didn't ever seem to get through. I'd tell her how she had the opportunity millions of people would die for, and she'd just shrug. I'd make suggestions as to how she might better balance her family life and her career. I'd talk to her about saying and doing the right things with the fans and with people in the industry, but nothing worked. She was quickly gaining a reputation of being short and snappy with the fans and uncooperative with the media. I'd talk to her about it until I was blue in the face, but most of the time it was like talking to a stone wall. She says now it was just a major case of insecurity, but I'm not sure I'd have believed that at the time. I didn't see how anyone with a voice like hers could be insecure about anything. The lady could flat-out sing.

By the time her second record was released, another song of mine called "Then and Only Then," she was booked constantly. The world was literally her oyster, yet she seemed to dwell in perpetual frustration. "I was stubborn," she says now. "I don't know why. I guess I was just born that way."

I remember clearly the day she was about to leave on a long tour to sing her first record and promote her second one, and I handed her a stack of several hundred postcards.

"Here, these are addressed to disc jockeys all over the country," I told her, "and they're all ready to mail. All I want you to do is send a few of them each day wherever you are on the tour. Just write a couple of short lines ... you know: 'Thanks, Tom, for playing "Once a Day." Sure hope you like my new record, "Then and Only Then." Love, Connie Smith.' And drop them in the mailbox at the hotel. That's all there is to it, and the guys will love you for it. You'll have another number one smash before you know it."

I thought she'd be thrilled, but she looked at me as if I'd just told her she had to go to Alaska without an overcoat. "I'm not going to do that," she snapped. "If I have to do that, I'll just quit this business and go back to Ohio."

Looking back on it now I realize I probably should have told her to go on back to Ohio. There was no way she'd have gone, and deep down I knew it.

As Connie's manager, my idea was to try to help her build a career that would last, one that would be more than a flash in the pan, and I knew that kind of a career needed roots, it needed a foundation laid not only in good music but in goodwill. And I continued to try and help her until her attitudes finally became more than I could handle. One day I just said to heck with it. I took the contract I had with her and tore it into tiny little pieces, laid the pieces in the palm of her hand, wished her well, and walked away.

It might sound funny after all I've just written, but Connie Smith is still and will probably always be my favorite female country singer. And she's one of my favorite people. She's more than paid me back for any help I might have given her in the beginning. At last count she had recorded forty-something songs of mine, including one entire album entitled *Connie Smith Sings Bill Anderson*. I saw her go through the unhappy phase of her life, failed marriages, repeated bouts with depression, and although she never knew it, I hurt right along with her. Then when she turned to her faith and sang nothing but gospel music for a while, I rejoiced with her. I hoped every day she'd somehow be able to find the peace she was looking for.

Today, she's there. She is married to the immensely talented Marty Stuart, and they have weathered many storms together, with love and grace. She's a Country Music Hall of Famer, a designation she cherishes. Connie Smith is the Rolls-Royce of country music, as dear a person as she is unforgettable a singer.

Bill Anderson's ascent to country music stardom came not with a bang but a whisper. Without a commanding vocal presence, he developed a style that was instantly identifiable. No one ever heard one of his records over the radio and asked, "Is that Bill Anderson?" He became, as Don Bowman said one day on WSM radio, "Ol' Whisperin' Bill Anderson. The one who says all those songs." Some people liked the way he said those songs. Others preferred the bluster of Faron Young, or the soaring vocals of Connie Smith. But by developing his own style, soft and sincere, he effectively removed himself from competition. He did not, as he explains in this chapter, remove himself from criticism or misunderstanding.

I read somewhere once that Anderson is the sixth or seventh most common last name in the United States. I know that in nearly every telephone book I've ever opened I've been able to find at least one Bill Anderson or William Anderson or John William or James William Anderson. I don't have an unusual name.

In the beginning of my show business career I thought that was an asset. I wouldn't have to try and come up with a stage name. My real name was easy enough to pronounce and easy enough to remember. But I have found out over the years that it's also easy to forget and easy to get confused. I've been called Bill Alexander, Bill Andrews, or Bill Henderson more times than I care to remember, and once in Wisconsin a lady from a local TV station was introducing me onstage and forgot my name completely.

"You folks are gonna love this next act," she told the crowd, nervously peering over at me in the wings, trying to get some kind of clue as to who I was. "He's real handsome, ladies," she stalled, "and he's wearing a gorgeous black suit." Finally, she realized she had no idea what my name was and it was not going to come to her. With a big sweeping gesture she turned toward me and said, "Come on out here, boy, and tell 'em who you are!"

Somehow I don't think that would have happened had my name been Engelbert Humperdinck, or Cleofis Thigpen, or Ferdly Crumpacker. That's why I'll always be grateful to Don Bowman, the little silver-haired comedian who joined my syndicated television show after Grandpa Jones departed. Don was the first person ever to call me "Whisperin' Bill."

In the spring of 1968 we had moved the production of our TV show again, this time from Canada to the General Electric Broadcasting Company facility in Nashville. GE had taken over ownership and syndication of the show, and since they also owned WNGE-TV, the ABC affiliate at the time, it made sense for them to bring us all together under one roof. And it didn't take me long to appreciate the fact that their studios out on Murfreesboro Road were a lot closer to my house than the studios had been in Charlotte or in Canada.

On taping days we'd usually begin wandering into the station around four o'clock in the afternoon, videotape two half-hour programs before a live audience that evening beginning around eight o'clock, and by ten or eleven o'clock that night we'd be through. Don was single at the time, he slept during the daytime, and he'd usually be wide awake and raring to go when our tapings were over. Many nights after we'd finished he would wander up to the studios of WSM radio where Ralph Emery was the all-night country music disc jockey. He'd join Ralph on the air over the fifty-thousand-watt, clear-channel station, and Ralph would ask him what he'd been up to.

"Oh, I've been out taping TV shows with Ol' Whisper," Don would reply.

"Who is Ol' Whisper?" Ralph would ask.

"Oh, you know, Ralph, Ol' Whisperin' Bill Anderson. The one who says all those songs."

And in those days I guess I did "say" a lot of my songs. Actually, I sang on most of them, too, but the sing-a-little, talk-a-little format that we began to develop on "Mama Sang a Song" and "Still" distinguished me from the other country singers of the day. I'd used it on "8 × 10" and on "Five Little Fingers," and I spoke all the lyrics on "Golden Guitar." I never made a con-certed effort to whisper, but neither did I want my records to sound like I was doing a commercial for a used car lot. I mostly wanted them to sound believable, and for me to do that it had to come out soft.

In those days, every disc jockey in the country listened to Ralph Emery late at night to find out what new songs he was playing (he often had advance releases from the major companies) and to listen to his personal interviews with the stars. And whatever Ralph played and whatever he said at night was repeated by the local DJs on the smaller stations all across America the next day. Therefore, when Ralph Emery began calling me "Whisperin' Bill," so did everybody else.

In the beginning, I was sensitive to it and wasn't quite sure how to handle it. I figured maybe if I'd ignore it, it would go away. Then several of the major stars took to impersonating me in their stage acts, and I had no place to hide.

I remember well a tour when I was opening for Ferlin Husky. I'd go out on stage every night and do my bit, then retreat to the side of the stage to watch him do his. And there has never been an artist in any form of musical entertainment who could entertain an audience like Ferlin Husky could when he was right. He'd sing his hits like "Gone" and "Wings of a Dove" and then launch into his alter-ego character, Simon Crum. And Simon would do impressions of other country stars. He'd sing like Ernest Tubb and Red Foley and even Kitty Wells. But his biggest hand and his biggest laughs always came when Simon imitated Whisperin' Bill. Ferlin would slide his right leg back behind him in an exaggerated imitation of my stance on stage and whisper real breathy into the microphone and do his own rewrites of my songs. And the people who had been applauding me just a few minutes before would then be sitting out there laughing their heads off. I laughed a lot myself because it was truly funny, but down deep inside it stung me a little.

I'll always love Ferlin for picking up on my sensitivity. He came to me one night after a show and he said, "That bothers you when I imitate you, doesn't it?"

I admitted that yes, sometimes, I guessed it did.

"Well, let me tell you something," he said. "In the first place if you weren't different I wouldn't have anything to imitate. Think of all the singers who are just plain singers, and there's nothing that makes them stand out enough for anybody to imitate them. You're different and you've got your own style and people recognize it. You should be grateful for that.

"And in the second place," he continued, moving swiftly from the deep, sincere voice of Ferlin Husky to the whimsical, whiny tones of Simon Crum, "Hell, if I didn't like you, I wouldn't give you the publicity!"

My attitude changed from that moment on. I became proud to be "Whisperin' Bill." It gave a special name and unique identity to someone with a very common name. It gave me a hook . . . a handle. There wasn't another Whisperin' Bill in a phone book anyplace that I knew of. I loved it. Nowadays when they imitate me, I laugh louder than anybody.

A distinctive voice like mine can also be a liability, as I have found out on more than one occasion. I lost my cool and snapped at a long-distance telephone operator out on the road one night when she couldn't get my call right. I didn't figure she knew me from Adam, but when the call finally did go through she said, "Thank you, Mr. Anderson." I had no idea she'd recognized my voice. I wanted to leave town on the next fast freight.

I've been told by some people in this business that I don't have enough of the temperament of a star, that I don't have a big enough ego. They suggest I should put more distance between myself and the public, that I sign too many autographs, meet too many of my fans up close, that I'm "too available." Maybe they have a point. But I have one as well.

Before I was a "star" I was a "fan," and I still remember what it feels like. I've stood in line for autographs only to be brushed aside by somebody I admired, and it hurts. I've written fan letters and watched my mailbox for days on end just to get a simple reply and have been crushed when none ever came. Once when I was in the seventh or eighth grade I wrote a letter to Hank Williams and asked him to send me a list of all the records he had ever made because I wanted to be sure I had them all. Maybe he never got my letter. Maybe I sent it to the Opry at a time when he wasn't even with the Opry. Maybe my dad forgot to mail it. I don't know. All I knew was I never got an answer from my idol, and I was hurt. So hurt, in fact, that I traded all my Hank Williams 78 rpm records to a friend for all his Spike Jones records. Wonder what those Hank Williams originals would be worth today?

I've tried hard never to break anybody's heart like some of the people I admired broke mine. I don't know that I've ever proved a thing by it, but I've done it this way far too long to think about changing now. The great Baltimore Orioles baseball player Brooks Robinson signed autographs at every request, so much so that his signature isn't "worth" as much as other, less-accomplished stars. But I'm pretty sure that each kind interaction he had with a fan was worth something more valuable to that fan than whatever the autograph could have been resold for on the Internet or at a baseball memorabilia show. Brooks and I both preferred kindness and availability over mystery and rarity. If that's a mistake, I'd make it again.

Having been both a disc jockey and a newspaper reporter, I have probably also had more of an understanding of the press and the electronic media than many entertainers. I've always tried to cooperate with them, too, realizing they have a job to do. Overall, the media have been good to me, but I was once burned awfully bad. It was in the midseventies, just after John Denver and Olivia Newton-John had won some major CMA awards, and several of the more traditional country artists were upset. In a move that was totally unrelated but awkwardly timed, George Jones and Tammy

Wynette called a large group of us together at their big Franklin Road mansion one night not long after the awards show to discuss the music business in general and to socialize a bit. Out of this meeting was born an organization called ACE, the Association of Country Entertainers. We decided we needed to be closer as a group and have some picnics and parties during the year, there was some talk about our trying to start a retirement home for country entertainers, and that's about all there was to it. However, the press was not invited nor allowed to attend our gathering. They had no idea what was going on, but some of them got together and decided we must be perpetrating some kind of evil against the pop stars who had won country music awards. And they had a field day.

They wrote that we were bitter and angry and that we'd had this secret meeting to discuss boycotting the Country Music Association, maybe even pulling out of the CMA to start our own organization. There was no foundation whatsoever for the things they were writing, but they began to get attention and attention sells newspapers. So they didn't let up. In an effort to combat the lies they were writing and saying about us, we met at George and Tammy's again and decided to hold a press conference the following day to set the record straight. The other entertainers elected me to be spokesman for the group.

I faced a battery of microphones and cameras early the next morning and read from a statement prepared by a lawyer who had been at our meetings as the invited guest of a major performer. I don't remember everything I said or exactly how I said it, but it was something to the effect that we weren't mad at anybody and we weren't bitter and we just decided this was a good time to organize all the entertainers into a group. After all, the music publishers had an organization and the talent agents had an organization, why couldn't the entertainers themselves have an organization? It was as simple as that.

After the press conference was over, however, a couple of reporters cornered some of the other stars who were there and asked them their personal opinions about the recent CMA awards. One of the artists supposedly made the statement, "Outsiders are coming in here and trying to take our music away."

When the papers hit the streets that afternoon, it was quoted all over the country that, "ACE spokesman Bill Anderson says, 'They're coming in here and trying to take our music away.'" Nothing could have been further from the truth. Not only did I not say it, I didn't even feel that way. And even if I had felt it, I wouldn't have been stupid enough to say it. You cannot imagine how upset I was.

I stayed up half the night calling the papers and the wire services pleading with them to print a retraction. Nowhere on any tape recorder (and there had been dozens of them at the press conference) could they produce a copy of my saying the words I was supposed to have said. But they realized immediately that they had created a newspaper-selling monster, they were getting tons of publicity from it, and they loved it. They weren't about to let something as relatively insignificant as the truth interfere with their fun.

But for me it was too late. By the next morning I was getting phone calls from people all over the country calling me everything from a fool to a pinko commie pig. Paul Harvey talked about me on his newscast. At the time I had a record that was number 5 with a bullet in the national charts, the "bullet" signifying that the song was still strongly on the rise. The next week it fell to number 11 with no bullet. The following week it disappeared from the charts forever.

A columnist for *Billboard* magazine wrote a lengthy piece taking me to task within the industry, and there were actually radio programmers who read her garbage and said they'd never play another Bill Anderson record. I wrote a personal letter to every major station in the country telling them my side. Most of them, once they heard the truth, believed me.

Tom T. Hall wrote me a very nice letter in which he said he really felt sorry for me "in the controversy over the good work you did with ACE and the bad publicity you received in return." He went on to say, "I am sure there are people who must look after their own interests in writing these press releases, but it's a pity that they must make someone else look small in order to make themselves look big." I appreciated his sensitivity to my plight and, more than that, the fact that he took time out to write and let me know.

In time it all blew over and things returned to normal, but I learned in that one episode how powerful and how vicious the press can sometimes be. And how helpless most of us really are to fight it. All of this, of course, has not improved in our new century of instant news, TMZ, and all of that.

Because I have never deliberately isolated myself from the public and because of my well-publicized role in the establishment of Connie Smith's career, I was also a target for every would-be singer and songwriter in America. They all seemed to think if they could just get a tape and a picture and a bio into my magic hands, I could wave a wand and make them all stars overnight.

"Please help me," a man once wrote me. "I want more than anything to be a songwriter but I only write the words. Can't you please take my words and write lyrics to them?"

Another gentleman cornered me one night at a rodeo in Texas and shoved a couple of copies of his new single record into my hand. His name was something like John Smith and his record was on the J.S. label, which was a dead giveaway that he'd paid for his session and his record pressing himself. But he had an unusual angle.

"I want you to help me," he pleaded. "This record was almost on RCA. Yes sir," he said in a whisper. "It was almost on RCA."

"What happened?" I asked.

"Well, they said they'd release it except I was too well unknown." As far as I know, he still is.

The late Tex Ritter, as kind, gentle, and benevolent a man as I've ever known, was like me in his attitude toward the press and the public. But like all of us, Tex also had his limits. Once he was approached during a private moment by a well-meaning fan who said, "Mr. Ritter, I hate to bother you . . . " whereupon, before the fan could finish, Tex snorted, "Then why do you?"

On the other hand, I often saw Tex display the patience of Job. Once he was being interviewed for a newspaper story while he was backstage getting dressed for a performance, and he invited the reporter to make himself at home. This he did, following Tex to the mirror as he tied his tie, sitting beside him on a wooden bench as Tex shined his boots, and finally trailing him right up to the urinal in the men's room. As "America's Most Beloved Cowboy" reached for his fly, the reporter asked, "Tex, what's the main difference between country music stars and pop music stars?"

Before Tex could answer, a fan burst into the room waving a piece of paper and a pen and demanding, "Hey, Tex, gimme your autograph."

Undaunted, Mr. Ritter calmly let go of his zipper, took the pen, wrote his name on the paper, affixed the date of the occasion underneath, and returned it to his admirer. He then turned back open-flied to the reporter and said, "In answer to your question, sir, we are accessible!"

In the coming chapter, Bill Anderson waters the seeds of his country music success by committing to close and near-constant contact with disc jockeys and fans. He also helps create Fan Fair, the annual country music festival that is now Nashville's signature event, under the less folksy moniker CMA Music Festival. And he enters the game show world, impressing television executives and famed actress Betty White. He lives underneath the city lights he wrote about back in Commerce in 1958, at a cost he wouldn't fully understand until later.

Most of my life I've been lousy at keeping secrets, but until about the time "Still" became a big hit, I didn't tell anybody in Nashville except my very closest friends that I had been to college. It wasn't that I was ashamed of it, but rather I was afraid my college degree might keep me from being accepted by others in the music business. Most of the pickers and singers from the late fifties and early sixties simply had not had the opportunity I'd had to attend college. Most of them came from rural or small-town backgrounds, many had no formal education past grade school or early high school, having had to drop out in order to work and help support their families. Music had been their magic carpet off the treadmill to oblivion, and I didn't want anybody thinking that I thought I was better than they were just because I happened to have been lucky enough to finish sixteen years of school.

In fact, when I first got to Nashville I didn't talk very much about my background at all. Besides my insecurities about my having gone to college, I was also very sensitive to the fact that I had not grown up on a farm. Or even in the country. Except for the short time we had lived with my grandparents in Griffin, I had been a city boy all of my life. How honest would they think it was in Nashville for a kid from the city to be trying to write and sing country music? Today it wouldn't matter at all, but back then I didn't want to take any chances. I figured the less that was known about me and where I had come from, the better off I'd be.

I don't know what role, if any, my education had to play in my initial approach to show business, but from the very beginning I was able to recognize this industry as being just what the name implies: half show and half business. And in my early days I spent whatever time I wasn't spending trying to absorb the show part attempting to learn all I could about the business itself.

I was left somewhat to my own devices, however, because for several years after I got into the business I did not have a manager. And in show business a good manager is almost a necessity. An artist can't go around telling people how good he is, but his manager can. Besides, a creative person should be free to create and let his manager worry about the day-to-day dealings with the business world, the contracts, the lawyers, the accountants. And, as my first manager told me, a good artist-manager relationship has to be almost like a marriage. It requires a lot of faith in the other person and a lot of give and take on both sides.

In the beginning I had a hard time finding very many people who believed in me as an artist. There was no doubt I could write hit songs and all the music publishers went out of their way to court me, but as a performer I was someone with a unique style as opposed to someone with a technically great singing voice. I was different, and sometimes difference has to grow on people.

Buddy Killen helped guide me in my early career decisions, introducing me to talent agents and promoters and helping me obtain my first appearances on the Opry, but Buddy was not in the talent-management business. He was a music publisher. Roger Miller and I both tried long and hard to convince Buddy to open a talent agency division at Tree Publishing because we both wanted to make a home there for all facets of our careers, but Buddy, probably very wisely, declined.

In those days in Nashville one person often functioned as both an artist's manager and his booking agent, and one of the most successful and well respected of these was a gentleman named Hubert Long. Hubert was a protégé of Colonel Tom Parker, having worked for the Colonel long before the Elvis days when Parker had managed country stars Eddy Arnold and Hank Snow. Hubert had left Colonel Tom to start his own talent management firm and booking agency in the early fifties, and when I arrived on the scene he was the guiding force behind the super-successful careers of both Ferlin Husky and Faron Young. Unlike most of the other talent agents in town, however, he didn't try to sign every artist who knocked on his door seeking representation. He was very particular about his artists, deliberately keeping his roster and his office staff small and manageable. It was an honor for an artist to say he was represented by Hubert Long. By late 1962 I had knocked around town working in and out of the various agencies long enough to know that I wanted Hubert Long to manage me and guide my career.

I knew Hubert was never going to sign to represent me based on my singing ability. But two other things caught his eye. First, my songwriting contract was about to expire at Tree, and Hubert was in the process of starting a new company called Moss Rose Publications. Obviously he wanted me to write songs for his company. In fact, in true managerial style he told me early on that if he were ever to agree to manage me he would want to manage every phase of my career. Translated, that meant he wanted to publish my songs. I wasn't too sure about that for a while. The second thing that worked in my favor, however, was the fact that Hubert Long was very attracted to my attitude toward country music as a business.

I remember well the day it all came to a head. I had been sitting in his office since early afternoon listening to him work his magic on the telephone, booking concert dates right and left for Faron and Ferlin.

Between a break in his phone calls, we started talking about what we'd each done the night before. Hubert, a confirmed bachelor who never spent very many dull moments in his life, was telling me about a party he'd attended and a special new lady in his life. He then asked me what I'd been up to.

"I stayed up until after midnight writing disc jockeys," I told him.

"What do you mean 'writing disc jockeys'?" he asked.

"Oh, I just drop short notes to all the radio guys I've met in my travels and thank them for playing my records. And then if I've got anything new coming out, I'll ask them to give it a special listen when it comes in. That's all."

"Who pays for all that?" Hubert asked.

"What do you mean?"

"Well, who pays for the postage?"

"I do."

"And the letterheads and the envelopes?"

"Same person."

"And who does the typing?" he asked, not sure of what he was hearing.

"I do," I told him truthfully.

"Boy, you sure must want to be in this business awfully bad," he said.

"More than anything else in this world," I confessed.

He sat there a minute and just looked at me. "Well, I've got a feeling anybody who wants it that bad is going to make it," he smiled. "And I think I'd like to be your manager."

Before I could thank him, laugh, faint, or jump up in the air, he reached into his desk drawer and pulled out a big roll of postage stamps.

"Here, use these next time," he said, tossing them into my lap. Then he stood up and we shook hands. That handshake was the only contract we ever had, and it lasted for ten years, until Hubert's death from a brain tumor in 1972. He was only forty-eight years old.

I'm not sure Nashville will ever see another Hubert Long. He was a big man physically, standing well over six feet tall and at one time probably tipping the scales at close to 250 pounds. He had slimmed down to around 185 or 190 by the time I met him, however, after having been diagnosed as diabetic and told by his doctors that he had to rid himself of the excess baggage. He had only a few strands of sandy hair left to comb across the top of his perpetually tanned head, but his quick smile and genteel, almost chivalrous warmth charmed everyone who ever met him. He was a shrewd businessman, but more important, Hubert Long brought class to our business at a time when many people looked upon us all as a bunch of hayseeds. He was impeccably honest, he'd bend over backwards to be fair to his artists and his clients alike, and he had a genuine affinity for the people he represented.

We artists were Hubert's family, and he was available to each of us twenty-four hours a day, seven days a week. Many's the time I called him in the wee hours from some tiny dot on the map with a problem of some sort, and he never failed to help me solve it. When I separated from my first wife, it was Hubert who scouted and found me a place to live on Old Hickory Lake. "Being close to the water will be good for you," he declared. Because he had lived high upon the banks of the Cumberland River for years himself, I knew he spoke from experience.

"The water will help you relax and give you a good frame of mind so you can create," he said.

He was right, and I lived in the house he found for me for twelve years. Some of my biggest hit songs were written inside those walls.

When Becky and I married, Hubert was my best man. But he didn't stop there. I always accused him of "producing" our wedding because he knew we needed dishes and silverware, and he told each of the invited guests just what gifts to bring. Had it been anybody but Hubert, such actions might have been considered gauche or ill-mannered, but everybody just laughed and went along.

Hubert, along with me, George Hamilton IV, and Bud Wendell, was in on the original conversation that eventually led to the establishment of the country music Fan Fair, the annual pilgrimage that in the new century became the CMA Music Festival, Nashville's signature musical event. The four of us were standing in a stairwell at the old Capitol Park Inn in downtown Nashville during the yearly Disc Jockey Convention complaining that we couldn't get close enough to the disc jockeys to talk and visit with them because of all the fans who'd come in.

"Maybe we need to have a separate convention just for the fans," one of us said.

Bud's eyes lit up.

"You know, that's actually not a bad idea," he said. "Maybe we should give it some thought."

Less than two years later, Fan Fair was a reality.

Hubert served as both president and chairman of the board of the Country Music Association and was one of the primary sounding boards used by the management of WSM in the planning and building of Opryland, the country music theme park that was a vital tourist draw from the 1970s into the late 1990s. He didn't live to see Fan Fair become a reality, much less the CMA Music Festival, or to see the doors to the new Grand Ole Opry House swing open on the Opryland complex, but he left an indelible mark on this business and on me personally. The night he was named posthumously to the Country Music Hall of Fame in 1979, I stood on the front row of the Opry House with tears in my eyes and cheered louder than anybody.

When Hubert died, I lost not only my manager but a business partner (I finally had signed to write for his Moss Rose Publications, and we also had gone into some other music publishing ventures together, including the establishment of my own publishing firm, Stallion Music, Inc.) and a dear friend as well. How would I ever be able to replace such a loss? Fortunately, someone was looking over me again.

In 1970, my close friend Dean Booth, a brilliant young attorney from Atlanta, had been in New York representing ABC Television in some kind of legal capacity. One night over dinner with one of the vice presidents of the network, Dean casually mentioned my name and my work in the music business around Nashville. "Bill Anderson is one of the most successful artists in the country music business today," Dean told the executive, "and he has one of the top syndicated television shows on the air. But everything he does comes out of Nashville. He very seldom appears on the networks. He needs to be seen on some of the bigger shows. I'd like to help him find somebody up here in New York, where all you heavyweights in the industry are located, to work with him and advise him and help him expand his career. Do you know of anyone here who might be able to help him?"

The ABC representative, who didn't know Bill Anderson from Bill Monroe, recommended that Dean contact a man named Bobby Brenner. Bobby, he said, had been a major talent agent in New York for years, working with large companies like Music Corporation of America and Ashley Famous Artists and representing such clients as Ed Sullivan, Eddie Albert, Peter Duchin, and others. But he had recently turned his back on the corporate life and gone into business for himself as an entertainment consultant. He might be just what Dean was looking for.

So Dean gave Bobby a call, arranged to go by his office in Manhattan the next day to talk with him, and then scheduled me to fly to New York in a couple of weeks to meet with Bobby myself.

From that very simple beginning came not only a whole new world of television exposure for me and a dozen or more new avenues for my career, but this energetic, brilliant little man from New York ended up becoming my manager, my business partner, my very close friend, and eventually even godfather to my son.

At first, he was not my manager but only a consultant in the area of television and worked closely with Hubert. Later, when the responsibility for my entire career came to rest on his shoulders, he devised a brilliant master plan.

"Your basic appeal, Will," he never called me Bill, always "Will" or "Kid" or, if he was mad at me, "James William," "is to women. Women buy most of your records, women are the ones who come to your concerts. Now, when do women watch television?"

Keep in mind, this was at a time before most women chose to go into the workplace. In any case, I wasn't real sure what he was driving at.

"Women watch television in the daytime," he said. "Now, here's my idea: Let's let all the other country stars keep chasing after guest spots on the *Tonight Show* and on the prime-time specials, and let's us go after getting you onto daytime television. I think it will work." I wasn't too sure.

But work it did. By this time my publicist, Bernie Ilson, had generated enough publicity for me to sink a battleship. Tons and tons of articles with my name, my picture, my dog's picture, and my mother's favorite recipes—anything to get Bill Anderson's name into circulation. I was having other country artists tell me that they'd go into a town for a concert and pick up the local paper to read about their show and instead all they'd find was a story about me. It was a bit embarrassing, but our mission was being accomplished.

It was only a matter of a few weeks until I appeared on NBC's *Today* show. I was the first country artist to appear on *The Mike Douglas Show* ("This will set our show back ten years!" I overheard one of the staff band members mutter when he saw me and the group coming into the studio lugging our guitars), and I probably appeared with Mike as much or more than anybody from Nashville during the years his show was on the air. Bobby booked me on all the top entertainment-talk shows with all the top hosts—David Frost, Dr. Joyce Brothers, Dinah Shore, Della Reese, John Gary, and so many others I can't remember them all. And then one day he really snuck up on my blind side.

"Will, I want you to start doing guest appearances on some of the daytime game shows," he said.

"Game shows?" I exclaimed. "What for, Bobby? I don't even watch game shows!"

"Well, start watching them," was his answer. "I've booked you a spot next week on *Match Game* at CBS in Hollywood. It's for six shows, five of the daytime programs and one nighttime shot. I think you should take it, but if you don't want it, I can probably switch them over to Tom T. Hall."

Bobby always had a way with words.

I flew to California and taped six episodes.

Match Game was a show where a contestant was asked to fill in the blank in a question and a panel of celebrities tried to anticipate and match the answer the contestant would give. It was a serious game in that the contestants had a chance to win some big bucks, but it was played in a none-too-serious manner by the panel. They told us to try our best to match the contestants but to have fun doing it. And if we could throw in something halfway witty in the process, feel free to do so. I don't remember how many matching answers I came up with that first time but it must have been a few and I must have acted semi-insane doing it, because they asked me to come back. And then back. And back again.

And then Bobby, having gotten my foot inside the Hollywood game show circuit door, carried his madness one step further. He turned my then-wife,

Becky, into a TV star. He booked us an appearance together on another CBS show called *Tattletales*, a program where three celebrity couples would try to match the answers their spouses or partners might give to personal questions about themselves and their relationships. The couple who matched the most answers in each daily half-hour segment was declared the winner. As with *Match Game*, we were contracted to six shows.

Becky was a little nervous before we went on *Tattletales* the first time, but it didn't take her long to relax and fall right into the flow of things. After about two questions and a couple of small giggles from the audience when she'd come up with a cute answer, she got to feeling her oats and didn't really care what she said. "Hey, it's not my career," she'd laugh, and then give some outlandish response to whatever the question happened to be. The more the studio audience and host Bert Convy would laugh at her answers, the more turned on she'd become and the crazier she'd act. Most of the time it was funny and I'd laugh too, but once we got into an argument over something she said.

The question had been, "Ladies, which one of the two of you will your husband say eats more junk food, you or him?" Well, Becky has always been a junk food junkie and I can either take it or leave it. Naturally, I answered that she ate the most. She had said that I did.

"Why, I don't eat junk food!" I exclaimed on nationwide TV. "You're the one who's always reaching your hand down in a sack of potato chips or into a can of cashew nuts. And you're always drinking a Pepsi!"

"Oh, no, you've got that all wrong. You're always making a turkey sandwich at midnight or eating an extra piece of lemon pie for dessert," she squealed.

"But that's not junk food," I protested. "That's nourishment!"

We had some good laughs over another incident that took place on *Tattletales*. Again the question was to the ladies: "Girls, what will your husband say was his most embarrassing moment?" The panel that day consisted of author Mickey Spillane and his wife, Sherri; game show host Allen Ludden and his wife, the marvelous Betty White; and us. When it came Becky's turn to answer, she launched into the story she'd heard me tell of the time in high school when I went onstage with my pants unzipped. However, when she came to the punch line about my having held my guitar in a rather unique position, she said, "He held his guitar down around his knees." The studio audience howled, where upon Betty White flashed the camera one of those patented astonished, dry looks of hers, raised her eyebrows, leaned forward and said, "Well, Becky, I have just gained a whole new respect for your husband!"

I had no way of knowing it at the time, but my appearances on *Match Game*, *Tattletales*, and later on *Password*, *Hollywood Squares*, and other daytime game shows were leading to something else—something a whole lot bigger—that was ultimately to have a profound effect on both my life and my career. For I found out in the early spring of 1977 that I was about to be asked by Mark Goodson, the king of the game show producers, if I'd like to audition for the role of host of a new game show he'd just devised, the pilot for which he had sold to ABC. When I first heard about it, I was told the show was to be called *The Stronger Sex* and would feature a male and a female as cohosts, something that up until this time had never been tried in game show television.

"Understand now, the show isn't yours to host by a long shot," Howard Felsher, the man who brought me to Mark Goodson's attention, emphasized. "All you're being offered is an audition, a chance for you to see and us to see if you can handle it. And all you'll win if you pass the audition is a chance to cohost the pilot, not the series, if in fact there's even going to be series. At this point that's not even for sure. But what do you say?"

I said, "Okay."

The first thing I had to do after saying, "Okay, I'd like to try," was to promise the producers I'd spend every available minute over the next few weeks in southern California learning the premise of the new game and how I might best negotiate the move from country singer to game show host. I caught a lot of red-eye airplane flights in and out of the Los Angeles International Airport, and I put in many long and tedious hours in the Goodson-Todman offices under the watchful eye of executive-producer-to-be Ira Skutch, learning just what it is that a game show host is supposed to do.

Finally, after several weeks, I hosted a mock version of the game with a former Miss America, Nancy Fleming, and she was very pleasant. In fact, I flew back to Nashville thinking she and I might make a good team, only to be called back to California almost immediately to try out with another potential cohost, author Joanna Barnes. Before it was over I must have done run-throughs with at least a dozen ladies, including Patty Duke.

The procedure as a whole was exhilarating, but at times it could also be very rough on my nerves. We'd play the game on a simulated set built in the Goodson-Todman offices with office staff members posing as contestants. After each half-hour run-through the production staff would leave without a word and disappear inside their private offices down the hall to talk about what they'd just seen and heard. Then they'd come back into the rehearsal room and give us their critiques, sometimes pages upon pages. Each time they'd return I'd feel like I should stand and address them as "ladies and gentlemen of the jury." They were mostly kind in their remarks, but I never received from them any indication of how my performance was stacking up against the others in the running. That only added to the intense pressure I was beginning to feel.

More than once I wondered if being the host of a network game show was really worth all the effort I was having to put into it, all the tension, all the stress. I'd sometimes close my eyes there on Sunset Boulevard in the middle of Hollywood and pretend I was back in Nashville listening to the ringing of an open E chord on my ole flat-top guitar. And I'd think about writing a song or climbing on the bus and heading out somewhere to perform for people who put no pressure on me at all. "I don't need to be a game show host," I'd tell myself. "I've already got a pretty good job."

Given the fact that I knew over two dozen other men had tried out for the job as cohost of this new show, including several who'd had network game show experience, I figured when it came time for Mr. Goodson and his staff to choose the host for the taping of the pilot my chances of landing the role rested somewhere between slim and none. I had, in fact, about given up hope of being chosen when my phone rang at home late one night and I got surprising but happy news: I'd been chosen to host the pilot.

I was determined not to worry about the series and whether or not it would ever get on the air. I planned just to relax and have a good time taping the pilot. And I did. My cohost turned out to be none of the ladies I had worked with in the run-throughs but rather a tall, striking blonde who at the time was hosting *Good Morning, Los Angeles*, sort of a local version of *Good Morning, America*, on KABC-TV in L.A. Her name was Sarah Purcell.

Sarah had never worked on a game show either, so in that respect we started out even. In fact, at that time, Sarah hadn't been working in front of a TV camera very long, period. She was a former secretary at a television station in San Diego who got pressed into on-the-air duty one night when the local TV weather girl didn't show up. The showbiz bug bit her so hard she never returned to her typewriter and steno pad. Mark Goodson hadn't met Sarah when he first spotted her either, but he liked what he saw on the local show and called her in for an audition.

Sarah and I more or less inherited one another, but we hit it off immediately and I can't tell you how relieved I was. She was lively, witty, just flaky enough to be real cute, and above all she was a lady. When she found national, prime-time stardom as one of the hosts of NBC's *Real People* a few years later, nobody was happier for her than I was.

I had to mark off an entire week on my schedule to tape the pilot. I flew into Los Angeles late on a Sunday afternoon, and on Monday morning we moved from our tiny make-believe studio at the Goodson-Todman offices into the honest-to-goodness real ABC-TV studios on Prospect Avenue. There we set up shop on a shiny new stage that I was told was the most expensive, elaborate set ever constructed for a game show. They said it cost over three quarters of a million dollars just to build. And then, with real cameras beneath real lights and with real contestants for what seemed like a hundred days and nights on end, I practiced making the rest of my transition from being a country music singer to being the host of a network game show.

"I'm sorry, Bill," producer Ira Skutch said to me over the long-distance wire from L.A. one Sunday afternoon about three weeks after the taping of the pilot. "We all thought you did a helluva job, all of us did, but the network just won't buy you. Mark, all of us, we've talked till we're blue in the face. ABC likes the show and wants it to go on the air in July, but I'm afraid we're going to have to go with someone else."

After thanking everyone for the opportunity, I hung up the phone and called Bill Goodwin, my booking agent. I told him to get busy booking me some concert dates for the summer. My brief career as a game show host was over.

A few weeks later, I was signing autographs inside my fan club booth at the country music Fan Fair in Nashville, the world of Hollywood and game shows a million miles from my mind. Suddenly, above the noise and commotion generated by ten thousand country fans who'd come to Nashville from all over the world to see and meet their favorite stars, I could hear my name being called over the loudspeaker system. Someone was paging me to come to the telephone.

Being totally surrounded by humanity, flashbulbs, and autograph books, unable to move more than a few steps at a time, I turned to Becky and asked her if she'd mind going to find out what it was and bring me any message.

She came back in about five minutes, out of breath and pale. "You'd better go to the phone quick," she said, and I conjured up all sorts of images of tragedy.

"What's the matter?" I asked anxiously, pushing the crowd aside.

"It's from California," she panted. "You've got the show."

By the time our show got on the air in July 1977, the name had been changed from *The Stronger Sex* to *The Better Sex*, but for some reason the general public always seemed to want to call it *The Battle of the Sexes*. I never cared what they called it as long as they watched it. Today I meet people who only vaguely remember the show who'll come up to me and ask, "What was that 'sex show' you used to do on TV?"

ABC gave our show a good time slot, the half-hour following the highly rated *Family Feud*.

The ratings on the show started off high, the result of a barrage of advance publicity and promotion. After the initial honeymoon period, however, they tapered off a bit before starting to build slowly but steadily back. We had been guaranteed only that we'd be on the air for thirteen weeks at the outset, which I learned is standard fare at the networks, but our first option was quickly picked up by ABC and we launched our second thirteen-week cycle. Everybody felt good about the future of the show, and I was having a blast. At first I missed my guitar, but I soon forgot it wasn't hanging around my neck and concentrated on trying to make *The Better Sex* an entertaining television show.

Basically, *The Better Sex* was a trivia game, and the premise was to see whether a team of five women captained by Sarah Purcell or a team of five men captained by yours truly could answer the most trivia questions. The winning team could then boast, "We are 'the better sex'!"

Trivia of all kinds was hot in those days, and our subject matter knew no bounds. We asked everything from "Which U.S. president once got stuck in the White House bathtub?" to "Who broke Babe Ruth's home run record?" I can't remember which president got stuck, but Henry Aaron of the Atlanta Braves broke Babe Ruth's home run record, on April 8, 1974.

Once we swung into production, I found that hosting a five-day-a-week game show, while perhaps not in the same league as laying concrete block or performing brain surgery, can nonetheless be very taxing. Most of the time we taped five half-hour programs in one day, although once or twice we got in a bind and had to tape as many as seven. Many times I was also having to face this grind on three or four hours sleep a night. I was living in Nashville trying to maintain a career in country music, which meant nonstop touring in the summer, and I had to hop many midnight flights to and from California.

I hadn't rented an apartment or a house on the west coast either, because I never had more than a thirteen-week guarantee of employment at any one time. I figured as soon as I signed a long-term lease on living quarters somewhere my show would get canceled.

The Better Sex stayed on the air until the early part of 1978 and was canceled then not because of bad ratings but because ABC had a lady named Jackie Smith in charge of daytime programming. Jackie saw that game shows in general were declining in favor with the public and that daytime dramas (affectionately known as "soap operas") were getting hotter and hotter every day. There were two soaps on ABC then, *General Hospital* and *One Life to Live*, which were only forty-five minutes each in length, and Jackie felt the rising tide for the soaps compelled her to extend those programs to one hour each. In order to do that, she had to recapture thirty minutes of program time from somewhere.

For me and Sarah and all the rest of the people who had worked so very hard to try and make *The Better Sex* come alive, it was a tough pill to swallow. The network gave us a little party backstage after we taped our last show, and there were a lot of us walking around the room wearing long faces. Jackie came to the party and moved graciously among us trying to console our wounded pride.

"Bill, you've just been marvelous," Jackie said to me, sensing, I'm sure, the disappointment in my face. "But you'll be back. In fact, if you don't come up with another game show, which I feel sure you will eventually, I want to use you in one of my soaps. How would you like that?"

"Me? In a soap opera?" I almost laughed. "Doing what?"

"I don't know right now. Let me think about it. I promise you'll be hearing from me, though."

She kept her word. Before I knew it, I was in New York on the set of *One Life to Live*, script in hand, ready to launch a whole new career as an actor in a daytime television drama. Show business had totally amazed me one more time.

"You don't have to act," said the *One Life to Live* director. "You're playing the part of yourself, Bill Anderson, the country singer. Just be natural and do what you'd naturally do under these circumstances. The great actors don't act anyhow, they react. Just calm down and let's have some fun."

In the story line, I was an old pal of a man who ran a small nightclub in suburban Philadelphia. This man had supposedly befriended me early in my career, and anytime I was on tour in the Philadelphia area I stopped by to see him. When the *One Life* viewers first saw me, I was presumably en route to a nearby concert engagement and popped into the club for a few minutes to chat with my old buddy.

My friend asked me to pull up a chair and started telling me about this young girl who'd just moved up from North Carolina and who was singing part-time in his club. "Her name is Becky Lee Abbott, and I think she's got real potential, Bill," he said. "I'd appreciate it if you'd take a listen to her and maybe give her some advice."

The director was right. This wasn't acting. This was doing something I'd been doing every day of my life for nearly twenty years. "Do I have to stick right to the script?" I asked, noting that the language they'd prepared for me seemed a bit contrived and stilted.

"Shoot, no," he said. "Just put it into your own words. We want this thing to be as realistic as possible."

So I sat backstage in the little club and told Becky Lee all about show business. How she needed to try and develop her own style of singing, how it would be helpful if she could write some of her own songs, the very same things I told aspiring performers every day of my life. And I just happened to have my guitar with me, and we just happened to sing a song or two together.

It must have come off all right because almost as soon as the first two episodes I taped hit the air they called me back for a couple more. In a few weeks they wanted me back again, and this time they said for me to bring my entire band. We all went and played a concert in the little club and had a ball. Suddenly I began to realize the writers were not only weaving me in and out of Becky Lee's life but slowly turning her into a major star as well. The next thing I knew they were telling me that I was going to bring her to Nashville and invite her to appear with me on the Grand Ole Opry. Except, not to worry, they were conveniently going to move the Grand Ole Opry to New York.

Right there in a television studio on West Sixty-Seventh Street they built a replica of the Grand Ole Opry stage that gave me chill bumps the first time I saw it. And for days Becky Lee moved in and out of crisis after crisis as the script built toward that magical night when the little girl from North Carolina would walk onto the most famous stage in all of country music to perform for the first time.

Not only did they construct a replica of the Opry stage and backstage area in New York City, but they also flew in Minnie Pearl and singer Jeanne Pruett for even more realism. They hired square dancers to dance and people to come and just sit on the stage and eat popcorn like they do at the real Grand Ole Opry.

There was really nothing to the "acting." We all just did the things we'd naturally do at the Opry any Friday or Saturday night. I'd introduce the acts, including, of course, Becky Lee, pick and sing a few songs, and cue the commercials. When the episodes went on the air, we were told that they brought in the highest ratings in the show's history.   Following the *Opry* scenes, the writers wrote me and the band into the script again, this time as featured entertainers at a big party thrown at a mansion out on Long Island. There was no make-believe involved here, however. We actually went to the mansion instead of their bringing the mansion to us. Even our bus and our bus driver, Joe Rose, got into the act this time, delivering us in style to the front door of this multimillion-dollar estate. These episodes took a week to tape, ran on the air for nearly three weeks, and once again the ratings went through the roof. From there they called us back into the studio almost immediately, and we started all over again.

It did finally all cool down, however, and the writers married Becky Lee off and sent her down to Memphis to live and do whatever newlyweds do in Memphis. By the time she left and the country music storyline began to subside, though, I had spent a large portion of nearly three years of my life appearing on *One Life to Live*. The promise I hadn't put very much faith in at the beginning had turned out to be a major reality.

In the mid-1970s, for the first time in his recording career, Bill Anderson's music began to slump. Or if the music didn't, then its chart performance did. Working hard to establish a television career, he spent many days away from Nashville, away from the studio and the songwriters and performers who had pushed and inspired him. Five straight singles came and went without a smash, and Bill felt himself flailing. Thus begat a new studio association with producer Buddy Killen, and an unforgettable, practically unbelievable foray into disco country.

At the same time I was flying back and forth to California and New York, some subtle winds of change were beginning to blow across the music business in Nashville. Even though I had been busy chasing new dreams, I hadn't detached myself from the old ones at all, and I was very aware of what was going on. It forced me to make two of the toughest decisions I've ever had to make in my life.

The hit records and hit songs had kept on coming. Songs like "All the Lonely Women in the World," "If You Can Live With It (I Can Live Without It)," "World of Make Believe," and "The Corner of My Life" all went to the top of the charts. Jan and I had gone to number one with "Dissatisfied," and Mary Lou and I had two smashes in a row, "Sometimes" and "That's What Made Me Love You." On the surface, my recording career appeared to be in good shape.

Yet underneath it all I was growing anxious. Country music itself was beginning ever so slowly to change. New artists were coming on the scene. New songwriters. The competition was beginning to stiffen. Nothing was as certain as it had seemed to be for so long.

And some strange things started happening to me. My follow-up to "Corner of My Life" had been a beautiful, modern country ballad called "Can I Come Home to You?" which I had recorded with high hopes. But MCA somehow mastered the tapes and pressed the records with too much bass on them. When the song was played on the radio, it sounded muddy and garbled. I was extremely upset. We asked the label to notify the radio stations that the pressings were faulty and assure them that a new pressing was on its way, but instead of solving the problem, that only seemed to intensify it. Some stations who had started playing the record as soon as they received it and probably had never noticed the muffled sound got nervous and pulled the record from their playlists. Other stations never got around to adding it, saying they were waiting on the new pressing. By the time the confusion settled down, we had lost three or four valuable weeks and the record never regained its momentum.

My next release after that was the ill-fated "Every Time I Turn the Radio On," the record that was killed by the ACE controversy. The next record, "I Still Feel the Same about You," just simply was not a hit. We pulled "Country DJ," an autobiographical ode to small-town radio announcers, out of my current album for the next single, and while it was a big hit with the DJs who could relate to all that it said, the general public didn't exactly throw their babies up in the air when they heard it. I next tried a song I'd found in England called "Thanks," and I quickly realized I should have said "No thanks" and left it over on the other side of the ocean. Five releases in a row without a killer. I was nervous.

Up to this point, Owen Bradley had produced every record I had ever recorded, and I knew I owed him more credit than I'd ever be able to give him in one lifetime. He had taken my simple recitation of "Mama Sang a Song" and created a musical masterpiece around it. I've already recounted how his meticulous production on "Still" made it so different, so unique, and so inimitable. And it was Owen Bradley who first helped me rewrite the melody and then created the signature "raindrops" sound on "I Love You Drops." And he who made Jimmy Colvard tune the big A string down two frets on my old flat-top Martin guitar and pick out the melody over and over and over again until he got it just right on "Golden Guitar." "You've got to make it sound golden!" Owen said relentlessly, until in fact it did.

I thought there was no record producer in the world who was in the same league with Owen Bradley, and time has certainly proven that to be the case. But at the same time it had been five record releases in a row since a Bill Anderson record had really clicked. That was more than a year's worth of records without a hit. Had we lost something? Had I lost something? Owen was like a father to me, but had time begun to pass us by? Was the magic not there anymore? Could another producer bring it back? And if so, who? I didn't know, and I began to agonize over it constantly. In the music business, if you're standing still, you're going backwards.

My trauma was compounded by the fact that Owen and I had not only our artist-producer relationship of nearly twenty years, but we had developed a very close personal friendship away from the music business as well. We lived in the same part of town and were often together at the Vanderbilt football and basketball games. No matter what professional decision I might have felt myself being forced to make, above all I did not want to jeopardize my friendship with this marvelous man.

Owen was under a tremendous amount of pressure from the parent MCA company in California about this time. There had been a lot of changes in the corporate structure out there, and his bosses were suddenly a whole new group of players. And as so often happens when changes are made, the new folks came in with their own sets of rules. Owen had not been in the best of health, either, and I think his mind was often on things other than producing phonograph records. I felt bad that I couldn't be part of the solution. Therefore, I guess I was part of the problem.

It finally reached the point where I knew I had to make up my mind one way or the other. Who would produce my records if I left Owen? Would I just be trading one set of problems for another? I was about to drive myself crazy with worry when I remembered something George Hamilton IV had said to me nearly twenty years earlier.

At that time I had been debating whether or not to leave Tree Publishing as a writer and sign with Hubert Long's Moss Rose Publications. I had been successful for over three years at Tree, and Moss Rose was a new, unproven company. At the same time I wanted Hubert to manage my career more than anything else I could think of, even though he had made it plain that his signing me as an artist would be contingent upon my also writing songs for his company. "You need to put all your eggs in one basket," he kept saying, even as he had tossed the postage stamps into my lap. But still I was having a hard time making up my mind. One day I would feel one way about it, and the next day I'd feel just the opposite. In the midst of my dilemma, I asked George to go to dinner with me between Opry spots one Saturday night and help me figure out what I should do.

Over a hot hamburger steak and a plate full of crispy French fries at the old Flaming Steer restaurant on West End Avenue, I explained to George as best as I could the rock and the hard place I felt like I was caught between. He listened carefully to all I had to say then said, "Well, here's how I've always tried to make major decisions in my life: I take a long time making up my mind about something. I try to look at all the angles, weigh all the pros and cons of whatever decision it is that I'm trying to make. And then when I've gathered all the evidence and examined it as carefully as I can, I make up my mind. Then—and this is the most important part—I never look back."

"I never look back." There's no telling how many ulcers and how many gray hairs that one little piece of advice has spared me over the years. "I never look back" has probably been one of the two or three most significant things anybody has ever said to me in my life. Because up to that point in my life I'd no sooner make a decision that I'd be right back stressing myself out over whether it had been the right decision or not. I guess I saw my dad do that to himself a lot during the years I was growing up, and I copied him. But that was wrong. George's advice was much better, and I continue to heed it today. It's the only way I've found to make decisions and keep from driving myself insane.

I told Owen the following week that I felt it was best for everyone concerned if I made a change. It was one of the hardest things I've ever done. It hurt me because I know it hurt him, but once I made up my mind I didn't, I couldn't, look back. I had to go on to the next step.

Buddy Killen had wanted to produce records for as long as I had known him. Although he was basically a music publisher, he got a kick out of moonlighting as a record producer and had actually produced quite a few hits. Perhaps the best known of these had come in the early sixties when he talked a bunch of studio musicians and background singers into helping him record a song he had written called "Forever." He got the record released on a small label, invented the name the Little Dippers for the group, and set out to have himself some fun. But suddenly the record started taking off around the country, and before Buddy knew what hit him he found himself with a pop smash on his hands.

I was hanging out around Tree a lot in those days and was there the day Dick Clark's office called and said they wanted the Little Dippers to fly to Philadelphia and appear on *American Bandstand*. "Lord, there's no such thing as the Little Dippers," Buddy moaned to me as he tried frantically to come up with a solution. In those days you just didn't turn down an appearance on *American Bandstand*. He ended up hastily putting a group of singers together, sending them to Philadelphia, and ultimately I think they even worked a few rock 'n' roll tours. And it whetted Buddy's appetite to produce more records.

He helped on nearly all the Roger Miller hits, he produced several records by soul singer Joe Tex that sold a million copies each, he cut country records by Dottie West, Diana Trask, Jack Reno, and several others, and when I decided to make my change, Buddy was the first person I knew to turn to.

"You really need to do some new, exciting things," Buddy said to me when I first brought up the subject of wanting to revitalize my recording career. "What you've been doing has been all right, but it's gotten stale," he said, and I agreed.

"Hey, I'll try anything once," I answered.

We shook hands, and as simply as that, nearly twenty years after our first meeting and our first successes together, Bill Anderson and Buddy Killen were back working on the same team again.

I have never seen a record producer work as hard as Buddy worked in selecting the material for our first session together. We must have listened to a thousand songs—"No, this one's not quite right"..."This one is OK, but we don't need one that's OK. We need one that's great!"—until we settled on the four best pieces of material we could find. Then and only then did he book the musicians and head me into the studio.

I was nervous recording with Buddy for the first time. I had been used to Owen's laid back approach, and Buddy was much more intense, maybe because we had something to prove. He spent hour after lengthy hour getting the musical tracks just the way he wanted them, then he made me sing the songs over and over and over again until I had them exactly the way he felt like they ought to sound. The more he'd push, the more uptight I'd become. Looking back, there's no doubt that he knew exactly what he was doing.

The first release to come out of those sessions was a Bobby Braddock song called "Peanuts and Diamonds." It was definitely different from anything I had ever attempted before. It went to number ten on the *Billboard* chart. Our second release, "Liars One, Believers Zero," came off that same first session and it went to number six. We cut a country version of Orleans' "Still the One," and it clicked. Buddy produced the entire second duet album with Mary Lou Turner, and in a 180 degree turnabout, it was his idea to ask Roy Acuff to sing with me on a song about an old-time musician seeking one last moment in the spotlight, the touching "I Wonder If God Likes Country Music." No matter what direction we tried to go in, the Anderson-Killen chemistry-music from a pair of Scorpios seemed to be working.

One of Buddy and my most discussed, beloved, and chuckled-about musical statements came about as the result of a very simple question I asked Buddy one day in conversation. Disco music was just beginning to take the country by storm, and the disco beat felt very exciting to me. I couldn't really relate to very many of the songs themselves, but those hard-driving, pulsating rhythms made me want to get up and move.

"Tell me something, Bud," I said innocently one afternoon in his office. "Is there any reason you couldn't take a country song and put a disco beat to it?" Frankly, I couldn't think of one.

"I don't know," Buddy answered. "I never thought about it. I guess you could. Why?"

"Well, I've just been thinking that it might make a pretty exciting sound. It might be something I'd like to try."

"You got any particular song in mind?"

"No," I said. "But I might just try to write one." And I left his office with the thought firmly planted in my mind.

I don't remember how many nights later it was that I was sitting around in my den, strumming on my guitar, when I began trying to write a country lyric and a country melody that I thought would lend themselves to a disco beat. I knew the lyric had to be just right. I couldn't sing about Mama or trains or gettin' drunk. It had to be a song about love, and the lyric had to be as pounding and as sexy as the beat behind it. I had never before set out deliberately to write a sexy song.

I don't know where the idea came from or how I happened to start writing it, but in a few minutes I was sitting at my typewriter, guitar strung across my shoulder, singing, "I can't wait any longer . . . This feeling's getting stronger . . . Satisfy my hunger . . . You're the only one who can." And the melody was as country as country could be. But in my mind's ear I could hear a hot, rapid-fire disco beat electrifying the words I was singing, and I knew the two would fit. I kept on writing:

> Where do I have to go
> What do I have to do
> Who do I have to lie to
> So I can lie with you?
> I can't wait any longer.

I called Buddy the next morning and told him I thought I had come up with a country lyric that would match with a disco beat, and he got as excited as I had been. I said, "I've gotta come down there and sing it for you!" and he said, "Come on!" but when I got to his office I suddenly got stage fright. Or whatever kind of fright it is that a songwriter gets when he's not sure his new song is really worth showing to anybody. Buddy almost had to beat me over the head to get me to sing it to him.

Finally I got up the nerve. "You'll have to use your imagination," I said as I sat there on a stool with just my guitar. "Imagine all the instruments, that disco beat."

"Willy, I've been using my imagination on your songs for twenty years," Buddy smiled. "Now sing it!" And I did.

He loved it. He walked over to his piano and began playing along with me. Then he started adding some chords I hadn't written. "It's going to need a little bridge of some kind," he said. "See how you like this." What he played sounded super to me. Suddenly I had a co-writer.

"Can we cut it?" I asked.

"How much nerve you got?"

"What do you mean?"

"I mean, have you got the guts to take the flak we're gonna get if it's a bomb? Heck, we'll probably get flak even if it's a hit," he said.

"I'm game if you are," I answered, and Buddy booked the session.

Nobody knew if a country song set to a disco beat would sell two copies or not, but we knew when it was finished that we'd done what we set out to do. That was to give it our best shot.

"What else does it need?" I asked Buddy after all the overdubs had been laid down and the mixing was in its final stages.

"Willy," he answered, resting his arm on my shoulder, "this record don't need nothin' 'cept out!"

I swore after "Where Have All Our Heroes Gone" that I'd never record anything controversial again, but "I Can't Wait Any Longer" made "Heroes" look like "Mary Had a Little Lamb." From the minute it hit the market, everybody and his brother had an opinion on it.

"It's the greatest, most original thing I've ever heard," some of the DJs were screaming.

"We'll never play that trash on our station!" others said with equal determination. "That's the filthiest, most suggestive song I've ever heard. Our listeners would run us out of town if we played it!" And every time I answered the phone or opened the mail, somebody was either praising me or lambasting me.

Surprisingly, a lot of people at my own record company were laughing at me and putting me down, especially some of those in the promotion department who were on the receiving end of many of the complaints. "Who does he think he is, coming out with all that heavy-breathing stuff?" they'd say. "A forty-year-old sex symbol? Don't make me laugh!" But while they were putting me down on the one hand, with the other hand they were writing orders from dealers buying as many copies of the record as they could get their hands on.

The fact that we'd taken a country song and set it to a disco beat, however, seemed to be lost on most people. Most of the ruffled feathers were from people who didn't like the plain-spoken lyric. "Our lives have touched . . . our minds have touched . . . and I can't wait any longer for our bodies to touch . . . and our souls to touch" seemed to turn off the people who had loved it when I whispered "My mama sang a song." But it sure seemed to turn a lot of other folks on.

"We get more requests for 'I Can't Wait Any Longer' than any other record we play," more than one perplexed disc jockey told me when the record was at its peak, "but we also get more complaints on it than any other song we play. One minute I say I'll never play it again, and the next minute the phones are ringing off the wall from people wanting to hear it. I don't know what to do."

I wasn't too sure what to do either. I didn't want to offend people or upset people who had been fans of mine for twenty years, but at the same time this was fresh, it was new, and it was exciting. MCA pressed up a twelve-inch version of the record that lasted nearly seven minutes and shipped copies to every disco nightclub in the country. I got booked on a nationally syndicated disco television show from an old warehouse in New Jersey called *The Soap Factory*, where I was singing and dancing and laughing with some of the loveliest ladies imaginable. And the record was a country smash.

The reaction to the single caused MCA to call for an entire album of similar material, which they titled *Ladies Choice*. It was a solid seller, but to this day people will tell me that it's either their very favorite album or their most unfavorite Bill Anderson album. It was, to say the least, polarizing.

In the fall of the year, *Billboard* magazine presented me with their Special Breakthrough Award for 1978, recognizing my bringing country music and disco together as "the most outstanding creative musical achievement of the year." Buddy and I were on top of the world, but we made one big mistake. We jumped down off our horse before the race was over.

We listened to what some of the promotion people at MCA who didn't like the record were saying, what a small handful of old-line, hard-core Bill Anderson fans were saying, and we allowed them to influence the songs we chose and the type of records we cut the next time we went into the studio. As soon as we finished *Ladies Choice*, we began to back away from the very thing that had made us successful. The momentum we generated with "I Can't Wait Any Longer" and the follow-up, "Double S," began to slip away. Within two years we had removed ourselves so far from it that we had allowed it to die out completely.

Buddy became totally frustrated with MCA. Here he had breathed new life into an artist who had been on their label for twenty years, given my career a whole new shot in the arm, and instead of appreciating it and building on it they were standing on the sidelines laughing at both of us and, in effect, telling us not to do it anymore. So Buddy quit. He didn't need the hassle. He quit producing my records; he quit producing any records at all for MCA. Instead, he took what we had started together and transferred it to the records he began producing for T. G. Sheppard on Warner Brothers. The same type songs, the same musicians, the same type arrangements. Warner Brothers didn't laugh, they believed in the concept, and T.G. became a star. I tried cutting a few more records for MCA under the direction of Jim Foglesong, a wonderful man who became the head of the company's Nashville operations following a big shake-up at MCA and their subsequent purchase of the ABC-Dot label, but nothing clicked. My contract expired at the end of 1981, and the label where I had hung my hat for twenty-three years put me out to pasture. I guess they couldn't wait any longer.

This is the part where the wheels come off. If you talk about the early 1980s with Bill Anderson, you'd best bring up the 1982 National League Western Division champion Atlanta Braves, a team that starred his knuckleball-throwing friend Phil Niekro. Otherwise, be prepared to hear the man they call "Whisper" do a lot of sighing. Bad radio investments. Terrible restaurant investment. No major label record deal. No hits at all. And as the early eighties became the mid-eighties, he was releasing unsuccessful, independent singles with apt titles like "Pity Party" and "This Is the Goodbye to End All Goodbyes." Add in his wife's severe head trauma after an automobile accident, and ... well, it got dark in there. And it would have been worse, but for the graces of God and Conway Twitty.

Have you ever noticed that there's something inside nearly all of us that drives us to want to succeed in an area of life where we have no expertise, no experience, and, more often than not, no talent?

A rich oil magnate invests his profits in the career of a country singer.

A rich country singer invests in oil. A ballplayer buys a restaurant. A wealthy restaurateur buys a sports franchise. And on it goes, the common denominator usually being that each person would have been well advised to stay within the boundaries of his own knowledge.

My venturing out from country music into the worlds of game shows and soap operas turned out alright. I probably should have quit right there while I was still ahead.

I'm an entertainer. A creator, perhaps, but my creativity has for the most part revolved around the business of entertainment. Maybe I can entertain in more ways than one, but I'm still an entertainer. Or a singer. Or a performer. Nowhere in the book does it say Bill Anderson is a businessman. Nor should it, unless the book is a piece of fiction.

I've tried to become a businessman a couple of times when I should have kept right on pickin' and grinnin'. And I've paid for it. Back in 1975 I heard of a little radio station in Provo, Utah, called KIXX that was for sale. Now, anybody who has ever worked at a radio station thinks he knows how to run a station better than anybody he's ever worked for. And every lowly disc jockey sits in the control room where he works and dreams of the day when he will own his own radio station. I was no exception. Owning a station had been my dream ever since the days back in Commerce, and I was determined to make it come true someday. Besides, not only was this station for sale, it was for sale cheap. That really caught my attention.

I found out quickly why the station had been on the market so cheap. It had a terrible reputation in the community. "KIXX is for hicks" was the rhyming local expression I kept hearing over and over after my name was on the dotted line.

The outside of the building was awful. There were potholes in the driveway so large that I didn't know, as Grandpa Jones once said about his driveway, "Whether to have them repaired or stock them with fish."

Having come out of the programming side of radio myself as opposed to being from sales, I was more concerned in the beginning with how my little radio station sounded than I was with how many advertisers we had. I thought if we sounded good the sponsors would stand in line to advertise. Since the selling of ads pays all the bills around a radio station, however, I would say I put the cart slightly before the horse. If I had it all to do over again, I'd have hired a crackerjack sales manager to bring some sponsors on board and then used the advertising money to hire some good programming people. But what did I know? I was just a hillbilly singer trying to rekindle the fire of an old love from his youth.

I finally gave up on the radio business after six years. The bad news is that the radio station business broke my heart. I was totally disillusioned by something I loved. The good news is I've gotten it out of my system. I don't love it anymore.

My second attempt at conquering a world outside my own came upon me more subtly than did the radio business, and I was, as a dear friend put it, "up to my butt in alligators before I remembered that my original intention was to drain the swamp."

In March 1981, a restaurant called PoFolks opened on Nolensville Road in Nashville. You will remember from several pages and twenty years ago that I had written and recorded a song by that very same title, "Po' Folks." And since 1964 when I began hiring musicians to work for me, I had collectively called them either the Po' Boys or the Po' Folks, each name a spinoff from the title of my signature song. When the PoFolks Family Restaurant (that's how they spelled it) opened for business in Nashville, it was naturally assumed by many in the community that I was only carrying my trademark name a step further and entering the food service business.

It wouldn't have been that unusual. Minnie Pearl had loaned her name to a fried chicken outfit one time and so had Eddy Arnold. Nashville was used to seeing Tex Ritter's hamburgers, Hank Williams Jr.'s barbeque, and

Boots Randolph's nightclub and eatery. Bill Anderson's PoFolks Restaurants wouldn't have shocked anybody.

I was surprised, however, when "When did you start running a restaurant?" was a question I began having to answer nearly every day. I just shrugged my shoulders because for quite a while I was not even aware that there was such a thing as a PoFolks Restaurant. Then I began seeing bumper stickers around town that read "I'm Po But I'm Proud," and I thought, "Hey, somebody's been reading my mail!"

I soon called a friend of mine, Rita Whitfield, at PoFolks's Nashville advertising agency.

"Rita, can you set up a meeting between me and the head honcho at that restaurant?" I asked. "I have a copyright registered in Washington, D.C., on the name Po' Folks, and I think I need to meet with the owner face-to-face. I might just have a lawsuit on my hands. Who knows, maybe I'll end up owning the place, and you'll be working for me."

Rita calmly told me that PoFolks was part of a chain of some fifteen or twenty restaurants scattered throughout the Southeast and headquartered in Anderson, South Carolina. She said she knew that the owner and president of the company, a Mr. Malcolm Hare, would be glad to meet with me the next time he was in Nashville. She'd be happy to arrange it she said. It turned out to be only a matter of a few days.

I met with Mr. Hare over a wonderful country dinner at PoFolks.

"Mr. Hare, where did you come up with the name PoFolks for your restaurants?" I asked.

"My name's Malcolm," he said, "not Mr. Hare." And he shifted his weight and slid forward in his seat. "Bill, I wish I could tell you I was riding down the road and your record came on my car radio and it inspired me," he grinned. "But I can't. I'm not really sure just how I picked out the name, but I'm glad I did. It sure fits."

"Well, it's been a pretty good name for me for about twenty years, too," I said. "Are you aware that I have it copyrighted?"

"No," he answered, "I'm not. But I have it copyrighted too. Do you spell yours P-o-apostrophe?"

"Yes," I replied, looking at the menu resting on the side of the table and realizing he did not.

"Maybe that's how I was able to copyright mine then," he interjected, leaning even closer and lowering his voice. "But, hey, let's don't get into that.

I'm interested in knowing if you'd like to become involved with us in some way since everybody seems to think you are anyhow. Is that something you might be interested in talking about?"

I was. And I became something Malcolm called the chain's national spokesman. PoFolks, Inc. (PFI), announced publicly that Bill Anderson, he of "Po' Folks" music fame, had signed a three-year contract to appear in radio and television commercials for PoFolks Restaurants and, in addition, had given the restaurants the right to use his photograph, signature, and likeness in the endorsement of their products and services.

I was also to allot PoFolks Restaurants a certain number of days each calendar year on which they could use my services as they saw fit. I would make myself available on those days to travel to the various restaurant locations around the country (of which there were exactly seventeen in four states at the time) and make personal appearances. For this PoFolks assigned to me a small amount of stock in the company, we agreed on an amount of compensation, and that's all there was to it. The contract was to run from June 1981 until June 1984.

I was happy as could be. I liked the people I'd met, I loved the food ("Just like eatin' off Grandma's kitchen table," I'd come to tell folks. "Not the dining room table but the kitchen table!"), and I especially liked the noncontrived feeling I got from being associated with something called PoFolks.

I soon learned my perception of what a restaurant is was wrong. My first mistake was in thinking a restaurant was a place to eat. I found out quickly a restaurant is a business.

The association between me and PoFolks was immediately good for business, too, both theirs and mine. Crowds flocked to the autograph parties where I'd go into the restaurants and visit with the guests at their tables and hand out free autographed pictures. Sometimes I'd put on an apron and go back into the kitchen to "help out." Sometimes I'd wait on tables. Other times I'd roam around the store with a portable tape recorder soliciting comments from the guests, which our advertising agency would later take into a recording studio and mold into radio commercials.

The chain began to expand. From seventeen units in four states the company grew to forty-seven units in ten states by the fall of 1982, and the parent company couldn't keep up with the demand for new franchises. Sales in the stores were averaging well over a million dollars a year per unit, and some were grossing as high as two million. The stockholders of PoFolks,

Incorporated, of which I had become one when I signed my contract, had a tiger by the tail, and we knew it. It forced us to make a decision.

Several large companies were watching us closely with an eye toward buying us out. The question was did we want to hang onto this monster and try to ride it through, or did we want to sell our interests to one of the available suitors and get out? We had to admit that in some places our manpower had become stretched painfully thin, and we couldn't bring good, qualified people on board and train them fast enough to keep up with the demand. We all feared that sooner or later operations within the restaurants would start to suffer. More capital investment was needed than we had available, and the very future of the concept seemed to be hanging precariously in the balance.

The Krystal Corporation of Chattanooga, the hamburger people, made a generous offer to buy us out, and right behind them stood the giant W. R. Grace Company expressing strong interest as well. At some point we had to give somebody an answer. From a personal standpoint, I faced the decision with very mixed feelings.

A few months earlier, a tragic sequence of events had enabled me to purchase a sizable amount of stock in PFI to add to that which I'd been given. Some of the original investors in PoFolks, a father and his son, had been killed in the crash of a private plane out in Texas, and the family's block of stock was offered to me. I purchased all I could afford and made the rest available to some of my friends. I became a member of the Board of Directors of PoFolks, Inc., I was given a corner office in the corporate headquarters building when operations were moved from South Carolina to Nashville, and now I wasn't sure I wanted to give up all the excitement. I was in pretty tall cotton for a hillbilly singer from Commerce, Georgia.

Common sense prevailed, however, and I finally agreed with the other owners that everybody's best interests would be served by our stepping aside. The newspapers reported that we sold PoFolks to Krystal for twenty million dollars, but we never saw anywhere near that amount of money. Krystal took over the operation of PoFolks in November 1982, and early the following year they took the stock public.

Had I been involved with PoFolks only as a stockholder and as their national spokesman, everything up to this point would have been fine. But a few months prior to the Krystal sale, I tried to conquer yet another world.

It turned out to be the single biggest mistake I've ever made in my life. I became a partner with Roy Jones, the vice president of operations for PFI, in some of the franchises themselves.

I had watched other franchisees making tremendous profits in PoFolks and when Jones, who had an extensive restaurant background, asked me if I'd like to join him in some franchising ventures, I didn't turn him down.

He and I formed a general partnership, sold shares to a group of limited partners who provided us with investment capital, and we went into the restaurant business. We selected a site in Clarksville, Indiana, that became the first PoFolks north of the Mason-Dixon line. We then bought a site in Louisville, and then purchased territorial franchise rights for the Charlotte, North Carolina, area. Next, we opened restaurants in east Tennessee, and, with Conway Twitty onboard as a partner, we went out to Oklahoma.

But it soon became painfully obvious to me and to Conway that there was more to running a successful restaurant company than serving good cornbread and flying around the country. We had built a lot of restaurants, but we hadn't hired a lot of good people to manage them. Some of the stores were starting to get into some pretty deep financial trouble. Roy Jones would give us pep talks, trying to keep us from becoming discouraged, and he'd tell us glowing tales about how many dollars were coming in the front door, but I noticed he never had much to say about all the dollars going out the back.

It had all seemed so easy in the beginning: Obtain from the parent company the franchise rights to a certain area. Sell some limited partnerships to investors who believed in us and in the PoFolks concept (and those were easy to find), and sign a few bank notes and equipment leases guaranteeing if anything went wrong and the company couldn't pay its bills that Conway Twitty and/or Bill Anderson and/or Roy Jones would step forward and pay them. That's all there was to it.

How could our company not afford to pay its bills? Weren't we making money every week in Louisville? Sure we were. Charlotte was lagging a little behind, but with all Jones's expertise he'd soon fix that. Besides, he explained to us, if we needed some cash in North Carolina, he'd just send some over from Kentucky. Somehow it never dawned on us to question a thing called "commingling of funds." There was a different set of limited partners in North Carolina from the ones in Kentucky, and taking money from one partnership and funneling it into another was as illegal as sticking your hand in the cash register drawer, pulling the bills out, and seeing how fast you could run. But somehow that never crossed my mind.

It wasn't long before the only people knocking on the doors were loan officers, finance companies, bank presidents, lawyers, and bill collectors. The stores in the Louisville market continued to do well, but it was taking all the money we could siphon off from there just to keep the doors open everywhere else. North Carolina, east Tennessee, and the one unit we'd opened in Norman, Oklahoma, were in dire financial straits. We had done a good job of expanding our little company but a lousy job of running restaurants.

Before Conway and I realized what hit us, we were personally signed to bank guarantees and restaurant equipment leases reaching well into the multimillions of dollars with no relief in sight. I didn't know whether to ride a bicycle or chop down a cherry tree because while Conway Twitty might have had many millions of dollars buried in the ground, I knew Ol' Whisperin' Bill didn't have anything of the sort. Our friend Mr. Jones left town and declared bankruptcy.

Enter the lawyers. Lots and lots of lawyers, and bankers, and financial advisors, and lots of hastily called meetings in all sorts of weird places and at all sorts of weird hours of the day and night. I couldn't recall everything that took place during those weeks now if I wanted to, and I don't really want to. Like a lot of other things in my life during this time, I've tried to forget.

The end result for me was that after much legal hassling and the payment of some exorbitant legal fees, Conway and I sold the parts of the businesses that could be salvaged and bit the bullet on the rest. It was a very large and very expensive bullet!

I found out throughout all these entanglements, though, that Harold Jenkins, aka Conway Twitty, was a hell of a man. Had he not been willing to step forward with a lot of long green folding money and been willing to accept large amounts of stock in the companies that bought us out, I might well have had to follow Jones into bankruptcy. Even as it stood, my little foray into the restaurant business wiped out a large chunk of my life's savings.

My PoFolks problems coincided with a downturn in my career as a recording artist. I had been working as a food industry maven and as a game show host and soap opera actor, but had unwillingly, perhaps unknowingly, ceded my position as a country music hit maker. "I Can't Wait Any Longer," the 1978 disco-country hit, was my final number one record as a solo artist.

In the 1980s, I scored only one Top 40 *Billboard* country hit, one called "Make Mine Night Time." In late 1980, I made the country Top 100 with a song aptly titled "I Want That Feelin' Again," but before long I was off MCA Records and onto my friend and hero Bill Lowery's independent Southern Tracks label. Bill and I had a regional hit with a song called "Southern Fried." By 1985, I was recording for Swanee Records, where I cut songs including one called "Country Music Died Today."

The best part of my 1980s came with the ascension of The Nashville Network, a cable television outfit that expanded the scope of country music. When TNN hit the marketplace in 1983, I was among the fortunate few who were invited onboard.

Elmer Alley, program director of WSM-TV in Nashville, was given the task of assembling the programming ideas for this totally new broadcast concept, and one of the things he felt would be successful with the viewers was a game show built around country music fans and their knowledge of country trivia. Because of my experience at ABC five years earlier hosting *The Better Sex*, I was the first person who came to his mind as a possible host for the program he later named *Fandango*.

It was the best thing that could have possibly happened for me. Since *The Better Sex* had gone off the air, I had been hosting a weekly syndicated series called *Backstage at the Grand Ole Opry* on a hundred or so stations scattered around the country, but I wanted to do more. The Nashville Network provided me with that opportunity.

After *Fandango* went on the air, producer Allen Reid invited me to join him and his wife, Mady Land, in the creation and development of his second TNN production, a competition show for up-and-coming young talent. The show was called *You Can Be a Star*.

I helped devise the format for *Star*, worked in the development of the scoring system, which was used to rate the talent, and suggested to Allen that my band, the Po' Folks, would be the perfect group to play the music behind the young artists performing on the show. He hired them and even made my band leader, Mike Johnson, musical director of the show. They worked in that capacity for the entire six years the show was on the air. I was pleased with the show's spotlight on young talent. In the new century,

Carrie Underwood, Kellie Pickler, and others came to popular attention through a similar show called *American Idol*.

At the time, people often asked me if I enjoyed hosting game shows more than I enjoyed making music, and my answer was no. Nothing surpasses the feeling an entertainer gets when he walks out on a concert stage and performs before a live audience, unless it's the feeling a songwriter gets when he finds his rhyming thoughts on the lips of millions of listeners. But I could rationalize: The game show viewership added to my audience, and the size of my crowds increased in the 1980s, even as my radio play decreased.

My happiness, though, did not increase in the 1980s. In some ways, I should have been sitting on top of the world, or at least feeling like it. I had spent a quarter century in the spotlight. I could count seventy-two charting singles that I had sung, and hundreds from my pen that had been voiced by others. I'd won more songwriting awards than any other writer in country music history. I'd been named country music's top male vocalist, half of the top duet (with two different singing partners), and, in several years, songwriter of the year. At one point, I was voted with Hank Williams and Harlan Howard as one of the three top country songwriters of all time, and I'd been elected to the Nashville Songwriters Association Hall of Fame and the Georgia Music Hall of Fame.

All good, then. Yes?

No.

For one thing, I'm never happy resting on laurels. In truth, I'm rarely happy resting at all. And the 1980s were about what I'd done, not what I was doing. Other than game shows, that is, and those were fun . . . but the kid who looked out at Commerce, Georgia, and imagined "City Lights" did not envision game show hosting in his future. That's not why I got into this thing. He also didn't envision losing much of his money in a dodgy restaurant investment. And he didn't envision losing his wife in an automobile accident.

Please understand, Becky did not die. But she nearly did, after being run into by a drunk eighteen-year-old. This was October 13, 1984. She was left with crippling brain damage, head injuries so severe that they changed her life, my life, and the lives of everyone else close to us.

I buckled, from physical and mental strain. I suffered a ruptured disk in my back, and for almost two years I winced from piercing pain that radiated from my back all the way down my left leg into my foot. Constant agony, even as I smiled for cameras. The painkilling medication helped in a way, and didn't help in other ways.

A few months after my wife's accident, I was standing at the bedside of my critically ill, twenty-five-year-old daughter, Terri, listening as doctors told me that the tumor they'd just removed from her body was malignant.

My wife and daughter ultimately got better, though my relationship with Becky—rocky, already, by the time of her accident—was forever changed by the incalculable alterations that brain injury brings into a life. Becky is a kind and brave person, and we are still friends, but we are no longer married. My daughter is a kind and brave person, as well. I treasure her. But all of this is explained in another book, for another time. Becky and I were married until 1997. Today, she lives a short way away from here. She's a great woman, and there's so much to admire about her, but it got to the point where we couldn't live together. It was very sad, and is very sad. I certainly accept my share of the blame. I was not perfect by a long shot. I did a lot of things that if I had to do over, I would not do.

So I'd like you to understand that, as the 1980s became the 1990s, I was not confident and I was not assured. I was broken, in many ways. I was thankful for what I had been given, but dreaded my personal, financial, and creative uncertainties. I've never been lower in my life than during that time. I had debilitating back pain, where I could hardly walk. When I was on tour, I'd sleep on my belly, on the floor of a Silver Eagle bus, riding down the road to some place I'd been dozens of time before, feeling worse for wear.

I didn't hang my head, and there weren't a lot of people who knew what I was going through. But I was scared. And I wouldn't have told you that then. But it would have been true then, and I'll tell you that now. My conversation with the country music audience began in the 1950s. It reached a pitched peak in the 1970s. And it grew awkward and forced in the 1980s, as my mind struggled to find peace in a broken marriage and tried to stay strong through my daughter's illness.

I was not strong. Thank God I'd learned to act by then. I smiled and shook hands and introduced old friends and new stars on the Opry stage. Inside, I felt like a relic. Yesterday's success does not obscure today's failure. What had I proven, other than that I used to be a songwriter?

"The Braves," Bill Anderson sometimes thought to himself in the months after the 1991 version of his favorite baseball franchise went to its first World Series since 1958, back when the team was still in Milwaukee.

Right, the Braves. If the Braves—his Braves, who had been so bad, so long—could rise from the ashes, why couldn't he? But he knew why. The Braves get to change players whenever management deems change to be helpful. Year to year, only the uniforms stay the same. A broken down pitcher doesn't have to keep trotting out there, getting shelled. He does something else with his life. Anderson didn't want to do something else with his life. He wanted to make his living writing songs, though the previous decade had given him no assurance—in fact, no encouragement—that he could keep on doing that. If he allowed himself even to voice the possibility of what would happen in his life over the next quarter century, someone would have called him foolish and everyone else would have nodded in silent agreement. No one in country music history had been down so far, so long, and managed to climb back to resounding contemporary commercial success.

But, as the 1992 Braves reported for spring training, country radio stations began to play Steve Wariner's version of Bill's "The Tips of My Fingers." A song that had been a hit four times prior, the first time in 1960, would become a hit again. And Bill Anderson would tentatively but willingly shake off his dinosaur outfit

I had never heard of a Number One party on the day in 1992 that someone called from Sony–Tree Publishing to tell me one was being held in my honor. Turns out a Number One party is where the songwriters, publishers, record label, promotional staff, publicists, and the recording artist get together to celebrate a big hit.

I had written that big hit, Steve Wariner's version of "The Tips of My Fingers." The song had already been a hit four times earlier, for me in 1960, for Roy Clark in 1963, for Eddy Arnold in 1966, and for Jean Shepard in 1975. Steve Wariner's hit recording of it was a great and welcome surprise. I thought people had forgotten that old song. Maybe they had, and that's why it became a hit again. That hit didn't bolster my confidence in my own creativity. Steve's recording was of one written by a young Bill Anderson, a man that burned to write and sing. Nothing I'd written in years had approached that song's vitality.

It wasn't the music industry that had changed and left me behind. It was me who had changed, taken my eye off the ball for reasons both necessary—the health and well-being of my family chief among those—and unnecessary (creeping cynicism, and the fear that I was washed up). But if I had changed, then maybe I could change again. Steve's version of "Tips" was some indication that words, melodies, and emotions can carry across decades.

For the nearly two weeks between the Sony-Tree phone call and the party, I didn't think about much else. I didn't think I'd know any of the movers and shakers on Music Row, and I thought I could easily wind up as the some kind of awkward, lurking presence, like an antique chair in the middle of a contemporary office space that clashed with the rest of the furniture but hadn't been tossed out for some reason or another. But when I got to the party and began to mingle, it turned out that I did know quite a few people there. And they knew me, from the Opry, from the record bins, and from history books that told them that my songs helped build that big Sony-Tree building.

What I didn't know was what a hit song meant in the 1990s in terms of royalties. The money I made from the first four major versions of "Tips" combined didn't generate nearly as much income as did Steve's record all those years later. Maybe the financial nightmare that I'd fried up with PoFolks could be mitigated by some more hit songs. I still felt bruised and bloodied, depressed about my marriage and my finances and my lack of viable new material. But, as I explained in this book's introduction, my hairstylist, Cheryl Riddle, insisted that I call her young friend, the country star Vince Gill.

The January morning dawned raw and cloudy, dry snow dusting the ground. I drove into town, took my guitar and a small briefcase from the trunk of my car, and climbed steps leading up to a small, gray stone house on Sixteenth Avenue that served as Vince Gill's management office. I was excited, and nervous. It was the first time I could ever remember being nervous about writing a song.

Vince greeted me with a smile and a handshake, and he introduced me to his manager, Larry Fitzgerald. We talked for a bit, and then Larry excused himself, and Vince and I retreated to his writing room. I told him about two song ideas I had, hoping he'd like one of them.

The first idea was not original to me but had been passed along by country music scholar Otto Kitsinger, who researched and wrote a radio show I hosted for a couple of years on the Nashville Network's radio division, TNNR. I was hesitant to mention Otto's idea because that would mean we'd be looking at a three-way split on the writers' credits—and the writers' royalties—rather than a simple co-write. But I felt the idea was strong and unique, and I brought it up.

"It's called 'Cold, Gray Light of Gone,'" I said. "Not 'dawn,' but 'gone.'"

Vince immediately picked up on the wordplay and said, "Let's write it." We did, for a few hours, interrupted only by a break for barbecue and cornbread at a nearby restaurant. Sometime that afternoon, Vince recorded a simple, guitar-vocal work tape of our new creation, and we put our guitars away.

> And there's nothing quite as lonely as the cold, gray light of gone
> Waking up and finding out, she's never coming home.

The note that said, "It's over," chills me to the bone.
No, there's nothing quite as lonely as the cold, gray light of gone.

There was nothing contemporary in the music or the lyric. That song could have been written in 1962. But it wasn't. It was written in 1994, and the emotions it conveyed still applied. People didn't stop leaving each other. Hearts still broke and mended, flew and stalled, sought and yearned. In 1994, Vince and I were both in the middle of all that. So were billions of other people. There was nothing contemporary in the music or lyric to "Cold, Gray Light of Gone," but nothing dated, either. Things become antique. Feelings never do.

When we were done, Vince said, "You say you've got another good idea we could write?" I told him I did and proceeded to tell him that I had heard a line a few days before, buried inside a gospel song that was playing on the radio. I thought it would make a great country title. He didn't ask for any more information, and I didn't offer any. He simply said, "Well, when do you want to get together and work on it? How about Thursday?" I had no idea what might be on my calendar for Thursday, though I assured Vince that I was totally clear that day. No problem.

Thursday morning, I was back in the gray stone house with my guitar, a writing pad, and a briefcase full of pencils. Just like before, only without the nerves.

"I see this idea as being a guy who is at a real crossroads in his life," I explained, as we tuned up and sipped coffee. He's being forced to make a decision between two women in his life. The hook is "which bridge to cross and which bridge to burn."

I looked in his eyes, hoping for a positive reaction. For the longest time, they didn't tell me anything at all. Did he like it? I had no idea. Couldn't tell. He just sat there, with no expression on his face. He stared at me, intently. Had I or the idea offended him? I didn't know, but I could feel something strange dangling in the air between us.

It wasn't until years later, long after we'd written the song, he had recorded it, and it had become a number one hit that I fully understood his initial reaction, or lack thereof. The idea had hit him right where he lived.

I didn't know much about Vince's personal life back then. I hardly knew him at all and didn't ask questions. I knew he was married to a lady named Janis, that she was part of the sister singing team known as the Sweethearts of the Rodeo, and that Vince and Janis had a daughter named Jenny. I had no idea his marriage, like mine, was in trouble, or that he was falling in love with the singer Amy Grant. I was trying to write a song, but we wound up putting a life's story on paper.

> I've got two loves in my life now:
> A true love and one that's brand new.
> I'm not really sure that I know how
> To love one and tell one we're through.
>
> I can't sleep at night, I toss and I turn.
> I keep losing sight of the lessons I've learned.
> I'm standing at the crossroads with just one concern:
> Which bridge to cross and which bridge to burn.

At the end of the day, after we'd finished writing our second song together, Vince told me he had a recording session coming up at the end of the month.

"I'll probably cut both of them," he said, smiling again. "I like them both." I thanked him profusely and left his office walking three feet off the ground.

I left for a working vacation aboard a cruise ship in the Caribbean at the time Vince headed to the studio. The whole cruise, all I thought about was Vince's recording session. Had he cut one of our songs? Had he held true to his word and cut both of them? I could hardly wait to get back to frigid Nashville and find out.

When I returned, the word I received was that he'd recorded "Cold, Gray Light," but that it didn't come off as well as he'd hoped. I was crushed. Then someone told me he'd gone back in later and cut "Which Bridge" on a separate session, and that it had come off much better. In fact, they said, it was probably going to be included on the album. I was bouncing off the walls again.

The album, *When Love Finds You*, was released on MCA Records later that year. Still today, it is regarded as one of Vince's finest albums, with superb songs like "Whenever You Come Around" and "Go Rest High on That Mountain." Oh, and a pensive ballad called "Which Bridge to Cross (Which Bridge to Burn)" that topped country charts. Deborah Evans Price, writing for *Billboard* magazine, wrote that the song "raises the chill bumps at every turn."

Suddenly, Bill Anderson wasn't an old songwriter who got lucky with a cover of one of his decades-old tunes, he was a force on the contemporary scene. "Bridge" knocked down a door that I'd thought was closed forever. I had written another hit song, my first on the charts in more than twelve years. And I'd written it with someone else, by setting an appointment, punching a time clock, and baring my soul in front of another songwriter.

Having written the song with an artist of Vince Gill's stature gave me instant credibility within Nashville's new songwriting community, with writers who had never before given Bill Anderson a second thought. I started calling them. More importantly, they started calling me.

Bill Anderson's unprecedented revival was a blindside hit that we should have seen coming. In 1991, the thought was, "He sure had a nice run, but those things always come to an end." By 1993, the surprise was less in the return to prominence and more in the fact that one of country music's greatest and most prolific songwriters had spent a decade under the commercial radar. For Bill, all of this was deeply satisfying, though there was the vaguely unsettling necessity of staying sharp, and keeping creative, at never showing up for a writing session without something palpable, and commercially viable, to contribute. Many writers try to assure that viability by tackling the same song subjects they hear on the radio hits of the day. Bill Anderson went another route, co-writing songs about talking teardrops and postcards from beyond the grave.

Writing with Vince Gill got me back in the Music Row rooms where hit songs were conjured, but it didn't mean I could stay in those rooms. I had to deliver ideas at each new session and had to help bring those ideas to fruition. Word travels fast everywhere, but no faster anywhere than in Nashville music circles. Once I started co-writing, I made sure to bring plenty of possibilities. "Don't wanna write that one? Here's another."

At this point, getting back into the songwriting game in a major way was what I wanted to do more than anything else in the world. I knew I needed to make some business changes to do that, the biggest of which was affiliating myself with a major music publisher. I needed as much muscle and might behind me as I could get.

Buddy Killen at Tree Publishing had given me my first shot at writing songs in Nashville, and, though I had left Tree years before, there seemed to be something pulling me back. I wrote there exclusively from 1958 until 1962, when my manager, Hubert Long, formed his own company, Moss Rose Publications. In an effort to put all my eggs in one basket, I moved to Hubert's stable both as an artist and a songwriter. In 1965, Hubert helped me form my own company, Stallion Music, Inc., and for the first time I was the owner of my own copyrights. That may sound like a small technical matter, but it was a big deal: A publisher takes 50 percent of a writer's proceeds. So if you're self-published and write your own songs, you keep the whole pie.

By the time Buddy sold Tree Publishing to the Sony Corporation in 1989 and it became Sony-Tree, the Stallion catalog was back at Tree, under an administrative agreement whereby they did a lot of the grunt work in exchange for a piece of the pie. Sony later purchased the giant ATV Publishing catalog, with songs by the Beatles and Michael Jackson, and the company became known as Sony-ATV-Tree. Now, it's just called Sony/ATV Music Publishing.

In the 1990s, most of the original Tree staff was still in place, including the lady in charge, Donna Hilley, who had for years been an administrative assistant to Buddy and the company's founder, Jack Stapp. Donna made me an offer to purchase Stallion Music, help me form a new publishing company under the Sony umbrella, and keep the lion's share of my music under one roof. I would own 50 percent of my new copyrights, plus have the muscle and power of Nashville's most successful music publisher at my fingertips. I signed on the dotted line, and in so doing I jumped back into the deep end of the songwriting pool. Sony/ATV was, and is, there to help arrange co-writes, to pitch material to producers and artists, to provide offices in which to write songs, and to do many other things to ease my load.

Steve Wariner became one of my first and favorite collaborators. He was coming off a smash record called "Holes in the Floor of Heaven," and his creative juices were flowing. Next to Garth Brooks, he was Capitol Records' top-selling male artist. We wrote several songs for his next album project, plus a hit song for a budding young star named Bryan White. Meanwhile, Steve's first three singles after "Holes" had not done particularly well, even his duet with Garth Brooks. He needed another hit in the worst way.

I don't remember where the idea came from, but I began working on a song by myself that I knew from the beginning was extremely unusual and unique. When I first told Steve about it, I said, "This is either one of the best ideas I have ever come up with, or you need to call the men in the little white coats to come and get me. I may have completely lost my mind."

He begged me to tell him more, but all I would say is, "It's the story of two teardrops having a conversation with each other." I was greeted by total silence on his end of the phone. I finally stammered, "Look, I'll bring it out and show it to you." More silence told me he was having trouble controlling his excitement or was thumbing through the phone book for the little white coat–clad mens' telephone number.

By the time Steve and I sat down together, I had written two full verses and a chorus to "Two Teardrops." I needed a better melody than the one I'd been using, though, and turned to Steve for help. He's a master of melody, and a virtuoso on guitar, and these things seem to come effortlessly to him.

The story I had crafted was nothing if not unusual:

> Two teardrops were floating down the river.
> One teardrop said to the other,

"I'm from the soft blue eyes of a woman in love . . .
I'm a tear of joy she couldn't carry.
She was so happy she just got married.
I was on her cheek when she wiped me away with her glove.
I could tell from the look on her face she didn't need me
So I drifted on down and caught me a ride to the sea."

The other tear said, "We've got a connection.
I'm a tear of sorrow born of rejection.
I'm from the sad brown eyes of her old flame.
She told him they would be lifelong companions,
Left him with questions and not any answers.
I was on his cheek as he stood there calling her name.
I could tell he had a lot of my friends for company.
So I drifted on down and caught me a ride to the sea."

Oh, the ocean's a little bit bigger tonight,
Two more teardrops somebody cried.
One of them happy and one of them bluer than blue.
The tide goes out and the tide comes in
And someday they'll be teardrops again.
Released in a moment of pleasure or a moment of pain
Then they'll drift on down and ride to the sea again.

So, that's different. And Steve's melody complimented the lyric perfectly. But both of us knew the song wasn't finished. It painted a neat little, incomplete picture. It had no purpose. It gave the listener an intriguing story, but no real reason to care. Our challenge was to give those tears a purpose in talking to one another, to make the listener feel something for them, and to give the song a conclusion worth waiting for.

After several hours of searching for the perfect way to craft a final verse, it hit me.

"We're writing about the cycle of life," I said to Steve. "The tears fall and float to the ocean. Then one day, as part of the osmosis process, or whatever, they rise up, become part of a rain cloud, and fall to earth again. They eventually end up as somebody else's teardrops, years, or maybe centuries, later. It's the cycle of life. Now, how do we put that to music?"

We wrote, re-wrote, and wrote some more, until we thought we had it. And just in the nick of time. Pat Quigley, who headed Capitol Records, was coming for dinner at Steve's house. I hung around, and we played it for

Quigley that evening. I expected to see Pat's eyes dancing and a big smile on his face. I saw neither.

When Steve finished singing, Pat stammered, "Uh, do the tears have to talk to each other?" It was as though he had missed the whole point.

After a pause, Steve said, "Yes, they do."

"Okay," Pat replied. "I was just asking. But I don't think the song pays off at the end. You guys can do better."

Initially, Steve and I took a "What does he know?" approach to Quigley's commentary. But at the same time, we'd been issued a challenge to take what we had and make it better. We had to make it pay off, to make Pat Quigley smile.

I drove back out to Steve's house, and we started trying again. He came up with the idea of the last verse being set in a hospital waiting room. A nurse comes in and tells the singer that his wife has just given birth to a baby girl. An old man sitting across the room has just been told that his wife of many years has passed away. The cycle of life angle that we had been searching for was right there in that thought. And then somehow I came up with the line that wrapped a ribbon around all that we had written, that made it complete. The old man is talking to the singer.

> You've got a brand new angel and I've lost mine.
> I guess the Good Lord giveth and the Good Lord taketh away.
> And we both wiped a teardrop from our face.

Pat Quigley smiled, big time, when we played it for him.

"That's it," he said. "Now, go cut a big hit record on it."

That's what Steve did. "Two Teardrops" rose to number two on the *Billboard* country chart, and it earned us a Grammy nomination for Best Country Song. Today, it remains one of Steve's true signature songs, right up there with "Holes in the Floor of Heaven."

On top of that, Steve and I had learned a lesson. We had resented Quigley's telling us that our song wasn't finished when we thought it was, but he had actually done us a favor. We'd been challenged to do better, and we did. I've learned over the years that creative people aren't always the best judges of our own material, anyhow. We can sometimes benefit from an objective outsider telling us when we've missed the mark.

While Steve and I had people trying to figure out how two teardrops could hold a conversation, two other writing buddies and I had just as many or more people wondering how a man could die in a plane crash and manage to mail a postcard to his wife, days later.

The working title of the song was originally "Postcards from Heaven," and the idea came to me from Debbie Moore, the twin sister of my booking agent, Carrie Moore-Reed. They sang together as Moore and Moore and were on their way to some concert dates in the Far East when Debbie was struck with the idea.

"What if I were to send a postcard home to my boyfriend, and the card made it back but I didn't?" she pondered. She began to work that thought into a song concept: The wife of a deceased man gets a postcard from him that was mailed after he died. She ran that idea by me at a party, and I told her that it sounded straight out of *The Twilight Zone* but that it appealed to me. I also told her I had absolutely no idea how or if it could be believably written as a song.

Enter a prolific young songwriter named Skip Ewing, who was riding a hot streak at the time. Debbie told Skip about her idea one morning at a Nashville landmark called the Pancake Pantry, and Skip liked the idea and asked if she'd shared it with anybody else. She said, "Only Bill Anderson."

Skip said, "Believe it or not, I'm writing with him this morning. Why don't you come over with me?"

She did, and Skip took the lead in crafting the story of a man who went on vacation and bought and sent a postcard to his love.

> On the front it just said, "heaven,"
> With a picture of the ocean and the beach.
> And the simple words he wrote her
> Said he loved her, and he told her
> How he'd hold her if his arms would reach.

She got the postcard after getting word that his plane went down. On the card, he'd written,

> Wish you were here
> Wish you could see this place.
> Wish you were near.
> Wish I could touch your face.
> The weather's nice . . . it's paradise
> It's summertime all year.
> There's some folks we know that say hello.
> I miss you so
> Wish you were here.

A fine country singer from Georgia, Mark Wills, recorded the song, and it became Mark's first number one record. For me, the timing couldn't have been any better. The royalties I earned from those songs could have bought a whole lot of country dinners. Instead, they bought me out of the hole I'd put myself in by investing in a restaurant chain that sold country dinners. But this was much more than a financial help. I had managed a career resurgence that was improbable, perhaps implausible to some, but also unmistakable.

In January 1999, "Wish You Were Here" hit number one. At the end of February, Steve Wariner's "Two Teardrops" peaked at number two. That meant I had co-written two songs that were roaring toward the top of the charts at the same time, giving the illusion that I was one hot songwriting son-of-a-gun. The songs weren't written at the same time—they were written almost a year apart—but they'd been released about the same time, creating an oversized Bill Anderson buzz in the Nashville music community. At the same time I was being nominated for membership in the Country Music Hall of Fame for the things I'd done as a writer and performer many years before, I was being cheered in Nashville as one of country music's top contemporary writers in town, twelve years after I'd become eligible to join the AARP.

When I started writing again—and started co-writing for the first time—I knew I was going to have to adapt, and I was willing to do that. I had conversations with three or four of my peers at the Opry who would say to me, "I wish I could still write." I'd say, "Well, you can. Get out there and learn from these new writers and expose yourself to what's happening now, and be willing to let your ego be stepped on every once in a while." They'd come back with, "Yeah, but I ain't gonna let no young kid tell me what to do." I let a lot of young kids tell me a lot of things, and I benefitted from that, greatly. There's no sense in worrying about what you've done in the past, or what the person in the room with you has accomplished. I've had a few young writers who came into a writing session with me a little bit nervous, but there's no reason for that, and it doesn't help either one of us. A blank sheet of paper is a blank sheet of paper, whether you've written one hundred hit songs or never written one. It's the great equalizer, and it's intimidating. But if you can transform that blank sheet into words and melody, rhythm and rhyme, that's a victory. That's the thrill of creation, and that edge of the knife never dulls.

Professional success, even the rarest and most fulfilling kind, does not dull the sorrow of loss. In July 2001, Bill Anderson received country music's highest honor: a spot in the Country Music Hall of Fame. A month later, his mother was dead.

Hot July 2001, and the central air-conditioning unit in my office had stopped working. My longtime assistant, Kathy Gaddy, told me that Ed Benson, who ran the Country Music Association, had called and asked me to ring him back. I figured Benson was calling to ask me to serve on the CMA's contentious Fan Fair committee. In the early 1970s, I'd helped brainstorm the original Fan Fair and served on the CMA Board's Fan Fair committee, and in the new century I was in no mood to go to regular meetings and argue about Nashville's prime summertime tourist draw.

Late that afternoon, I called Ed Benson back and began by saying, before he had a chance to ask, "Ed, I can't do it."

He sounded stunned and said, "I'm sorry. You can't do what?"

"I can't serve on the Fan Fair committee for next year. I really don't have the time right now. I appreciate your thinking of me, but I'll have to take a rain check."

Ed told me he wasn't asking me to serve on that committee. He then said he was calling to tell me I'd been elected to the Country Music Hall of Fame, the highest honor someone can be given in our music.

I was stunned. And a little bit mistrustful. The year before, a reporter from the *Tennessean* left a message on my voice mail, asking how it felt to have been elected to the Hall of Fame. Before I could return his call, I found out that Charley Pride was actually the winner. I learned later that the reporter had called everyone he thought might have been on the final ballot (there's a lengthy nominations and voting process) and asked each one how it felt to have been elected. Not anything my journalism professors at the University of Georgia would have considered above board, and it left me a bit upset.

But Ed assured me that this was for real. And with his assurance, waves of emotion swept through me. I didn't get into the business to seek recognition and win awards, I got into it because I was obsessed with country music. In the moment, I thought of all the people with whom I wanted to share the news. I thought of my small town radio disc jockey days, which signaled the beginning of my career in Georgia. I recalled honky-tonks in Texas when nobody came to hear me sing, only to drink and dance. I remembered long bus rides, and, before that, even longer rides at the steering wheel of a car, as I struggled to take my songs to any place where someone might listen.

I wanted to call everyone I knew and tell them the good news. More than anyone, though, I wanted to talk to my mother and dad.

It wasn't until almost two hours after Ed Benson had called that I was able to get them both on the phone at the same time.

"I just want y'all to know that I've been elected to the Country Music Hall of Fame!" I announced once we had said hello and I had assured them there was no pending family emergency.

"Who?" Mom asked. She had a great sense of humor, but I wasn't sure whether she was attempting to use it or not. I started to laugh, but didn't.

"Me, Mama. Your son. Your first-born child. Bill. Remember?

"That's nice," she offered, quietly.

My dad, meanwhile, listening on an extension phone in the back bedroom of their small house, began to cry. That wasn't unusual. We Andersons tend to cry a lot. He cried when I graduated from the University of Georgia, and when each of his grandchildren were born. He cried when he and I fulfilled a lifelong dream, watching an in-person World Series game together at Atlanta Fulton County Stadium.

"Bill's been elected to the Hall of Fame, Mama," he said softly, between sniffles, with an underlying tone of pride in his voice.

"That's good, Bill," confirmed my mother, and his wife of sixty-seven years.

More silence. Then, "I'm going out to dinner tonight. I'm going to eat mattaconi."

She meant "manicotti."

Six weeks later, Mama was gone.

Many is the time I heard people say to Mama at the Opry or at one of my concerts, "Oh, Mrs. Anderson, I know you must be so proud of Bill."

Mama would invariably smile and say, "I was proud of him the day he was born."

It wasn't any successes or brushes with fame that had impressed her. She loved me just for being.

"I've had a wonderful life," she told me, not long before she died. "And you've been a big part of it."

Mama died August 19, 2001. A Sunday night. My band and I were playing shows that afternoon in Flat Top, West Virginia. In the first show, we sang and cut up with the audience for the better part of ninety minutes and then took an intermission. Prior to the break, I told the crowd I'd be signing autographs for a while at a tent-covered table to the left of the stage.

"If we haven't done the song or songs that you came to hear," I said, "write out your requests and give them to me or to one of the band members when you come through the autograph line. When we come back for our second show, we'll be glad to try and sing your requests."

The song I got the most requests for, by far, was one I'd written for and about my mother, nearly forty years before: "Mama Sang a Song."

That song is a narration about how my mother sang old-time gospel songs when I was a boy, and how the sound of those songs in her plaintive voice touched and inspired me. It's my favorite of all the songs I have written.

I'd been back onstage for half an hour in the second set, when I began to feel the edges of a stiffening breeze across the front of the open-air platform where I stood. Soon, the wind was whipping through West Virginia pines, and the blue sky from earlier in the day was a menacing gray.

I finished the song I was singing and told the crowd, "This next song is our most requested of the day. Looks like some bad weather is on the way, so I want to get it in while we can."

With that, the singers in my band broke into the opening refrain—"God put a song in the heart of an angel, and softly she sang it to me."

Halfway through the first verse, lightning cracked in the distance, thunder boomed, and the audience ran for cover. It began not just to rain but to pour. I stepped off my platform and sought a dry spot alongside the band, where there was cover. But not for one split second did anyone stop playing. The lyrics, the melodies . . . nothing wavered. There was nobody left in the audience to hear, but for some reason none of us could bring ourselves to stop in the middle of "Mama Sang a Song."

The band played and the voices sang until, finally, nothing was left but the echo of my voice whispering, "This old world's a better place because . . . one time . . . my mama sang a song."

When the song ended, there was complete silence, save for a clap of thunder. Water raced down across wooden benches that had been filled with fans, down the hillside toward the stage. An hour later, we were back on the bus, our driver easing the lumbering coach back out to the highway. None of us could remember having such a torrential downpour wash out one of our concerts.

Around eleven p.m., I was asleep on the bus. Someone knocked loudly on the door to the rear stateroom where I was resting. It was my longtime guitar player and band leader, Les Singer.

"Bubba, you awake? Wake up. You need to call your dad in Atlanta, right away."

I reached for my cell phone and turned it on, fearing the worst. When Dad came on the line, he confirmed my fear.

"We've been trying to reach you for hours," he said. "Mama died tonight."

We rolled into Nashville around five a.m. Shortly before seven, I was on a plane to Atlanta. Sitting by the plane window, it dawned on me that the last song I sang while my mother was alive on this earth was the song I wrote for her when I was barely out of my teens.

When Mom died, Dad's whole world died with her. He insisted on going to visit her grave every single day. It was heartbreaking to sit there on the small granite bench with "Anderson" chiseled across the front and hear him sob.

That's not how I like to remember my dad. Sorrow did not define him. Kindness and honor and faith came closer. But I can't help but recall that scene from time to time.

"You don't know about lonely, till it's chiseled in stone," sang Vern Gosdin. And that's true.

Athletes don't enter halls of fame until their careers have ended. Recording artists don't tend to enter until their careers have cooled. But in 2001, Bill Anderson found his name called twice in a month's time: first as a Country Music Hall of Fame member and next as the winner of a Country Music Association Vocal Event of the Year Award. The CMA designation was the first of his career, and he shared it with fellow Hall of Famers George Jones and Buck Owens and with modern-day star Brad Paisley. The CMA-winning song sprung from a producer's baffling pronouncement: "Too country."

What's that?

The Country Music Hall of Fame's official induction is held during what's called the Medallion Ceremony. Former Opry manager E. W. "Bud" Wendell said some nice things about me and presented me a beautifully engraved bronze medallion that proclaimed me a member of country music's most esteemed club. And then I stood behind a microphone and read some notes I'd prepared. Fighting back tears, I thanked Bob Tanner, the music publisher in San Antonio who encouraged me to send him some songs I'd written when I was eighteen years old. He told me, "You never know where the next hit is coming from." In less than a year, I sent him a song called "City Lights."

I thanked the friend I met back when he was in the army, stationed near Atlanta. He and I shared dreams of becoming songwriters and recording artists, and when he was discharged from the service, he came to Nashville, knocked on doors, and told me to do the same. Once I got to Music City, there were doors I didn't have to knock on, because he'd already opened them for me. His name was Roger Miller, and now my plaque and biography hang in the Hall of Fame's rotunda, along with his. And Hank Williams's. And Roy Acuff's. And Eddy Arnold's. And all my other country music heroes, the ones I'll never be able to consider peers.

I thanked my first Nashville publisher, Buddy Killen. And my producer, the legendary Owen Bradley. And my first manager, Hubert Long. And Bobby Brenner, the manager who came to me after Hubert's death and introduced me to the world of game shows and soap operas and network television and all that. This Hall of Fame designation was for all of them, for my family, for my band members, for every fan who came to see a show, and for every disc jockey who played a record.

As I wrote in a song, "I can do nothing alone."

The late summer and early fall days of 2001 combined to create the best and worst times in my life and career. I lost my mom in August. Our whole country went through the shock, horror, and sadness of the terrorist attacks in September that took lives and destroyed the World Trade Center. I was inducted into the Country Music Hall of Fame in October, and just a few weeks later, I won my very first CMA Award.

The Country Music Association didn't start giving awards until 1967. Many of my biggest hits came along well before that. When my career cooled in the 1980s, I assumed I'd probably never win a CMA prize. But in 2001, a very creative songwriter named Chuck Cannon and I combined to write a protest song of sorts that finally enabled me to bring home an elusive CMA trophy.

Not long before writing with Chuck, I'd written a traditional, three-chords-and-the-truth country song with Sharon Vaughn, one called "When a Man Can't Get a Woman off His Mind." That song was the talk of Music Row. Everybody professed to love it, but nobody would step out and record it. I presented it to one of the top record producers of the day, and he listened to it a half-dozen times. He kept raving, "Man, that is the perfect country song." Finally, he took the demo out of his CD player and handed it back to me across his wide wooden desk.

"I'm glad you like it," I beamed. "Who do you think you might get to record it?"

"Nobody," he replied.

"But I thought you liked it?"

"I do. In fact, I love it. But I can't ask one of my artists to record it. It's too country."

So, I had an answer. But not one I could understand. What was his definition of "too country"?

A few days later, Chuck Cannon and I got together to write. I told him about my experience, and Chuck listened intently.

"So, he said the song was 'too country'?" he asked, in disbelief.

"Yep. His very words."

Chuck hit a chord on his guitar and said, "Too country . . . what's that? Is it like too Republican or too Democrat?"

I laughed, but he said he was serious.

"Let's write this," he said. "This is something that needs to be said."

Next thing I knew, we were spitting out music business commentary, and social commentary.

> Too country ... what's that?
> Is it like too Republican or too Democrat?
> Is it too far to the left?
> Too far to the right?
> Too straight down the middle?
> Is it too black or too white?
> Are the biscuits too fluffy?
> Is the chicken too fried?
> Is the gravy too thick?
> Are the peas too black-eyed?
> Is the iced tea too sweet?
> Does it have too much tang?
> Are there too many lemons
> In mama's lemon meringue?

We ended on this note:

> Is the message too real?
> Too close to the bone?
> Do the fiddle and steel
> Remind you too much of home?
>
> Is honest and true
> Just not in demand?
> Too country ... Too country ...
> Too country?
> I don't understand.

I didn't understand, and still don't. I've never heard anyone say a rock 'n' roll song was "too rock," a jazz song "too jazzy," or a rap song being "too hip-hop." Can you imagine a classical piece being called "too classical"?

I was choosing songs for a new album I wanted to release about that time, and I thought, "What the heck? Nobody else is going to record 'Too Country,' so why don't I just do it?"

I don't remember if Brad Paisley heard me perform the song on the Opry, or if I played it for him one night when we were cruising around town listening to new music in his pickup truck. But somehow he heard it, he understood the message, and he wanted his fans to hear it. And Brad Paisley had, and has, a bunch of fans.

I'm not sure I believed him at first when he told me he wanted to cut it.

"And I want you and Buck Owens and George Jones to record it with me," he said.

Somehow, he pulled it off. On Brad's *Part Two* album, you can hear me singing "Too Country" with contemporary superstar Brad Paisley and country legends Buck Owens and George Jones.

The song was apparently too country to be a radio single, but it grabbed enough attention to win the CMA Vocal Event of the Year for 2001. I was laughing like a hyena when someone snapped a photograph of the four of us receiving our trophy onstage at the Grand Ole Opry House.

Not long before Buck passed away in 2006, I was able to get a copy of that photograph autographed by all four artists. A copy of it hangs on my office wall today.

Dean Dillon. Hollow-eyed howler. Drinking man's song-poet. Swashbuckler. Hillbilly Hemingway.

Bill Anderson. None of that stuff.

The two were set to write together, and it made both of them nervous. They met and found common ground in familiar things: country music and inevitable regret.

I barely knew Dean Dillon.

I knew about him. Knew he was George Strait's favorite songwriter and had written a bunch of hits for George. And I knew he had a reputation as a wild child. At various points in his career, he was talked about as a genius spinning out of control. And I knew I was a little nervous about writing with him, because I didn't know what to expect.

Until he called me a couple of days before we were scheduled to write, I didn't know he had some of his own insecurities about writing with someone he barely knew. He suggested we meet for breakfast at seven-thirty in the morning before our ten a.m. writing session. At the Pie Wagon in Nashville, I walked into the best and most rewarding breakfast of my life.

Dean sat across the table from me and began asking questions about my family, about my upbringing, and about my father. He told me he'd never known his dad, much less had a relationship with him, and I began to get a clearer picture. Our backgrounds were completely different, but we seemed connected by a common, if invisible, thread. We were bound by music.

Just before ten, we left and went to a small, upstairs office just off Music Row, where Dean kept a writing room. Following up on our breakfast conversation, I told Dean that, in a way, I envied his lifestyle.

"I should have spent more time out in the rain without an umbrella myself," I confessed. He reached for his guitar and began to sing:

> I'd have spent a lot more time out in the pouring rain
> Without an umbrella covering my head.
> And I'd have stood up to that bully when he pushed and called me
>   names
> But I was too afraid.

Neither of us knew what the song was going to be called at that point, but it was obvious that we were going to write about the things in our lives that we would do differently if we were given the chance to do this again. I loved this concept. People are forever telling each other that they'd do everything all over again the same way. And we wouldn't. None of us would. If we're to be anything but foolish, we'd use our twenty-twenty hindsight to make better choices, say kinder things, and lift each other up higher. Every day, I do things wrong and every night I wish I'd done them right. Or I mean one thing and convey another. Or I hurt someone unintentionally. Or I order the chicken when I should have ordered the fish.

"Elvis came to Knoxville once when I was growing up in east Tennessee," Dean said, as we talked. "And I begged my mama to let me go see him. But she wouldn't. If I could live that over again, I think I'd go anyhow."

Suddenly, that thought became a part of whatever song it was that we were writing.

> And I'd have gone on and seen Elvis that night he came to town
> But Mama said I couldn't.

Except that Dean said, "I'd have gone on and "saw" Elvis, instead of "seen" Elvis. I knew it was grammatically incorrect, but I wasn't about to make a fuss over it. I had learned early on that when you co-write songs, you've got to be prepared for a certain amount of give and take. I figured if and when our song were ever to be recorded, the artist or producer would pick up on the grammatical error and correct it, but that never happened. Kenny Chesney sang it just the way Dean wrote it, which, looking back, added to the song's authenticity.

Then from out of nowhere, Dean sang, "And I'd have gone skinny-dippin' with Jenny Carson that time she asked me to, but I didn't."

I loved it, but offered, "That should be 'dared' me to, not 'asked' me to," and Dean agreed. And then he came up with the title line.

> Oh, I . . . I'd have done a lot of things different.

I don't think we could have written the next line without our having had our talk over breakfast.

> I wish I'd have spent more time with my dad when he was alive . . .
> Now I don't have the chance.

My dad was still alive at that point, but I was going through the agony of not being able to see him as often as I'd like and dealing with the knowledge that he wasn't likely to be around that much longer. Dean had never known his father, so I knew I was at least a little better off in that regard than he was. I saw the pain in his eyes as we etched those words onto our sheets of paper. We continued to dig deep and tap into our emotions. We were two strangers, sharing things we hadn't shared with close friends.

> And I wish I'd have told my brother just how much I loved him before
>   he went off to war
> But I just shook his hand.
> And I wish I'd have gone to church when my grandma begged me to
> But I was scared of God.
> And I wish I would have listened when they said, "Boy, you're gonna
>   wish you hadn't."
> But I wouldn't.
> Oh I . . . I'd have done a lot of things different.

Dean and I interpreted that last point differently, and it briefly became a sticking point.

"No," I insisted. "It should be 'had' instead of 'hadn't.' He wishes he 'had' listened."

Kenny Chesney sang it Dean's way. In my recording, I sang it my way. Kenny's version is heard by a lot more people than mine was. Maybe I should have done that different.

That day, Dean and I disagreed on one other point, as we wrote the chorus.

> People say they wouldn't change a thing
> Even if they could.
> Oh, but I would.

Dean started reaching for the next line. "No, no, no . . . we don't need another line," I insisted. "This is all we need to say."

"But that don't make sense musically," he argued. "We need a four-line chorus."

"No, we don't," I said, and this time I was determined to stand my ground. "That's what will make this song stand out. Don't explain a thing. Let the listener fit what we've said into his own life. Leave it hanging." And I turned to my guitar and tried to show him how it would make sense musically. Eventually, though not without a struggle, he came around.

At this point, we were only a few lines away from an exceptionally good song. A writer never knows if he or she has written a hit, but good writers instinctively know if they've gotten everything out of an idea. Sometimes, I think knowing that one simple thing separates the good writers from the mediocre ones. Or the great writers from the good writers. Dean and I both sensed we were on the verge of creating something special.

But how to wrap it up? So many songs knock my socks off in the first verse and chorus, or the first two verses and choruses, then sound as if the writers broke for lunch and then wearily threw their last verse together before a three p.m. tee time. But the last verse of the song should be its strongest part. A good song should continue to build toward its climax.

Dean sang the song down from the top, so we could get a full grasp of what we had written up to that point. After listening, we both knew the song should end with love, with a personal, one-on-one relationship. We had admitted to generalities and family issues that we would handle differently if we had the chance, but nothing had been said about the mistakes the singer might have made in his love life. Or in his marriage. Or, as the case would have been with me and with Dean, marriages. Plural and difficult.

> There was this blue dress she wanted one time so bad she could taste it.
> I should have bought it, but I didn't.

The words rolled off of Dean's tongue like he'd been singing them all his life.

"Let's make it a red dress," I suggested. "I think that's more vivid." Dean agreed, but he got his "blue" into the next line.

> And she wanted to paint our bedroom yellow and trim it in blues and
>   greens
> But I wouldn't let her.

Dean's words again. And I knew I was in the presence of a master when he added, almost as an afterthought:

> It wouldn't have hurt nothin' . . .

That thought was so great and so humanizing. So true. But I knew we still had one more thought to convey. It needed to be an admission of regret and wistfulness. I thought back to the days in my own marriage, when my wife wanted me to take dancing lessons. I was totally opposed, and I refused. But it wouldn't have hurt nothin'. Suddenly, I knew where we needed to go with our last line:

> And if I'd known that dance was gonna be our last dance
> I'd have told that band to play on and on . . .
> And on and on and on.
> Yes, I . . . I'd have done a lot of things different.

Kenny Chesney's version became a Top 5 single that was nominated for the Academy of Country Music's Song of the Year Award. And when Kenny recorded the song, he added a spoken line at the end that tied all the pieces together, saying, "I think we'd all do a lot of things different."

Lord knows, I would. Every success story carries with it a million failures.

My heart hurts for Dean and others like him, who never knew the joy of having a relationship with their father. My father was my hero. He was a man of integrity, honesty, character, and compassion. He was a self-made man who started his own insurance company and spent a lifetime helping people.

After Mama passed away, I became even more conscious of making time to go to Georgia and be with my dad. I would phone him at least every other day, no matter where in the world I was. My last conversation with him took place late on a Friday afternoon, from a motel room in North Bay, Ontario, Canada. The sun was beginning to go down and I was about to leave the room and ride the bus to the auditorium for our concert that night. But I felt a strong urge to call my dad, just to hear his voice. We talked about the Atlanta Braves and about University of Georgia football. He asked me how the weather was in Canada. I told him I loved him, he told me he loved me, and we never had the chance to speak again.

My sister called that Sunday afternoon in the early fall of 2003. I was touring with Kitty Wells; her husband, Johnnie Wright; their son, Bobby Wright; Jean Shepard; and George Hamilton IV. I had just arrived in Brandon, Manitoba, when the phone rang.

"Bubba," she said, "Daddy died this morning."

She said he'd been sitting in his easy chair in the living room, reclining and relaxing with the Sunday paper, when he closed his eyes and went to sleep.

Jean Shepard's husband, Benny Birchfield, had just driven their van over two hours from Winnipeg to Brandon. As soon as he heard the news about my father, he climbed back in the van and drove me back to Winnipeg so I could catch a south-bound plane. That act of kindness will remain with me forever.

I guess it sounds funny for a man in his seventies to say he misses his parents, but I can't help it. I still miss mine. Not a day goes by that I don't think about them and thank God for letting me be born to and raised by such special people.

There was just no place for it.

No place for a song about chronic alcoholism and double sui-cide. Or was that what it was about? It seemed unclear. For sure, it was about sadness, and about the burial of flesh and bone and spirit. Anyway, there was just no place for it, so it found its own.

20

In the publishing company parking lot, I asked Jon Randall Stewart how he was doing.

I probably shouldn't have asked.

"So far today, I've lost my wife, my publishing deal, and my recording contract," he said, looking at his watch. "And it's only two-thirty. I'm scared to think what else might happen between now and six."

He was serious, though with the slightest trace of a grin on his face. Almost a smile of resignation. He seemed to be saying, at least to himself, "This isn't good, but it is what it is."

Before I could gather my thoughts and offer him condolences or encouragement, he asked, "We still on to write in a couple of weeks?"

"Yeah, so far as I know. But I think it's more like three weeks."

"Well, I should have a whole lot of good new ideas by then," he said. "We'll write the saddest song in history."

Then he paused, and then he added, "But that's one thing I like about writing with you. You're not afraid to go dark with me. Some guys only want to write happy little songs. You don't mind digging into the dark places."

"It's just the bluegrass coming out in both of us," I offered. "With all that you're going through, we'll write one that'll make 'Knoxville Girl' sound like 'Walkin' in the Sunshine.'"

We laughed, neither of us realizing that was exactly what we were about to do.

The morning of April 12, 2000, Jon and I were assigned Sony/ATV Publishing's Writer Room number 3, in the little brick structure that used to be a Metro Nashville fire station. Room number 3 is the smallest of all the writer rooms, and one of only two with no windows. Once we got inside, we had no idea if it was sunny outdoors or pouring rain. And we saw none of the other writers as they came and went from the building. It's a good thing, too, because as deep and dark as we were about to go with the song we were writing, we didn't need distractions.

I showed up that day with the idea to suggest to Jon that we write a song called "Midnight Cigarette." I envisioned a relationship or a marriage that had slowly died or burned out gradually, like a lighted cigarette would do if left burning in an ashtray in the middle of the night.

This was not our first writing session together. We had written a song called "Cold Coffee Morning" ("It's gonna be a cold coffee morning / And a warm beer afternoon") that Jon recorded for Asylum Records. It had been his current single release when the label unceremoniously dropped him from its roster. It was actually in the charts and climbing steadily when the company pulled the plug on the relationship.

We had also written a ballad that both of us recorded, called "I Can't Find an Angel," so we knew we had a songwriting chemistry, in spite of the differences in our ages and our experiences.

We opened up guitar cases, sipped coffee, and began to play catch up on the things that had happened since we saw each other in the parking lot a few weeks before.

"I'm doing a lot better than I was the last time you saw me," Jon said. "Boy, you really caught me at a bad time."

I told him I'd felt for him and was glad to know he was doing better. At the same time, I didn't feel it was my place to push him for details. As it turned out, he would offer them soon enough without my asking.

I told Jon about "Midnight Cigarette," and he picked up on the concept right away. "I love it," he said. Then he stopped and looked at me. "I've got an idea, too," he said. "But I don't know if it's any good or not."

He sheepishly hit a chord on his guitar and sang, "He put the bottle to his head and pulled the trigger."

"Good Lord," I said. "Where did that come from?"

"Oh, it's a long story."

Then he told it.

Right after I'd seen him in the parking lot, Jon had decided to remove himself from the radar screen of life for as long as it might take to grieve over his losses and put his life back together. He told me that he went to a friend's house, "crashed" for two weeks, drank heavily, and wasn't inclined to stop. He'd been married to singing star Lorrie Morgan, and the news of their impending divorce had become public knowledge. It seemed easier to run away and hide.

His manager had flown to New York in hopes of securing more support from Jon's record label but had only angered some of the top brass there, causing the company to exit the Jon Randall Stewart business. He hadn't been producing hit songs for his music publisher and owed them more money than they thought he was worth. His contract expired, and they chose not to renew it.

He said that after a couple of weeks, he apologized to his buddy for crashing at his place and drinking so much.

"But before I could get out everything I wanted to say, my buddy interrupted me and put his hand on my shoulder," Jon told me. "He said, 'That's alright. I've put the bottle to my head and pulled the trigger a few times myself.'"

"God, what an unbelievable line," I said, shaking my head at its sheer brilliance. "But can we use it in a song?"

Jon had been thinking about it, I could tell.

"No problem," he said. "I told my buddy I probably would." He reached for his guitar and said, "But I really like your line, too. What if we said something like, 'She put him out, like the burning end of a midnight cigarette'? Maybe that's our opening line."

I flipped to a clean sheet of paper on my lined white legal pad. I penciled in the date in the upper left-hand corner of the page. And I wrote "Jon Randall" underneath. Then I wrote "the key of E" beneath that and drew a circle around it. That had long been my method of identifying the songs that I co-wrote. I wrote the opening line near the top of the page, but saved room above it to insert the title if and when we came up with one.

It didn't take long.

Jon said, "What if we made the song like a lullaby? A 'la la la la' kind of thing?"

We both began to doodle, searching out chord progressions and a rhythmic pattern that we thought might fit. I began searching for a line to follow the one about the midnight cigarette. Jon was busy honing in on the lullaby idea. All of a sudden, he said the words, "Whiskey lullaby." We had our title. All that was left to do at that point was write the song.

> She put him out, like the burning end of a midnight cigarette.
> She broke his heart, and he spent his whole life trying to forget.
> He finally drank his pain away a little at a time
> But he never could get drunk enough to get her off his mind.
> Until the night . . .

We decided early on that the song had to be written and sung in the third person. We had to say "he" and "she" and not "you" and "me." Why? We weren't sure at first, but it seemed right. Later, we realized why.

> He put that bottle to his head and pulled the trigger
> And finally blew away her memory.
> Life is short but this time it was bigger
> Than the strength he had to get up off his knees.
> We found him with his face down in the pillow
> With a note that said, "I'll love her till I die."
> And when we buried him beneath the willow
> The angels sang a whiskey lullaby.

I couldn't remember having ever been part of writing such an unusual song. And I wondered if it was something really good or just something really different.

The second verse took some careful thought and planning. Should we continue with his story, even though he was now six feet under, or should we tell the story from the perspective of the woman? And, while her view seemed the logical thing to explore, how should we go about it?

One of the benefits of writing song lyrics out by hand, as opposed to creating them on a computer, is that there's no delete button on a pencil. Sometimes when you're using a pencil, it's easiest to mark through something you've written and move on. That's what I did when we started trying to create a second verse, and from that original sheet, which I now have framed on my office wall, I can tell you that the second verse initially began with:

> Sometimes at night
> She can almost feel him in the dark
> It hurts so bad.

We didn't get any further. We realized quickly that line of thinking wasn't going to get us where we needed to go. But perhaps this would:

The rumors flew, but nobody knew how much she blamed herself.
For years and years, she tried to hide the whiskey on her breath.

But now what? We sat and stared and struggled.

"What if we go back to the same lines we used in the first verse?" Jon asked. "That way, we can show that both of them were feeling the same emotions."

> She finally drank her pain away a little at a time
> But she never could get drunk enough to get him off her mind.
> Until the night . . .
> She put that bottle to her head and pulled the trigger
> And finally blew away his memory.
> Life is short but this time it was bigger
> Than the strength she had to get up off her knees.
> They found her with her face down in the pillow

And here, we felt we needed a new line. I suggested:

> Clinging to his picture for dear life.
> They laid her next to him beneath the willow
> While the angels sang a whiskey lullaby.

We'd definitely gone dark, and Jon's largely minor-key melody perfectly matched the lyric. We sang it over several times, adjusting the phrasing here and there, and then put it down on a simple guitar-vocal work tape. The song was finished, but what had we written? Was there anybody in contemporary country music who would dare touch a song like this? In the spring of 2000 . . . or 1990, or 1980 or 1960 or 2010, people weren't running up and down Music Row yelling, "Write me a double-suicide drinking song!"

For the longest time, Jon resisted recording a full-blown demo on "Whiskey Lullaby." He didn't have much faith in the song getting recorded and didn't want to waste time and money. On the other hand, the more I lived with the song, the more I felt we should do a demo. I kept badgering him until he gave in. I booked a small studio and hired my friend Rex Schnelle to engineer the session. Late night seemed to be the only time that fit everyone's schedule, so we gathered one evening around ten o'clock.

Rex is a great musician who can play guitar, bass, keyboards, mandolin, drums, and just about anything else you'd need, so I saw no sense in hiring a band. Jon is a superb guitarist who was a key member of Emmylou Harris's Nash Ramblers band, and he brought his guitar. The song didn't lend itself to a huge arrangement. We just needed to communicate the feeling and tell the story.

Jon sang the song through a couple of times, and I could sense that his excitement was beginning to rise as he relaxed and recaptured the feeling that we had the day we wrote the song. Rex recorded a performance with just Jon's vocal and guitar, and Jon listened to the playback. All of a sudden, he jumped up and yelled, "This song needs a Dobro!" Within a half hour, legendary picker Al Perkins—who had also contributed to the Nash Ramblers—walked in, Dobro in hand.

For the next couple of hours, we recorded guitar and Dobro, bass, lead vocals, and harmonies. The finished demo was, in my opinion, a masterpiece. I told Jon we should release it as it was, and he reminded me he didn't have a record deal anymore.

Everybody who heard the demo loved it. But no one was confident that it could play well in the marketplace and find a home on the radio. Finally, I got a call one day telling me that it had been put on hold—"on hold" is an industry term for, "we're considering this"—by the Dixie Chicks. But before the Dixie Chicks had the chance to record it, they exited the country music mainstream after making critical comments about then-president George W. Bush.

Fortunately, a secretary for a Music Row publishing company had obtained a copy of Jon's demo and filed it away in her desk drawer. She remembered and pulled it out at just the right time.

I was in the offices of Sea Gayle Music, a publishing company owned in part by Brad Paisley, trying to write a song with him on the day it happened.

We had left our writing room in one of the rear offices and walked up front for some reason when Liz O'Sullivan, seated at her desk by the front window, began bragging on me as a songwriter. She asked Brad if he'd ever heard a song that I co-wrote called "Whiskey Lullaby." He admitted he hadn't, and she slid open the center drawer of her desk and removed a CD containing the demo. I was totally shocked, because I had no idea she had even heard the song. She led us into an adjoining office where she slid the CD into a player and turned up the volume.

Brad listened intently, and when it was over he said, "I want to record that."

I told him the Dixie Chicks had it on hold, and he said if they didn't record it that he would. They didn't, and when it became clear that they wouldn't, he began scheming.

"What would you think about 'Whiskey Lullaby' being sung as a duet?" he asked. "What if I brought in a woman and had her sing the verse that tells the story from the woman's point of view. I think that could be effective."

"I don't know," I answered. "Who do you have in mind?"

"I don't think there are but two people who could really pull it off," he said. "One would be Alison Krauss and the other would be Dolly Parton." "I think it's brilliant," I said. "You couldn't have chosen two better people or better singers than Alison and Dolly. Go for it."

Keep in mind, Brad didn't need my opinion on any of this. But I loved the conversation.

"Well, I think I'm going to go after Alison first," he said. "I think she'd be great, and she's had some radio play and some chart action lately. That wouldn't hurt."

I told him to keep me posted, and I called Jon.

Alison sang the song, requesting and receiving one small lyrical change: Instead of singing that she "blew" away his memory, she opted to say she "drank" it away. That softened the song a bit, and I think it was a wise choice. To conform his lyric to hers, Brad made the same change in the chorus that he sang. And when I heard the record, I was the one blown away. It was perfect. But I still had some lingering doubts as to whether it could be successful in contemporary country music.

New York City. I was staying at the Waldorf Astoria Hotel on Park Avenue. A long way removed from the Hotel Andrew Jackson in Commerce, Georgia.

I'd been fortunate enough to perform at London's Royal Albert Hall, and at New York's original Madison Square Garden. But none of that prepared me for the experience of performing at Carnegie Hall.

I shared the spotlight with Brad Paisley, and we sang "Too Country." The audience rewarded us with a huge ovation. The entire cast, which included Alison Krauss, Alan Jackson, Little Jimmy Dickens, Vince Gill, Trisha Yearwood, Charley Pride, Ricky Skaggs, and others, closed the show by singing "Will the Circle Be Unbroken?" It was cause for chill bumps.

The next night was the CMA Awards show, at Madison Square Garden. The only time that show has been held outside of Nashville. As Song of the

Year nominees for writing "Whiskey Lullaby," Jon Randall and I had been assigned seats on the third row, just to the right-hand side of the stage. Brad Paisley and his wife, Kim, were seated directly in front of us. Willie Nelson strode onstage to read the list of best song nominees. My heart pounded at the mention of our song, and when he opened an envelope and said "Whiskey Lullaby" had won, I jumped up and hugged Brad and knocked his white western hat from his head.

The rest of the evening is a blur. I know Jon and I went to a press conference backstage. Afterward, we attended some parties and soaked up handshakes and hugs. Somewhere after midnight, I found my way back to my suite at the Waldorf. I stood at the window gazing across the "bright array of city lights," thinking I must be the luckiest human being in the world.

I had just won the top award given for songwriting. All I had ever wanted to be was a songwriter. As a kid, I had dreamed of writing hit songs. I had written many of them before, but this was the first of my creations to be validated in such a major way.

And I was less than twenty-four months away from my seventieth birthday.

The songs were pouring out now. How could they not? It was all about empathy and clarity of emotion, and about mining seemingly incongruent minds and personalities for cohesive artistic ideas. Bill Anderson's stories about the creation of hit songs "Give It Away" and "I'll Wait for You" are lessons in collaborative creativity, in seeking consensus while holding to well-reasoned opinions.

I was in Georgia visiting my sister, Mary, the afternoon I learned George Strait had recorded one of my songs.

She was ailing, and sleeping, and I'd gone for a walk on the cracked sidewalks near her house when my cell phone rang. It was Sony/ATV Publishing's Terry Wakefield, saying George had cut my song, one that I'd co-written with Jamey Johnson and Buddy Cannon. The song had been born on a morning when none of us came to the writing session with any idea of what we might write about.

We'd gathered at ten a.m. around a glass-top coffee table in Buddy's office on Nineteenth Avenue in Nashville. We were drinking coffee and swapping stories when it dawned on us that we should probably start thinking about what we might create that day.

Buddy turned to Jamey. "You got an idea?"

"Nope."

"How about you, Whisper? You got another 'Peel Me a 'Nanner' in your brain somewhere?"

"Lord, I hope not," I replied. "One of those in a lifetime is enough."

"No, it's more than enough," Buddy jabbed. He has been convinced for years that my old song "Peel Me a 'Nanner," is the worst country song ever written.

"Well, I don't have anything, either," Buddy admitted. We'd come to co-write, but now we were co-staring.

"Well, I am going through a divorce," Jamey finally said. Buddy and my ears perked up. When was a divorce not grounds for a country song? Jamey leaned over and picked up an Epiphone guitar.

He began to strum and sing aimlessly, about a picture that had been taken in San Francisco, on his honeymoon. According to his singing, his wife pulled that picture down from the wall and told him to give it away.

"Is that a true story?" I asked.

"Naw," Jamey said. "But it sings good."

One of the cardinal rules of songwriting is never to let the truth get in the way of a good story.

I suggested that if she were giving away meaningful pictures from the wall, she might also be giving away furniture. Next thing I knew, he was singing about a big four-poster king-sized bed where the couple once made love.

"We're getting to the heart of the matter now," I said.

But it was Buddy who saw something in the idea that neither Jamey nor I would have seen. Buddy suggested, "What if we talk rather than sing the first part of the song? You know, to set it up."

My initial reaction was, "You making fun of me?"   I would never have thought to suggest such a thing. Even though recorded narrations had been a staple of my career for years, and other artists like Jimmy Dean, Porter Wagoner, Bobby Bare, and Jimmy Dickens had flourished with them as well, I couldn't remember the last time a talking song of any kind had made an impact on country music. And I would have been the absolute last person ever to suggest anybody write or record one.

"No, man, I'm serious," Buddy said. He played a guitar chord to illustrate his point. I wasn't sure.

"Everybody will hear this and think I talked you guys into it," I said.

"Well, if it's a flop, we'll tell them that you did," Buddy laughed.

Next thing I knew, we had created a short spoken intro to our song, and I was beginning to scribble thoughts and words onto my ever-present sheet of lined white paper. The song began with a spoken-word section.

> She was storming through the house that day, and I could tell she was leaving. And I thought, "Aw, she'll be back." Then she turned and pointed to the wall and said . . .

(Here's where the melody kicks in.)

> "That picture from our honeymoon that night in 'Frisco Bay,"
> She said, "Give it away, just give it away."
> "And that big four-poster king-sized bed where so much love was made,
> Just give it away," she said. "Give it away."
>
> Just give it away.
> Ain't nothin' in this house worth fightin' over
> And we're both tired of fightin' anyway.
> Just give it away.

In the first verse and chorus, we'd already violated one of the unwritten rules of modern country songwriting. We had used the title to the song five times.

The great writer and Country Music Hall of Famer Hank Cochran used to say he tried to get the title into his lyrics as often as possible, so that no one would wonder what the name of the song was. I tended to subscribe to that theory myself, but that had come to be viewed as old-school writing by many of the more rock-influenced young writers who were beginning to make their voices heard. I was a bit skeptical of trying to get a song with a heavily repeated title into the current marketplace myself, but at the same time I had to admit it was refreshing. When I brought up my reluctance, Buddy and Jamey assured me that they liked the path we were taking, and we tore into creating a second, although shorter, talking section: "So I tried to move on, but every woman that I held just reminded me of that day."

> When that front door swung wide open and she flung her diamond ring
> Said, "Give it away. Just give it away."

I stopped the proceedings.

"Flung? Can we say 'flung'? Is that even a word?"

"It is now," one of them said.

"Well, based on my own divorces, I know what needs to come next," I offered:

> I said, "Now, honey, don't you even want your half of everything?" She
> said, "Give it away. Just give it away."

"No real woman would ever tell you to give away her half of everything," I said.

"This one would," Jamey inserted. "She's really pissed." I got the feeling by now he might be talking from personal experience.

We left the line as it was, then decided to repeat the chorus again. We discussed the idea of writing a second musical part, to bridge the gap between the second chorus and the third verse we knew we needed. We voted unanimously to plow straight ahead with a third spoken section instead: "So I'm still right here where she left me . . . along with all the other things she don't care about anymore."

When George Strait recorded the song, he added a bit of emphasis by grunting sort of an "umph" in that spot. I loved it.

Like that picture from our honeymoon that night in 'Frisco Bay
She said, "Give it away." But I can't give it away.
And that big four-poster king-sized bed where all our love was made
She said, "Give it away." But I can't give it away.
I've got a furnished house, a diamond ring,
And a lonely broken heart, full of love
And I can't even give it away.

We had used the title of the song sixteen times inside the three verses, two choruses, and the short section at the end. The song had three separate places where the words were spoken rather than sung. And we had used a total of only three musical chords to play the melody.

Conventional wisdom said this song didn't stand a chance.

We finished writing before lunch, and none of us could get the song out of our heads. Buddy had me put in a call to my guitar player, Les Singer, to see if he might come over to Bud's office about four o'clock that afternoon to help us lay down a simple guitar demo. We all thought the song was perfect for George Strait, and we wasted no time in getting it to him.

Les brought his old Martin guitar, Jamey sang a straightforward, uncomplicated vocal, and before dark we had a finished demo of the song none of us had come to the writing session that morning expecting to create.

At the time, Jamey was managed by Erv Woolsey, Strait's manager, and he made a beeline straight from the demo session over to Erv's office, with a CD in his hand.

The next word I got was that both Erv and George loved it and that it would be part of their upcoming recording session in Key West, Florida. I joked and told Buddy I was heading to Wal-Mart to buy something on credit. But I knew better than to spend the royalty money before I received it. In this business, I had seen many a slip between the cup and the lip.

But, walking along the suburban sidewalks of Atlanta, I got the call from Terry Wakefield, who told me there'd been no slip.

I heard George's recording for the first time when I went to Dallas for a Country Music Association Board of Directors meeting. And it was the first time I had ever heard one of my songs played on an iPod. They didn't have iPods back in Commerce, Georgia, in the 1950s, when I looked out and imagined a bright array of city lights.

Little Jimmy Dickens and I had been invited to this particular board meeting as "honorary guests" of the CMA, and all the industry heavy-weights were there. Someone from George Strait's camp came up to me during a break in the proceedings and whispered, "Would you like to hear George's cut of your song?" I replied, "Well, if you insist."

The person led me into a corner of the meeting room, handed me a pair of earbuds, and cranked the volume on his iPod. For the first of what would eventually be hundreds of times, I listened to George's right-on interpretation of something I'd helped to create. It was stunning.

I asked to hear it again, and then again. Then I called Little Jim over and played it for him. Might have been his first time to use an iPod, too: I'm not sure that Bolt, West Virginia, was rich with such technology when he was growing up there in the 1920s.

By the time they called the board meeting back into session, I was floating somewhere above the room. I could not believe how good this recording was, but I had no idea whether the label would release it as a single. I could only whisper a prayer or two.

I learned a long time ago, God's always listening, even if you're whispering.

In July 2006, George Strait's recording of "Give It Away" was released as the first single from his *It Just Comes Natural* album. It soon became his forty-first number one country single, and it peaked just as voting was beginning for the Academy of Country Music Awards show. We suddenly found ourselves with an ACM nomination. I had never won an award from the academy, and I was thrilled when "Give It Away" was announced as the ACM's Song of the Year in 2007. The show was held in Las Vegas, and it was fun to have networking opportunities out there with people I didn't often see in Nashville. A chance Vegas encounter with Jennifer Nettles and Kristian Bush of the group Sugarland led to our discovering that she lived in my hometown of Decatur, Georgia, and he lived in Avondale Estates, where I went to high school. We decided on the spot that the three of us needed to combine our Georgia-ness and write a song together. We later did, creating a song called "Joey," a Top 20 country hit in 2009.

"Give It Away" went on to win the Song of the Year Award from the Country Music Association as well. In his speech from the winners' podium, Jamey Johnson thanked his ex-wife for divorcing him and thereby providing him with ideas from which to write the song.

I should have thought of that myself. After all, it's best to be generous and offer credit where credit is due.

I had yet another song rising up the country charts on the heels of "Give It Away." It never made it all the way to the top, but Joe Nichols's recording of a ballad I co-wrote with Harley Allen was a story unto itself.

"I'll Wait for You," the story of a man trying to get home to his dying wife in the midst of a "three-foot high" snowstorm, was Harley's brainchild. He shared the concept with me the first day I went to his house to write.

> The snow out in Montana was three feet high.
> The lady at the counter said there ain't no flights.
> And so he called her on the telephone.
> He said, "I'll rent a car and I'll drive home."
> And she said, "I'll wait for you."

I said, "Harley, I don't think the lady at the airline counter would have said, 'There ain't no flights.' I think she would have said, 'There are no flights.'"

The son of bluegrass legend Red Allen, Harley was having none of that.

"I don't care if it's correct or not," he said, puffing from one of his ever-present cigarettes. "In this song she's saying 'ain't.' We ain't even goin' to discuss it."

I knew if I wanted to be part of what had the makings of a good song, I would allow the airline counter lady to say "ain't." And so I did.

We plowed on.

> And she said, "I'll wait for you, like I did last year
> At Christmastime with your family here
> And your car broke down out in San Antone."

I interrupted again.

"I think this guy would have been driving a truck and not a car."

Harley didn't argue, and our hero traded in his car for a truck.

> "And the gifts stayed wrapped till you got home
> Oh, this ain't nothing new . . . Sweetheart, I'll wait for you."
> Now he's on his cell phone in a Coupe de Ville . . .

Silently, I questioned whether a car rental company in the middle of Montana would have had a Coupe de Ville in its fleet, but I kept my mouth shut. It rhymed beautifully.

> Talking to the one he loves and always will.
> His heart is breaking 'cause she's there alone.
> Her heart is aching 'cause she wants him home.

And she says, "I'll wait for you like back in '68
When our child was due but I said, 'He'll have to wait
Until his dad gets here and stands by my side.'
Remember, dear, our son's first cry?
Oh, this ain't nothing new.
Sweetheart, I'll wait for you."

He didn't stop all day to eat a bite
And he finally got there about midnight.
The doctor said she's in a better place
She said to give you this note just in case.

And it said, "I'll wait for you at Heaven's gate.
Oh, I don't care how long it takes.
I'll just tell St. Pete that I can't come in
Without my love and my best friend.
Oh, this ain't nothing new.
Sweetheart, I'll wait for you.
P.S. I love you, too.
Sweetheart, I'll wait for you."

The problem was that when we first wrote that last chorus, it was nowhere near lyrically tight and succinct. I knew we were chasing some elusive emotions right there and felt, much like Pat Quigley had felt when Steve Wariner and I were trying to craft the ending of "Two Teardrops," that at first Harley and I hadn't nailed it. He seemed to be happy with whatever it was that we'd written, but I wasn't. I felt . . . no, I knew . . . we could do better.

"Hey, man, let's get together one more time and see if we can't tie that ending together a little better," I said to him one day on the phone. "This song is too good not to give it the best we can." Harley grew defensive and said the lyric was good enough the way it was. I kept insisting that it wasn't.

"Look, it's almost an hour's drive from my house out to yours," I said. "But I'll be glad to come back out if you'll work with me on this. Please, I don't think you'll be sorry."

He reluctantly agreed. I drove back out a few days later, and when we finished the song, he actually thanked me.

"Guess I get lazy sometimes," he said, as we munched on his wife's home-made chocolate chip cookies.

"We all do," I admitted, watching as he took another cigarette out of his shirt pocket and lit up.

Fewer than four years later, Harley Allen—a multitalented singer, song-writer, and musician from Dayton, Ohio, was dead at age fifty-five.

Lung cancer.

The expressive, soulful country singer Joe Nichols cut a terrific record on "I'll Wait for You," not long after Harley and I finished writing it. But it seemed to take forever for his record to secure a solid foothold on the charts. There was quite a bit of inner turmoil at Joe's record label at the time. Long-time employees were leaving, with new people filtering in. The old guard there decided to film and release a video. The new people didn't like the way the video looked, and they ordered up a different one. New record producers got involved with the album project, scrapped some old songs and replaced them. I was worried, because I thought a really good song was going to get lost in all this transition.

Enter Anna Nicole Smith. There's a sentence I never thought would be part of my memoir. Anna Nicole Smith was a long-legged, buxom, blond model and actress who married an octogenarian oil tycoon, to much tab-loid speculation. She had a sad, star-crossed life, and she was addicted to prescription medications. One night, she came to the Opry. I was onstage trying to sing a song when she and her entourage swept in, turning every head in the house and claiming several seats that had been held for them in the front row. Nobody at the Opry heard a note I was attempting to sing. They were too busy gawking at this outrageous-looking woman.

I was neither pleased nor impressed. But Joe Nichols was on my portion of the show that night, and he sang "I'll Wait for You." It suddenly became Anna Nicole Smith's favorite song, Joe Nichols became her favorite singer, and when she died in February 2007 at age thirty-nine of what doctors called "combined drug intoxication," the people in charge of her funeral flew Joe to the Bahamas to sing "I'll Wait for You" at her nationally televised funeral service.

Joe's single came out in July 2006, but it became a Top 10 country hit in 2007, after Smith's death.

Everybody ought to get to visit Commerce, Georgia, with Bill Anderson. You can learn a lot that way. A lot about gratitude and remembrance and dedication, and a lot about how music and art can be passed through generations, through kindness and stubborn goodwill. On a Saturday in 2014, I walked with Bill through the halls of Commerce High School and saw theater students—there on a Saturday to rehearse in a lovely new performing space—rush up to hug and thank him. Most of those kids couldn't have named you one Bill Anderson–penned song. But they knew enough about him to know that he'd gotten his start in Commerce, and that his name was on their building because he cared for them.

In the summer of 1997, the little Georgia radio station where I began my broadcasting career celebrated its fortieth anniversary. I had been standing in the control room of WJJC in Commerce on the June morning in 1957 when engineer Bill Evans pulled the switch and general manager Grady Cooper spoke the first words that ever went out over our airwaves. A little over an hour later, I sat down with a stack of country music records and hosted the station's first-ever disc jockey show.

To celebrate the anniversary, the station's new owners threw a big, free outdoor concert at the local high school football stadium. They invited me to come back as the show's headline attraction.

I arrived in Commerce a full day ahead of the concert, to reconnect with the town and its people. I'd known the station's owners, Gerald and Rob Jordan, since they were rug rats crawling around the radio studio floor while their parents, R. L. and Bonnie Jordan, sang live gospel music over the airwaves. I was pleased and proud that Gerald and Rob thought to bring me back to town, and I was a little overwhelmed with the emotion of being in Commerce again for the station's birthday party. That emotion swelled when I got onstage for the concert, and my mouth took control of my brain.

"Ain't we having fun?" I hollered into the microphone, and I took the crowd's roar as affirmation. "How would y'all like to do this again next year?" I continued. "Okay, here's the deal: I'll come back next year about this time, and I'll bring some friends of mine from Nashville with me."

Another roar, thankfully, because I was making this up off the top of my head and I needed a moment to come up with the grand plan.

"And we'll put on a benefit concert and raise some money for a charity that will be decided on later. I'll let you people here in the community decide what charity you want to help. But there will be one requirement: The money we raise will have to stay here in Commerce and Jackson County. You people here have helped me and supported me so much over all these years that I want to give something back to you. Have we got a deal?"

In fact, we did.

The Jordans and I burned up the phone lines and mail routes between Nashville and Commerce for the next several months, trying to wrap hearts and minds around this monster I had enthusiastically and accidentally created. The moment I began talking on that stage, it was too late to turn back.

Gerald and Rob went before the city leaders and told them about my offer. The Jordans asked for guidance in selecting the charity that our show might benefit. It seemed the city of Commerce needed and wanted—had wanted for some time, as it turns out—a small but modern performing arts center that could be used by the schools and the community to host plays, concerts, and other fine arts events. The old junior high auditorium that I had used in the 1950s when I brought Hank Snow to town had burned down, and nothing had adequately replaced it.

The question became, "What if we used the money from Bill Anderson's concert to start a fund aimed toward building the auditorium we need?"

The answer became, "Then that would make things better, and encourage artistry and music and achievement."

The last Friday in June 1998, I was back at the football stadium, this time with Opry stars Jimmy Dickens, Johnny Russell, and the Whites. The response was fantastic, and we decided to do it again in 1999, by which time the show had been named the City Lights Festival. People were coming to Commerce from other cities and states, booking hotel rooms, and dining in the local restaurants. Soon enough, our big show on Friday night was preceded by a Thursday golf tournament, a Dinner with the Stars meal, and an acoustic show on Thursday night. After the Friday concert, there were local talent shows and other related events lasting into Sunday. This all turned into an annual thing, and our little bank account, earmarked for the construction of a performing arts center, steadily grew.

"My" City Lights Festival went on for ten years. My favorite festival came in the seventh or eighth year, when the headliners were Vince Gill and Ray Price. Vince was at the height of his popularity, and his name alone was enough to fill the stadium. Add to that the presence of Ray Price, the man who had taken my song "City Lights" to the number one spot in the country in 1958, and the billing was magic.

A television crew from Nashville came down to cover the happenings, focusing on the angle of Ray Price coming for the first time to sing in the shadow of the little hotel where one of his signature songs had been written. I led a camera crew through the hallways of the old hotel building— now a bank—and up onto the roof where I had gone that hot August night in 1957, when I plopped down across a lawn chair and composed the lines that would change my life.

Thirty minutes into his performance, Ray muttered softly, "This is for you, Bill," and twin fiddles broke into their trademark introduction to "City Lights." I stood motionless, straining to try and see the top of the old hotel, a half-mile away. Tall trees and their summer leaves blocked the view from my eyes, but not from my heart. For three minutes, I was nineteen years old again.

> A bright array of city lights
> As far as I can see.
> The great white way shines through the night
> For lonely guys like me.

Those words had found their way all around the world, and now they were back home again. Tears fell from my eyes, across my cheeks in what felt like a sacred moment. If I could have stopped time at any one point in my life, it would be then and there.

Ray ended his set and left the stage to a massive standing ovation. There were those in the crowd, I'm sure, who had felt the tingling just as I had. The life of that song was now part of the life of that town.

"I feel like I just went to school," Vince Gill said quietly to me, as he turned to prepare for his own segment of the show. I caught the glimpse of a tear in his eye.

The City Lights Festival, with help from local governments, made the auditorium a reality. It's located inside Commerce High School. I went back for the official dedication on September 11, 2011. Kids in the community finally had a place to perform. The first year the place was open, Commerce High School's group went to the state drama competition finals for the first time in school history. The drama teacher publicly credited their achievement with their having had, for the first time, a legitimate place to rehearse, practice, and hone their craft.

That "legitimate place" is called the Bill Anderson Performing Arts Center, and I'm as proud of that as I am about any hit record.

As Bill Anderson winds up his story, we learn a valuable lesson from Cowboy Jack Clement. We learn Bill's connection to a superstar who was born when Bill was fifty-two years old. And we find something out about the value and endurance of Moses's pencil.

When I was recording top-charting records, I didn't often allow myself to enjoy it. I regret that now, but at the time it was, "Oh, God, what'll the next one do?" I put all this pressure onto myself. I remember driving to a session to record the follow-up to a chart topper, thinking all along the way, "What if this one's not as good as that one? What if it's a bomb?" That's no way to go through life, but I spent a lot of years doing that.

At the Opry these days, I often find myself talking to performers more than fifty years younger than I am. When they ask me for advice, I ask them right back, "Are you enjoying yourself?" If they say, "Yes," my advice is to keep right on doing that. If they waver, my advice is to start enjoying. As the great Cowboy Jack Clement used to remind everyone at recording sessions, "We're in the fun business. If we're not having fun, we're not doing our jobs." Usually when he said that, everybody in the room would laugh, except Cowboy. He was serious about the fun business, and he was right. We're all in the fun business. If we're not having fun, we're not doing our jobs. These days, I'm doing my job.

I know it's unusual, this thing where I'm in my late seventies, interacting and writing songs with people so much younger than I am. Sometimes I'm self-conscious about that, and on at least one occasion I've neglected significant opportunity because of that self-consciousness. There's a guy in Nashville named Scott Swift, who from childhood has been a big fan of mine. His mother was a gigantic Bill Anderson fan, and she told Scott's daddy one night, "If Bill Anderson were to knock on our door, I'd run away with him."

Scott told me he lived in fear every time somebody knocked on their door that it'd be me, coming to take his mother away. In any case, every time I came within a couple hundred miles of Reading, Pennsylvania, where the Swifts lived, they'd be at the shows. One time, Scott even helped my band unload the instruments and sound equipment off the bus.

When Scott came to Nashville as an adult, he reached out to me and said he had a daughter who wanted to be a singer and a writer. He asked if there was anything I could do to help her. Now, I'd seen that particular dog and pony show a bunch of times, but he was a nice man and when he introduced me to her I could see she was a nice young woman. Sweet as she could be. I said, "This isn't very much, but I'm going to have a dinner and do a short concert for a couple hundred fan club members. If she wants to come over and sing a song, we'll feed y'all a free dinner."

So Scott, his wife, the girl's brother, and the girl all came out, and I introduced her . . . this fourteen-year-old girl who'd moved from Pennsylvania. She played to an audience that looked like her grandparents, and instead of doing a Kitty Wells or Connie Smith song that the crowd might have recognized, she sang a couple of songs she wrote. She was a good guitar player and there was something very likable about her, though what she was doing wasn't really meant for the people in my fan club.

I was impressed, and Scott told me that she was writing songs most every day. He said, "You ought to come out to the house and write with her." I thought, "What in the world would I have in common with a fourteen-year-old girl? What could I say that would relate to what she's saying? What life experiences has she had that would relate to any of mine?"

I'll never know the answer to that, though I wish I did.

Scott's daughter is named Taylor Swift. As I write this, she's the biggest singing star in the world. And she has remained as kind and sweet as she was when she was literally singing for her supper. I'm glad I could provide an early stage for her, though I'm pretty sure she would have conquered the world even without restrained applause from the Bill Anderson Fan Club.

The new century country stars that I've worked with have treated me with ease and respect. In most cases, they were comfortable with me from the outset, even when I wondered if they'd take me seriously, or if they'd think of me as a relic. Brad Paisley calls me "Moses" and kids me about writing with a pencil, but then he calls and says, "My computer crashed, have you still got that song?" My pencil and paper have never crashed. And Brad reminds me a lot of myself. Not as a singer or as a guitar player—he sings instead of whispering, and I could never play a guitar half as well as he can—but his tenacity and compulsion to try new things seem familiar to me, as is the "Gee whiz, who, me?" look in his eyes. It's as if he can't believe all the stuff happening to him. I know I never could.

I still can't. In 2015, a marvelous singer named Mo Pitney recorded a song I wrote with him and my good friend Bobby Tomberlin—called "Country." The song's success meant that I have written songs that have charted in seven consecutive decades. No other songwriter has done that before. Ray Price recorded "City Lights" in 1958. Sixty-seven years later, country singers are still voicing my words and melodies. I'm told that has never been done before. I'll admit that I'm vain enough to have looked it up. And it's never been done before.

AFTERWORD

I once wrote in a song that "nothing ever grows where the sun always shines."

I guess that was my way of explaining the reasoning behind the old saying "Into each life, some rain must fall." In spite of the glorious sunshine that has bathed, and continues to bathe, my career, I've had a few dark clouds pass over my personal life, pausing just long enough to rain from time to time on my parade.

After losing my mom in 2001 and my dad in 2003, my only sibling—my sister, Mary—passed away from ovarian cancer in the summer of 2006. She left behind her husband of over forty years and two grown sons. One of the last things she said to me was "Bubba, when I'm gone, promise you'll take care of my boys." I assured her that I would.

I didn't do a very good job, though. Her oldest disappeared in a tropical storm off the coast of Florida not long afterward, and his body was never found. The youngest ran afoul of the law and went to jail.

My first wife, Bette, the mother of my two daughters, died of lung cancer in June 2010.

My son-in-law, Chuck Robeson, succumbed to a malignant brain tumor in the spring of 2014, leaving behind his wife—my daughter Jenni—and four children, ages nine to twenty. Chuck was only forty-nine years old. Jenni is stronger than I've ever had to be.

My grandson, Gary William (Gabe) Anderson, was diagnosed with a very rare form of cancer at the age of six and continues to battle it today. His sister, Sophie, adopted from China in 2011, has had several health issues as well.

These things pain me. I worry about them, cry about them, and pray about them. We are all troubled. If we're not, something's wrong. And if we are, something's wrong. No matter what, something's wrong. And yet so much has been right for me in my life.

I recorded a song years ago that said:

> Sometimes I wonder when things go so wrong
> Has God forsaken me and left me alone?
> And then I remember in times of distress
> He's always with me . . . I'm most richly blessed.

If I could use one word to describe my life and my career, that's the word I would use. Blessed.

Looking back across all the years and all the miles, I realize that in spite of my battles, my trials, and my losses, I have been incredibly blessed. It started with a mother and dad who loved me unconditionally and provided me with the foundation on which to build my own life and chart my own course. It continues with three children who love me to this day, and eight grandchildren who are mostly still in the process of figuring out who this guy they call PawPaw really is and what he's all about. Maybe this book will help. The friends and the fans have been steadfast and loyal. The enemies have been few.

As the song says toward the end, "Almost despite myself, I . . . among men . . . am most richly blessed."

I probably should have added, "Amen."

DISCOGRAPHY

(does not include all compilations or re-issues)

ALBUMS

Decca Records

4192	Bill Anderson Sings Country Heart Songs	1961
4427	Still	1963
4499	Bill Anderson Sings	1964
4600	Bill Anderson Showcase	1964
4646	From This Pen	1965
4686	Bright Lights and Country Music	1965
4771	I Love You Drops	1966
4855	Get While the Gettin's Good	1967
4886	I Can Do Nothing Alone	1967
4859	Bill Anderson's Greatest Hits	1967
4959	For Loving You (with Jan Howard)	1968
4998	Wild Weekend	1969
3835	Bill Anderson's Country Style (Vocalion Label)	1969
5056	Happy State of Mind	1969
DXSB7198	The Bill Anderson Story (double album)	1970
75142	My Life / But You Know I Love You	1970
75161	Bill Anderson Christmas	1970
75184	If It's All the Same to You (with Jan Howard)	1971
75206	Love Is a Sometimes Thing	1971
75254	Where Have All Our Heroes Gone	1971
75275	Always Remember	1971
75315	Bill Anderson's Greatest Hits, Vol. 2	1971
75293	Bill and Jan or Jan and Bill (with Jan Howard)	1972
75339	Singing His Praise (with Jan Howard)	1972
75344	All The Lonely Women in the World	1972
75383	Don't She Look Good	1973

MCA Records

MCA24001	The Bill Anderson Story (re-issue)	1973
MCA320	Bill	1973
MCA416	Can I Come Home to You?	1974
MCA454	Every Time I Turn the Radio On	1974
MCA2182	Sometimes (with Mary Lou Turner)	1975
MCA2222	Peanuts and Diamonds and Other Jewels	1976
MCA2264	Scorpio	1976
MCA2298	Billy Boy and Mary Lou (with Mary Lou Turner)	1977
MCA2371	Love and Other Sad Stories	1978
MCA3075	Ladies' Choice	1978
MCA3214	Nashville Mirrors	1980
MCA80006123-02	The Definitive Collection	2006
MCA80007008-02	The Millennium Collection	2006

Southern Tracks Records

STL001	Southern Fried	1983

Swanee Records

SW5007	Yesterday, Today, and Tomorrow (double album)	1984

RCA Records

AHLI-4350	Bill Anderson Hosts Backstage at the Grand Ole Opry	1982

Curb Records

D2-77436	Best of Bill Anderson	1991
D2-77593	Country Music Heaven	1993
D2-77871	Greatest Songs	1996

Independent Records

NR11316	On the Road with Bill Anderson	1980
BAPF001	Bill Anderson Presents the Po' Folks Band	1984
BAPF002	A Place in the Country	1986
BAPF005	Yesteryear	1990 (cassette tape only)

Reprise Records

9 46695-2	Fine Wine	1998

TWI Records

also issued on Varese-Sarabande Records

TWI100	A Lot of Things Different*	2000
TWI104	Softly and Tenderly*	2004
TWI105	The Way I Feel*	2005
TWI106	Nothin' But Hits (2 CD package)	2010
TWI107	Songwriter	2010
TWI108	No Place Like Home on Christmas*	2002
TWI110	The Atlanta Sessions (with bonus DVD)	2013
TWI111	God Is Great—God Is Good (2 CD package)	2015

Madacy Entertainment Records

MEG253394	Whisperin' Bluegrass (2 CD set)	2007

Varese-Sarabande Records

VSD5643	Bill Anderson's Greatest Hits	1996
VSD5843	Bill Anderson's Greatest Hits, Vol. 2	1997
302-066-391-2	Bill Anderson Twelve Classics	2002
302-066-718-2	Forty Years of Hits (DVD)	2001

Bear Family Records

BCD17150	The First Ten Years (1956–1966) (4 CD box set)	2011

Red River Records

RRECD096	Life	2015

Decca/MCA Records—Po' Boys (1965–1973)

DL74725	Bill Anderson Presents the Po' Boys
DL74884	The Po' Boys Pick Again
DL75278	That Casual Country Feeling
MCA337	The Rich Sounds of Bill Anderson's Po' Boys

SINGLE RECORDS

TNT Records

| TNT-165 | "Take Me" / "Empty Room" | 1957 |
| TNT-9015 | "City Lights" / "No Song to Sing" | 1958 |

Decca

30773	"That's What It's Like to Be Lonesome" / "The Thrill of My Life"	1958
30914	"Ninety-Nine Years" / "Back Where I Started From"	1959
30993	"Dead or Alive" / "It's Not the End of Everything"	1959
31092	"The Tips of My Fingers" / "No Man's Land"	1960
31168	"Walk Out Backwards" / "The Best of Strangers"	1961
31262	"Po' Folks" / "Goodbye Cruel World"	1961
31358	"Get a Little Dirt on Your Hands" / "Down Came the Rain"	1962
31404	"Mama Sang a Song" / "On and On and On"	1962
31458	"Still" / "You Made It Easy"	1963
31521	"8 × 10" / "One Mile Over Two Miles Back"	1963
31577	"Five Little Fingers" / "Easy Come—Easy Go"	1964
31630	"Me" / "Cincinnati, Ohio"	1964
31681	"Three A.M." / "In Case You Ever Change Your Mind"	1964
31743	"Certain" / "You Can Have Her"	1965
31825	"Bright Lights and Country Music" / "Born"	1965
31884	"Time Out" / "I Know You're Married" (with Jan Howard)	1966
31890	"Golden Guitar" / "I Love You Drops"	1966
31999	"I Get the Fever" / "The First Mrs. Jones"	1967
32077	"Get While the Gettin's Good" / "Something to Believe In"	1967
32146	"Papa" / "No One's Gonna Hurt You Anymore"	1967
32197	"For Loving You" / "The Untouchables" (with Jan Howard)	1967
34490	"Stranger on the Run" / "Happiness"	1968
32276	"Wild Weekend" / "Fun While It Lasted"	1968
32360	"Happy State of Mind" / "Time's Been Good to Me"	1969
32417	"Po' Folks Christmas" / "Christmas Time's a Coming"	1969
32445	"My Life" / "To Be Alone"	1969
32514	"But You Know I Love You" / "A Picture from Life's Other Side"	1970
32511	"If It's All the Same to You" / "I Thank God for You" (with Jan Howard)	1970
32643	"Love Is a Sometimes Thing" / "And I'm Still Missing You"	1970
32689	"Someday We'll Be Together" / "Who Is the Biggest Fool?" (with Jan Howard)	1970

32744	"Where Have All Our Heroes Gone?" / "Loving a Memory"	1970
32793	"Always Remember" / "You Can Change My World"	1971
32850	"Quits" / "I'll Live for You"	1972
32877	"Dissatisfied" / "Knowing You're Mine" (with Jan Howard)	1972
32930	"All the Lonely Women in the World" / "It Was Time for Me to Move On Anyway"	1972
33002	"Don't She Look Good?" / "I'm Just Gone"	1973

MCA Records

40004	"If You Can Live with It" / "Let's Fall Apart"	1973
40164	"World of Make-Believe" / "Gonna Shine It on Again"	1974
40070	"The Corner of My Life" / "Home and Things"	1974
40243	"Can I Come Home to You" / "I'm Happily Married"	1974
40304	"Every Time I Turn the Radio On" / "You Are My Story"	1975
40351	"I Still Feel the Same about You" / "Talk to Me Ohio"	1975
40404	"Country DJ" / "We Made Love"	1975
40443	"Thanks" / "Why'd the Last Time Have to Be the Best?"	1975
40488	"Sometimes" / "Circle in a Triangle" (with Mary Lou Turner)	1975
40533	"That's What Made Me Love You" / "Can We Still Be Friends?" (with Mary Lou Turner)	1976
40595	"Peanuts and Diamonds" / "Your Love Blows Me Away"	1976
40661	"Liars One, Believers Zero" / "Let Me Whisper Darling"	1976
40713	"Head to Toe" / "This Ole Suitcase"	1977
40753	"Where Are You Going, Billy Boy?" / "Sad Ole Shade of Gray" (with Mary Lou Turner)	1977
40794	"Still the One" / "Love Song for Jackie"	1977
40852	"I'm Way Ahead of You" / "Just Enough to Make Me Want It All" (with Mary Lou Turner)	1977
40893	"I Can't Wait Any Longer" / "Joanna"	1977
40964	"Double S" / "Married Lady"	1978
40992	"This Is a Love Song" / "Remembering the Good"	1979
41060	"The Dream Never Dies" / "One More Sexy Lady"	1979
41150	"More Than a Bedroom Thing" / "Love Me and I'll Be Your Best Friend"	1979
41212	"Make Mine Night Time" / "The Old Me and You"	1980
10473	"Rock 'n' Roll to Rock of Ages" / "I'm Used to the Rain"	1980
51017	"I Want That Feelin' Again" / "She Made Me Remember"	1980
51052	"Mister Peepers" / "How Married Are You, Mary Ann?"	1981
51150	"Homebody" / "One Man Band"	1982

51204	"Whiskey Made Me Stumble" / "All That Keeps Me Going"	1982
52290	"I Wonder If God Likes Country Music" / "Ride Off in the Sunset"	1983
60059	"I Love You Drops" / "Still" (re-issue)	1983
60115	"Five Little Fingers" / "Mama Sang a Song" (re-issue)	1983

Southern Tracks

1007	"Southern Fried" / "You Turn the Light On"	1982
1011	"Laid Off" / "Lovin' Tonight"	1982
1014	"Thank You Darling" / "Lovin' Tonight"	1982
1021	"Son of the South" / "Twentieth-Century Fox"	1983
1026	"Your Eyes" / "I Never Get Enough of You"	1984
1030	"Speculation" / "We May Never Pass This Way Again"	1984
1067	"Sheet Music" / "Maybe Go Down"	1986
1077	"No Ordinary Memory"	1987
2011	"Love Slippin' Away" (with Toni Bellin)	1989

Swanee

4013	"Wino the Clown" / "Wild Weekend"	1984
5015	"Pity Party" / "Five Little Fingers"	1985
5018	"When You Leave That Way" / "Quits"	1985

INDEX

Tree Publishing Company, 1, 50–51, 55–56, 184;
    Sony and, 225–26, 233–34
Tubb, Ernest, 18, 48, 77, 165
Turner, Grant, 74
Turner, Mary Lou, 162–63, 201, 205
Twitty, Conway, 56, 218–19
"Two Teardrops," 234–36, 238, 277

Underwood, Carrie, 220

vaudeville, 129
Vaughn, Norman "Sleepy," 32
Vaughn, Sharon, 248

Wagoner, Porter, 91, 92, 153, 272
Wakefield, Terry, 271, 274
Ward, Sela, 13
Wariner, Steve, 2; "The Tips of My Fingers" and,
    223, 225; "Two Teardrops" and, 234–36, 277
Warner Brothers Records, 209
Waters, Bob, 44–45
Wayne, Don, 97–98
Welk, Lawrence, 167
Wells, Kitty, 114, 257
Wendell, E. W. "Bud," 247
West, Dottie, 165, 205
"What Good Would It Do to Pretend?," 20, 31
"When a Man Can't Get a Woman off His
    Mind," 248

"When Two Worlds Collide," 71, 95–96
"Where Are You Going, Billy Boy?," 163
"Where Have All Our Heroes Gone?," 75, 127,
    130–32, 207
"Which Bridge to Cross (Which Bridge to
    Burn)," 227–29
"Whiskey Lullaby," 262–68
White, Betty, 190–91
White, Bryan, 234
Whitfield, Rita, 215
Wiggins, Little Roy, 59
Wilburn Brothers (music group), 153
Wil-Helm Agency, 166
"Wild Weekend," 92, 130
Williams, Hank, 18, 27, 101, 114, 176; awards of,
    221, 247; on songwriting, 94
Williams, Hank, Jr., 115, 214
Wills, Mark, 238
"Wish You Were Here," 238
Womack, Burl, 33
Woolsey, Erv, 274
"World of Make Believe," 201
Wynette, Tammy, 145–46, 176–77
Wynn, Charles, 19

Yearwood, Trisha, 267
You Can Be a Star (TV show), 220–21
Young, Donny, 57, 59
Young, Faron, 71, 85, 114, 171, 184